THE CARING ECONOMY
BUSINESS PRINCIPLES FOR THE NEW DIGITAL AGE

About The Author

Gerry McGovern was born in Longford, Ireland in 1962. He was educated in St Mel's College, Longford and the College of Marketing and Design, Dublin. He holds a Bachelor of Science in Management from Trinity College, Dublin. He was was extensively involved in sports, playing Gaelic football for Longford for a number of years.

Gerry has had a varied career. After leaving college in 1984, he worked in business for a while, before leaving to write fiction and travel. He has had a number of plays published, as well as some short stories and poetry. He is working on a science fiction novel. He has two children, Aonghus and Fionn, and his partner is the poet, Máighréad Medbh.

In 1994, Gerry wrote a report for the Irish government entitled "Ireland: The Digital Age, the Internet". In 1995, he founded Nua, an Internet development company, with Niall O'Sullivan and Antóin O'Láchtnáin. Among the many accolades Nua has received was the 1996 Best Overall World Wide Web Business Achievement award from the European Commission.

One of the first development projects Nua undertook was Local Ireland, a portal for all things Irish. In 1998, Telecom Éireann, Ireland's national telecom, invested US$8 million in Local Ireland and Nua. Gerry is currently Chief Executive of both Nua and Local Ireland.

Gerry is a frequent speaker on Internet issues on the worldwide circuit. He writes a free, weekly e-mail newsletter entitled 'New Thinking', which seeks to contribute to a philosophy for the digital age.

To subscribe, send an email to:
newthinking-request@nua.ie
with the word
subscribe
in the body of the message.

gerry@nua.ie
www.nua.ie
www.local.ie

The Caring Economy

Business Principles For The New Digital Age

Gerry McGovern

BLACKHALL
Publishing

This book was typeset by
Artwerk for
BLACKHALL PUBLISHING
26 Eustace Street
Dublin 2
Ireland

e-mail: blackhall@tinet.ie

ISBN: 1 901657 61 2: hbk
1 901657 60 4: pbk

A catalogue record for this book is available
from the British Library.

Printed in Ireland by
Betaprint Ltd

For *Máighréad, Aonghus* and *Fionn*

"In dreams begins responsibility"
Old Play

Contents

Acknowledgements

This book is about the phenomenon that is the Internet. In itself, it is a product of the Internet. Much of what I have learned about the Internet over the years has been as a result of using it, and observing and participating in its discussion forums. Most of the research for the book itself was done using the Internet. A 'beta' version of the book was published on the Internet in late-1998, and very valuable feedback was received. It has made the finished product a much better book.

I have always had a great respect for writing and for writers. Before the Internet, I had believed that all great writing was a solitary art. With the Internet, I recognise that great writing and great communication will become much more participatory and co-operative in the coming years. I am by nature a solitary person, but I have learned with the Internet that we are all dependent on each other, that co-operation can bring rich rewards, and that thinking is the shared experience of a human race yearning to know itself better, its world and its universe.

I wish to acknowledge the great spirit of co-operation that has driven human knowledge forward. I wish to acknowledge the tremendous individuals and groups that worked together to make the Internet possible. I wish to acknowledge the following people in particular for their various contributions in helping me directly or indirectly to put this book together. I hope I don't leave anyone out, but if I do, let me say that it is not intentional.

Máighréad Medbh, Niall O'Sullivan, Antóin O'Láchtnáin, Ossie Kilkenny, Barry Murphy, Terry Maguire, Dick Peck, Billy Glennon, Al Bredenberg, John Audette, Mary Morris, Ann O'Donnell, Avi Nahir, Janus Boye, Brian O'Driscoll, Steve Cisler, Clint Hyer, Clyde McConnell, Paul Gerbino, Colin Dunbar, David Fickes, Dee Edwards, Doug Schmidt, Eoghan O'Regan, Fergal Lawler, Frank O'Dwyer, Craig Johnston, George Zuberbuehler, Gerard O'Connor, Tony Mason, Claire Rourke, Jerry Fairbridge, Jim Bottomley, Joe Katzman, John O'Farrell, Joseph P Cothrel, João Magalhães, Nicholas Negroponte, Esther Dyson, Juan Carlos Burruezo, Justin van den Berg, Kang Xiaoning, Kevin O'Reilly, Sjako Cu, Larry Gardiner, Martin A Schell, Mary Rickman-Taylor, Neal Howard Brodsky, Philippe Scheimann, Olwyn Leo, Emilio Cerri, Pratik Vithlani, Ing. Brenda de Vries, Robin Sircus, Rolf von Behrens, Stephen Cole, Stephen

Synnotts, John Perry Barlow, Kevin Kelly, Vint Cerf, Kevin Sweeney, Michael Nugent, Brendan Tuohy, Noel Treacy, everyone at Nua and Local Ireland.

Gerry McGovern
June 1999

© Fergal Lawler 1999

I
The Caring Economy:
Internet Business Principles

In the digital age, it pays to care.

Let's face it, many of the products made today are becoming commodities with the same basic components and performance levels. How different is one bank's ATM machine from another? How different is the performance and reliability of one car from another? Nearly all computers have 'Intel Inside' and many are made from the same essential parts.

How will business differentiate itself in a world becoming increasingly commoditised? In a world that is becoming increasingly automated? For some products and services, the lowest price will always be the focus. But there hasn't an economy in history that has been ruled by price alone.

To differentiate itself, a company can start by using the Internet to engage with its customers more, seeing them as partners so as to develop solid, long-term, mutually profitable relationships. By developing products that truly match customer needs. By focusing on service. By being friendly and helpful.

Because human relationships cannot be automated, cannot be commoditised. Machines, at least for now, cannot be programmed to care. People care. And let's not forget, in this haze of technological change and often illusory promise, it is people who buy our products and services.

Why do we do the things we do? Why do we get up in the morning? Why do we go to work? Why do we save? Why do we buy and sell things? What are the things that make us happy? What do we want from life? What do we really care about?

Today, as we move from the industrial age to the digital age – as we cross from one age to another – it is important that we ask these time-honoured questions. In fact, it is vital.

It is vital that we are able to look at the world with fresh eyes and are willing to learn new things, new business practices. It is vital that we take nothing for granted. That we assume nothing. That we question everything. That we particularly question the things that we believe to be absolutely true.

We should examine the philosophical foundations of our lives and not be afraid to find that they are crumbling. We should be ready to build new ones. Because we can. Because we must. Because there is no other choice.

The Caring Economy is based on a number of fundamental beliefs. These beliefs are that:

- the digital age demands new thinking and a new philosophy;

- the digital age requires a new set of business principles, governing everything from research and development to customer interaction;

- the digital age is about technology finally becoming transparent and people becoming paramount;

- in the digital age people have never been more educated, self-confident and empowered;

- people care. They care about themselves. They care about their family, their friends, their community, their country, their environment;

- business needs to care about people if it wants long-term success;

- the Internet is a revolution primarily in communication, not technology.

The Caring Economy is not a book about computers or the Internet. It's not about information technology and e-commerce. It's not about more bandwidth and faster processors. It's not about digital television or video-on-demand. It's not about nerds and hackers. It's not a book about cost savings and downsizing and automating people out of the picture. The Caring Economy may cover and explore all these technologies and issues, but it is not about them.

Rather, it is a book about people (business people and consumer people) and how we all interact on the Internet. It's a book that explores the relationship between people and the tools they make and use. It's about how people are impacted by, and impact on, new technologies and issues. It's a book that seeks to establish some philosophical foundations and basic principles for living in the digital age. It's a book about how we all need new attitudes, new rules and new business principles for success in a digital age economy and society.

It's a book that puts forward the belief that community and

commerce are inherently intertwined; that you can't have one without the other. It goes deep into the meaning, function and potential of communities. It explores the whole meaning of what a 'network' is, what 'networking' is about and how best to live and work within a networked environment. *The Caring Economy* believes that perhaps *the* fundamental principle for success in the digital age is to *think network*.

The Caring Economy is about attempting to give a map to people on a journey to a new age, a new world. It says to the business person not to get so scared, not to overreact; that things are not all that different. That when it all boils down, the digital age will still be about people communicating, interacting and trading with other people.

The Internet is one of the most important developments in human history. I feel very lucky to be alive at a time of such a momentous change.

The Internet is not about technology, it's about people communicating, people offering and searching for information. Technologically, the Internet is very basic. Electronic mail (e-mail), the most powerful and most used tool the Internet offers, does not require powerful computers to be sent or received. In many ways, the Internet slows, if only temporarily, the onwards and upwards race to make faster chips and fatter software.

Think of communication for a moment. Think of language, writing, books, radio, television, the Internet. Whenever there is a major change in communication, there is a major change in society.

The marriage between computers and communication is long overdue and badly needed. You have heard of the phrase, "art for art's sake". Well, I think it is has very often been true to say of the computer industry that it has followed an ethos of "computers for computers' sake".

In the early years of computer development, the idea that computers would be used for communicating would have been anathema to many computer engineers. The concepts of the 'end-user' and 'computers-made-easy' were simply not on the horizon of people developing computer hardware and software. Computers were designed to solve the 'great' problems of the world. They were not designed to be understood, or used, by us mere mortals, they were designed by computer engineers for other engineers.

The general result of this ethos for the last 30 or 40 years has been an information technology industry focused on the machine and the process, rather than on people and the needs of people. It's been an industry focused on cost-cutting and getting rid of people, rather than growth and empowering people. Thus, we have had a flow of hardware and software that you needed a degree to understand. People were supposed to adapt to technology, rather than technology adapting to people.

We never accepted buggy cars or buggy washing machines, so why do we have to accept buggy software? A general excuse is that software development needs to be rapid and constantly moving forward. Why? Could it be possible that the computer industry has deliberately created a technology trap? That faster chips and fatter software feeds onto itself leaving business and consumers running to stand still? That it is really the computer industry that needs new computers and new versions of software to feed its voracious bottom-line?

It is not surprising the Internet was not invented by Microsoft, Intel, IBM, or any of the other major players in the computer industry. It is not surprising that while born out of a military need, the Internet evolved and grew strong as a result of multi-disciplinary co-operation and sharing. It is not surprising that the Internet has thrived as a result of being bare bones but useful, rather than being a multimedia feast for the senses.

The Internet has taught us all a valuable lesson: that simple – in the form of e-mail – can be the most powerful of all. With its emphasis on communication and information, the Internet is changing – and will change even more fundamentally in the future – how those who design computers see and think about them. It will change how those of us who use, or who are about to use, computers, see and think about them. As a result of the Internet, computers are now truly interacting with consumers, truly interacting with society.

The Internet opens up the possibility for the computer to be a tool for people to use, rather than a machine that is obsessed with computing things, automating things and replacing people. The Internet is for young people, for old people, for people at work and for people at play. The Internet is for people who want to find information on a rare illness, for people who want to check up stock quotes and sports results, for people who want to buy and sell things, for people who want to find out about sex and sexuality, for all sorts of people in all sorts of places. The Internet lets us communicate and raise our voices.

The Internet has the potential to be a bridge that connects a number of fundamental trends that are occurring in very many of the societies of our world. In such societies, people are living longer, women are gaining increasing purchasing power and influence, children are for perhaps the first time in history knowing more about fundamental aspects of society (computers) than many of their parents do. Old people, women and children are three powerful engines that will drive *The Caring Economy*.

I remember once having a conversation with a senior executive from what used to be Digital Corporation. He was nearing retirement and he got into telling me stories about his career. He told me that when he was younger he worked for a very enlightened company who regularly sent him and other executives off on courses. One of the courses dealt with how people were going to manage their increased leisure time in the fast approaching 'leisure society'. We had a good laugh at that one.

For all their power, all their potential, all their promise, computers have not delivered 'the leisure society'. Quite the opposite. Those who have jobs today work harder and longer than they ever did. Computers have not exactly driven up productivity growth either. In fact, until the last few years, American productivity growth, for example, had been more than sluggish over a 30-year period. And where is the paperless office?

If the computer industry has not delivered the leisure society, what has it delivered? Perhaps it has delivered the *adrenaline society*; the society that never sleeps, the society that is constantly bringing out new versions of itself, that never lets its products (or its people) get old.

I don't think the rest of the world is all that interested in the adrenaline society. Sure, we all like a bit of the excitement, however, by and large I believe that most people prefer a caring society. Because that's the type of society most people *already* live in and I believe want to continue to live in.

I mentioned to a couple of associates in the computer industry, that I was calling this book *The Caring Economy*. There was a silence and then a look of puzzlement. "Caring is such a *weak* word," one person replied. I find it interesting that some feel that to care is a sign of weakness.

We are an intelligent, often logical and driven species; that is accepted. We are also a sentient species. We feel. We care and like to be cared for. We care about our food, we care about our clothes, we care about our family, our community and our nation. We care about our children and we'll work hard to give them a good education and the best possible chance in life.

We care about the cars we buy and are seen driving. We care about relaxation; we go to the movies, sports games, we go on holidays. We care about the environment and try to buy products that are not harmful to it. We care about the clothes we wear. They're about much more than keeping us warm; they're about making us look good and feel good.

Yes, we belong to a caring society. We care about ourselves and we like to think that others care for us. When we are sick and old we want and need to be cared for. Having said all that, it has to be accepted that we live in a society where caring is increasingly self-centred. Families are not as strong as they used to be. People used to rear large families who would then look after them in old age. Now they have fewer children and invest in pension plans.

Communities are not as strong as they used to be. Life-long employment created stability and was thus good for holding communities together. Twenty years ago, if someone told you they had worked with a certain company for 30 years and would be loyal to that company to the end, you would have held them in high esteem. Today, such statements would be met with raised eyebrows, if not open contempt. Downsizing has taught us that it's every worker for themselves.

Today, loyalty is for fools. The educated consumer sees the so-called 'relationship' marketing and its "Dear Gerry" *personalised* letters as no more than trick marketing. Consumers are suspicious, and rightly so, of marketing efforts that try to get personal with them. They don't get warm feelings when asked to have a relationship with a wordprocessor's mail-merge function.

A society that stops caring is a society that is in for trouble in the long-term. Computers, instead of contributing to a more cohesive, content, happier society, have, on balance, destabilised society. The focus of information technology on cost-cutting and getting rid of people, the mania for downsizing, the obsession with 'bigness', is degrading the values and structures of society. In many ways, information technology knows the cost of everything and the price of nothing.

Downsizing has downsized our values. Information technology is creating an unstable society. An unstable society leads to an unstable population, an unstable customer base and ultimately an unstable economic and business base.

Think about this for a moment: if our children don't learn and practice values, such as co-operation, decency and loyalty, how does business expect them to be brand-loyal as adults?

Let's be very selfish here for a moment. What I'm saying is that caring is good for business. That a company which genuinely cares for its customers will keep more of them longer, particularly in a digital age environment where many customers are at their most educated. As has been well proven, it's much more profitable to do business with an existing customer than to get a new one.

The Internet has the potential to focus the undoubted power and potential of computers on communication, on the needs of people, and thus contribute to a more cohesive society, thus laying the foundations for long-term growth and profitability. As already stated, the Internet has achieved its phenomenal success as a result of the caring principles of co-operation and sharing. The Internet is a reflection of *The Caring Economy*.

There's nothing corny about caring. There's nothing weak about caring. It's what is going to differentiate many of the successful from the non-successful companies in the digital age. The days of cutting costs and milking companies for short-term gain are numbered. In this war of change, we need a long-term vision more than ever.

We need to focus on the basics again: the customer. If we genuinely care about them and deliver to them products that reflect this caring attitude, they will in time care about us and become loyal to our brands. Together, we will have created a mutually profitable relationship.

© Fergal Lawler 1999

2
War of Change

THE TIME CRISIS AND THE WAR OF CHANGE

We are living through a war – a war of change. We are fighting to understand it all, fighting to adapt with the change. We are fighting for our time. This war will hopefully end and the digital age will settle into more predictable slower changing patterns. For now, though, individuals and companies must be on a war footing.

The advances in computers and communications bring about tremendous change and instability. So very little is dependable. So very little holds firm. It is as if the ground has begun to shift underneath our feet. Standing still means moving backwards.

In the 1970s it took ten years to develop a car. By the 1990s it took five years. Talking about cars, an IBM report[1] made the point that:

> If we took a 1985 Cadillac and applied the computer industry's price/performance curve, it would today get 2,100 miles on a gallon of gas, have a top speed of 230 mph and cost $42. (Luckily though, cars don't crash as often as computers.)

Following Moore's Law, new computer processors are developed roughly every eighteen months that are twice as powerful and half the price. New Internet browsers emerge every six to nine months. A substantial website development should be completed within four to six months.

As *Upside*[2] magazine put it:

> Moore's Law is the defining factor in all modern industry. No one ever lost betting on it or won betting against it. And it is a template by which one can judge the behaviour of even the most cutting-edge companies.

For more than two decades, the capacity of the basic integrated circuit, the dynamic random-access memory (DRAM) chip, has doubled consistently in intervals of less than two years: from 1,000 transistors (1 kilobit) per chip in 1970 to 1,000,000 (1 megabit) in 1987, 16 megabits in 1993, and 1,000,000,000 (1 gigabit) predicted for the year 2000. A gigabit chip has the capacity of 125,000,000 bytes, approximately equivalent to 14,500 pages, or more than twelve volumes of *Encyclopædia Britannica*.

According to *The Emerging Digital Economy*[3] (a major report published by the US Department of Commerce in 1998):

The Internet is growing faster than all other technologies that went before it. Radio existed for 38 years before it had 50 million listeners, and television took thirteen years to reach that mark. The Internet crossed the line in just four years.

In 1995, *The Economist* magazine reported that:

Relentless technological change is driving down many of the elements in the cost of a telephone call. Already, the cost of carrying an additional call is often so tiny that it might as well be free. More significant, carrying a call from London to New York costs virtually the same as carrying it from one house to the next.[4]

Indeed, technological change is the most relentless of all. By 1997, information technology companies, while making up only 8 per cent of US firms, were accounting for 33 per cent of economic growth. By 1998, there were 7 million information technology jobs in the United States, with an average salary of $46,000, compared with an average salary of $28,000 for all jobs. The 1998 American inflation rate of 2.1 per cent would have been 3.2 per cent were it not for declining prices for computer equipment.

The time crisis is all around us. "Do you know the average amount of time we invested in shopping for and preparing the family's main meal in the mid-1930s?" Morris Tabaksblat[5] (Chairman of Unilever NV) asked in *Smart Routes to the Smart Consumer*, "2.5 hours. By the mid-50s that was down to one hour...half an hour in the mid-70s...a quarter of an hour in the mid-90s…and we estimate it will be down to less than ten minutes by 2005."

The average working week in America has risen from 40 hours in 1973, to 50 hours in 1997, according to a Harris Poll.[6] A Cornell University study (published in 1999)[7] found that more than four in ten men and three in ten women work more hours than they would like. The study also stated that between 1972 and 1994, the total amount of time the average American couple worked increased by seven hours per week.

Already we are seeing marketing approaches on the Internet which literally *pay* people for their time. CyberGold, for example, is a company that pays people to view online advertisements. They have stated that advertisers are "happy to pay for the attention of users".

Change can be exciting. Change can be frightening. Constant rapid change becomes a war, a time when everything is uncertain. For the majority of people, living through a war of change is an unnerving experience.

For a period, not understanding how to use a computer did not matter that much. The related tasks could always be got around or delegated. Some might have thought that they could still do their job by remaining computer illiterate.

Today, if we want a decent job we have to be able to use a computer. If we want to embrace the potential of the digital age, we have to be on the Internet. Those who can't, or won't, use computers and the Internet will become digital age illiterates.

This war of change will surely end. It is a result of the friction caused as the digital age moves in and the industrial age grinds out. Hopefully, in another five or ten years, the world will have settled into a more predictable and slower pattern of development.

For now we have to deal with the rapid change and all the stress that comes with it. Learning to cope with it is no easy task, but learn we must. There is no going back to that old, more predictable world. The only constant – the only thing we can totally rely on today – is that nothing is reliable, that everything can and will change. Like it or not we need to get used to it.

To put today's change into some context – and to show just how dramatic it is – let us compare it to the pace of species change. As Freeman Dyson explains:

It takes 1 million years to evolve a new species, 10 million

years for a new genus, 100 million years for a new class, 1
billion years for a phylum.

How many generations of computers have we seen in the last 50
years?

President Bill Clinton, during his 1998 trip to China made the
following statement.

> In the world we live in, this global information age, con-
> stant improvement and change is necessary to economic
> opportunity and to national strength. Therefore, the free-
> est possible flow of information, ideas and opinion, and a
> greater respect for divergent political and religious convic-
> tions, will actually breed strength and stability going for-
> ward.

The point I believe he was making was that in a world of constant change, that which is static or static-minded is doomed to
the economic and political dustbin of history. That which
changes with the times at least has the possibility of surviving
the times.

There is no point in hanging around in a world of change. You
need ideas, sure, but the only way you can really protect them is
by acting upon them. As John Perry Barlow wrote in his *Wired*
article "The Economy of Ideas":[8]

> As we become fixated upon information commerce, many
> of us seem to think that originality alone is sufficient to
> convey value, deserving, with the right legal assurances, of
> a steady wage. In fact, the best way to protect intellectual
> property is to act on it. It's not enough to invent and
> patent; one has to innovate as well. Someone claims to
> have patented the microprocessor before Intel. Maybe so.
> If he'd actually started shipping microprocessors before
> Intel, his claim would seem far less spurious.

This is a genuine new age and we are witnesses and participants
in one of the key shifts in human society. It is as fundamental and
far-reaching as that. It is as big as we can imagine 'big' to be.

The digital age will change the way we live, the way we think,
the way we relate, the way we work. It will change us and our
world. Nothing will remain untouched.

As, Ira Magaziner, then senior adviser to President Clinton, stated in 1998:[9]

> None of us knows where all this is heading, but if we get it right, we have an opportunity that only comes once every couple of hundred years. If we get it right, we can drive enormous changes in our economical and social structures.

A NEW AGE – A NEW PHILOSOPHY

If we do not understand the fundamentals and underlying themes of the age we live in, then we will have great difficulty living and working in a successful and fulfilled manner.

This is the beginning of the digital age. As we have invented the age itself, by inventing the computer and telecommunications (along with all their by-products), so now we need to 'invent' a way to understand and live in it.

We need a philosophy for the digital age.

The creation of a digital age philosophy requires us firstly to understand what the underlying fundamentals are that make this age what it is. What makes this age different?

Some readers might wince a little at the word 'philosophy', thinking that it belongs in academia, not the real world. I make no apologies for using it because I believe that it is exactly what we need. Going forward without a digital age philosophy is going forward blind.

Those of us over 30 were born and reared in the industrial age. We ate, slept and drank its philosophical tenets. They were in front of us every day, in our homes, in our workplaces, in the newspapers, in our conversations, in our classrooms and playgrounds. In our social and economic structures. We understood terms, such as the 'working class', the 'five-day week', '9-to-5' and 'lifetime employment'.

Our children will imbue a digital age philosophy in a natural day to day manner, but we of the older generations must work much harder. We need to shed much of the skin of our industrial age philosophy and thinking, and then learn to wear the philosophy and thinking of the digital age. We need to understand new terms, such as cyberspace, e-commerce, globalisation, teleworking and virtual organisations.

This is not an easy task by any means. It can be both frightening and unnerving. But whether we like it or not we have no choice. If we do not move forward willingly then we will be moved sideways. If we do not become students again, regaining a child-like curiosity and capacity to learn, then we will increasingly find that we are living in a world that we do not understand. If we cannot embrace the digital age, then the digital age will push us aside and pass us by.

As Morris Tabaksblat (Chairman of Unilever) has stated:

> Change: Regard it as an ally and not as an enemy. Understand the process that drives change and you can use it, instead of being used by it. Change: use it, or be used.

Of course, this is not to say that everything changes. The industrial age and all its factories and physical, mechanical things will of course not disappear. People still need cars and televisions and houses to live in. However, the role and importance of such physical products will diminish in absolute value terms as the digital age matures. As has happened to agriculture in the industrial age, so too will happen to industry in the digital age.

It's important to understand that we are all caught up in this change, and that this is not by any means the first time that such dramatic change has impacted on humanity. (Nor, in all likelihood, will it be the last.) Think of the drama of the change from the agricultural age to the industrial age. Think of the shock to the system that somebody from a rural area received when they first arrived in a sprawling city. For many, life was lived in slums and work was in dreary, polluted factories.

BACK TO THE AGRICULTURAL AGE?

"There is nothing new under the sun" may not be an absolutely true saying, but it is well worth pondering. Revolutions are often vastly overrated events. They tend to arrive with a big bang, but when the dust settles, much remains the same.

Have you read Tom Standage's book, *The Victorian Internet*?[10] Commenting on the book for Amazon.com, he wrote that:

> We like to think of things like online weddings, hackers, secret codes and information overload as peculiarly modern phenomena, but it turns out that they could all be

found on the telegraph networks of the 19th century too. So what? Well, I think that tells us something important about our attitudes to technology: that as new inventions come and go, the ways people react to them stay pretty much the same.

Telling the story of the telegraph, an old-fashioned but paradoxically modern technology, is also a fun way to stick a pin in the Internet balloon. Sure, I like the Internet, I use it all the time, but I don't think it's the answer to the world's problems. People said the same about the telegraph in the 19th century, and they were wrong. My message, then, is one of historically-informed scepticism. When you're using the Internet, browsing the Web, sending e-mails – ordering my book, even – remember that even though it seems to be cutting-edge technology it is, in many ways, old hat.

The digital age is a revolution, but then revolutions, tend to turn a full circle. For most people, the world has always been about themselves and their interaction with other people. The world has always been, to some degree or another, a caring society and economy. In communities throughout the world, people have always co-operated and shared.

In time, patterns of business and living in the digital age will have a lot more in common with agricultural age patterns, than they will have with industrial age business and living patterns. Entering into the digital age may indeed be like going 'back to the future'.

For starters, we are nearing the height of cities particularly in the Western world. Mega-cities were a phenomenon of the industrial age and the necessity of having people close to the wheels of production and consumption. In a digital age economy, increasing numbers of people will not have to travel to their work, instead, their work will travel to and from them.

The Internet, and networks in general, are more reflective of organic systems than of industrial mechanisms. In many ways, you grow and cultivate a network and business within that network, than in the traditional sense, build and construct it. Co-operation and sharing are an inherent part of economic and social life in agricultural societies. These behavioural patterns are often absent in large, bristling cities.

In 1998, Thomas Malone (head of MIT's Center for Co-ordination Science) told *Wired*[11] magazine that:

> The classic management phrase is 'command and control'. If we believe that top-down, centralised management will become less and less common, the question becomes: What could take its place? The notion of *cultivation* [my emphasis] provides perspective from which we can legitimately think it's fine if we're not in control.

Digital age thinker and philosopher, John Perry Barlow, writing in *Wired*[12] in 1998 stated that:

> It is my belief – originating in my own personal leap from the 19th century to the 21st – that the mental habits of agriculture are much more conducive to understanding the essentially biological qualities of information economy than is the mechanical skull vice of the industrial worldview.

In *New Rules for the New Economy*,[13] Kevin Kelly has written about the digital age as a very organic place.

> As networks have permeated our world, the economy has come to resemble an ecology of organisms, interlinked and co-evolving, constantly in flux, deeply tangled, ever expanding at its edges. As we know from recent ecological studies, no balance exists in nature; rather, as evolution proceeds, there is perpetual disruption as new species displace old, as natural biomes shift in their make up, and as organisms and environments transform each other. So it is with the network perspective: companies come and go quickly, careers are patchworks of vocations, industries are indefinite groupings of fluctuating firms.

To borrow a computer term, the industrial age encouraged, if not forced, people to 'stand alone'. As a result, neighbourhoods and communities have gradually lost a lot of power and value, certainly in relation to the communities that existed within an agricultural age society.

The 1980s and 1990s have seen the absolute triumph of 'me' values in much of Western society. Communities have been

under constant threat, and in many countries have been seriously weakened.

In the agricultural age, people *had* to work together and co-
operate, since their very survival depended on it. Families and
extended families lived together. Children learned skills from
their parents. Everyone helped out on the farm, and when the
hay needed to be put in cocks, the neighbours all joined in,
because nobody knew when the rain was coming. In the agricultural age, people operated in 'community networks'.

What goes around, comes around, they say. It could also be
said that we move forward only to return, at least partly, to some
place in the past. The Internet is a network – an organic place. It
makes sense to co-operate. It makes sense to cultivate.

A LONG-TERM VISION

Why have so many business people become so narrow in their
view of the future? Can we lay all the blame on the stock market? But the stock market invests heavily in Yahoo and Amazon,
and those are very long-term plays. Has downsizing become a
disease, rather than a solution? Has this war of change made us
dizzy and short-sighted?

We need to make sure that we don't become another victim of
this war of change. The fact that we need to react very quickly,
means that there has never been a greater need to have a longer
term vision for ourselves and our organisation. We need to figure out what we truly believe in, what we truly stand for, where
we really want to go?

Otherwise, we will be pulled and dragged by the change. We
will turn into a mish-mash of short-term reactive strategies,
which will ultimately fall apart under the force of their own
contradictions. We can deal with the change if we have that
vision.

REFERENCES

1. IBM White Paper, *Banking in the Network Economy*
    http://www.ibm.com/ibm/publicaffairs/banking/intro.html.
    The quotation about the 1985 Cadillac can be found at:
    http://www.ibm.com/ibm/publicaffairs/banking/emerging2.html

2. M S Malone, "Upside: The First 100 Issues" (August, 1998) *Upside*
    http://www.upside.com/texis/mvm/story?id=35805d070

3. "The Emerging Digital Economy" US Department of Commerce (1998)
    http://www.ecommerce.gov/emerging.htm

4. F Cairncross, "The Death of Distance" *The Economist* (30 September 1995)
    http://www.economist.com/

5. M Tabaksblat, Chairman of Unilever NV, *Smart Routes to the Smart
    Consumer*, http://www.unilever.com

6. Harris Poll Online, http://www.harrispollonline.com/

7. C Laino, "*Couples feel the Time-squeeze*" *MSNBC* (1999)
    http://www.msnbc.com/news/234573.asp

8. J P Barlow, "The Economy of Ideas" *Wired* (March 1994)
    http://www.wired.com/wired/archive/2.03/economy.ideas.html

9. D Joachim, "Internet paves way for Mass Deregulation" *Internet Week*
    (December 1998), http://www.techweb.com/wire/story/NIN19980612S0001

10. T Standage, *The Victorian Internet: The Remarkable Story of the Telegraph and
    the Nineteenth Century's Online Pioneers* (Walker & Co) 1998

11. P Schwartz, "Re-organization Man" (Interview with Thomas Malone) *Wired*
    (July 1998), http://www.wired.com/wired/archive/6.07/malone.html

12. J P Barlow, "Africa Rising" *Wired* (January 1998)
    http://www.wired.com/wired/archive/6.01/barlow.html

13. K Kelly, "New Rules for the New Economy" Wired (September 1997)
    http://www.wired.com:80/wired/archive/5.09/newrules.html.
    Now available in book form: K Kelly, *New Rules for the New Economy*
    (Viking Press) 1998

© Fergal Lawler 1999

3
Cyberspace: The New Space

A NEW SPACE

One of the most significant changes that the digital age has brought about is the introduction of a new 'space' within which we will live, socialise and do business. What exactly we call this space – the Internet, cyberspace, virtual space – is not that important. However, it is important that we understand what constitutes this new space, what its characteristics and rules are, and how best to behave within it, because, whether we like it or not, this new space will become an increasingly important part of our lives.

OUR PHYSICAL SPACE

Before we can attempt to gain a deeper understanding of the Internet and cyberspace, we need, firstly, to stand back and reach a more clear understanding of what constitutes the physical space we now inhabit. This has rarely been necessary up until now, as we have taken the space we live in as a given. However, by understanding what constitutes our physical space, we will find clues with regard to the tools and structures required to consolidate and live within cyberspace.

Structures of Physical Space
In my opinion, the physical space we inhabit has both 'natural' and 'artificial' structures.

Natural Structures

Natural structures occur naturally, without any human intervention. These include the following.

1. *The entity that is the earth and its atmosphere*: land, mountains, sea, air – its geography.

2. *The natural resources that are found on the earth*: oil, iron, stone, gold, etc.

3. *The life forms that are found on the earth*: fish, birds, insects, animals, humans.

In the industrial and previous ages, physical geography had been the great definer of cultures and economies. Mountains, rivers and lakes walled tribes, which settled within these walls and created cultures and nations, which mapped their borders along these physical boundaries.

Natural resources dictated how economies and business would evolve. In general, those countries that had rich natural resources and the capacity to exploit those resources were those that led economically.

Geography has defined how and where we live in so many ways. We used to take it for granted that where somebody lived was where they would do most of their purchasing and where they would pay most of their taxes. That is no longer necessarily the case in the digital age, where someone might live in Ireland, work for a company in America and get their mortgage from a German bank.

Showing a recognition of these new emerging realities, in 1997, American vice-president, Al Gore, was quoted as saying that:[1]

> Time zones, not cost, will become the biggest barrier to keeping in touch. It will become possible to site any screen-based activity anywhere; and to tap into all sorts of information and advice – from crop prices to university courses to medical help – from anywhere in the world.

In 1995, Francis Cairncross wrote an interesting article for *The Economist* entitled "The Death of Distance".[2] It dealt with the impact the advances in telecommunications and the Internet were having on distance.

The death of distance as a determinant of the cost of communications will probably be the single most important economic force shaping society in the first half of the next century. It will alter, in ways that are only dimly imaginable, decisions about where people live and work; concepts of national borders; patterns of international trade.

This is not to say that geography will become irrelevant anytime soon. Perhaps in some ways, the opposite will occur. As people communicate and businesses trade more and more on an international rather than national and local basis, ultimately more, not less, international travel will occur.

At the same time, the role that geography has played in human life and business will definitely change. In the not-too-distant future, children in most of rural Ireland will probably not think twice about the fact that their Japanese teacher actually lives in Japan, and is teaching them through video conferencing and e-mail.

Artificial Structures

The artificial (made by humans) structures of physical space are those that humans have created. They can be broadly broken down into two types: public and private.

Public Artificial Structures

1. The civil service, political and legal structures that humans have established which facilitate governing and planning.

2. The 'free' services and public utilities that governments and public entities provide: government and planning, policing and armed forces, certain education, health care, environmental protection, road networks, water, street lighting, public parks, etc. (These 'free' services are, of course, funded through taxes.)

3. The charged-for services and public utilities governments provide: electricity, public transport, telecommunications, certain health care and educational services.

Private Artificial Structures

This is where the private sector community, and the individual come in. It includes the following.

1. Private industry and capitalism: everything from private houses and buildings to Coca-Cola and Kellogg's Corn Flakes.

2. Communal services and structures that are provided by private citizens for free or minimal charge in the interest of the larger community. These include everything from local committees to promote tourism or employment in an area, people who help organise youth activities, people who visit old people, people who contribute to the building of a community centre, etc.

These artificial structures tend to come under different categories depending on the country and political philosophy. (In some countries, for example, water is a free resource, in others it is charged for.) There is, of course, a major European trend with regard to the privatisation of public utilities, with a particular focus on telecommunications services. However, no matter where a particular service or utility might fit, there are basic entities and divisions as described above within practically all human societies.

THE URBAN AND THE RURAL

Tools, of course, are what we use to create our artificial world, and when major new tools arrive, the whole structure of some societies can change.

"Who could have foreseen in Michael Faraday's time," Francis Cairncross wrote,[3] "that electricity would eventually release women to go out to work, transforming the shape of the family, or allow the development of cities such as Manhattan and Hong Kong, whose skyscrapers could never have been built without the lift?"

Cities developed when advances in transportation (the invention of the wheel) and agricultural techniques began to create surplus crops and a capacity to store such surpluses. By 3000 BC, cities had been established in Mesopotamia and Egypt. Although cities would play very important roles down through the ages, it was the Industrial Revolution, with its factory-driven economies, that began to transform them into the massive entities that we know today.

As the *Encyclopaedia Britannica*[4] states:

In 1850 less than 7 per cent of the world's population lived in urban centres of more than 5,000 inhabitants. By 1950, 30 per cent did, and the figure was over 60 per cent in the fully industrialised countries of Europe, Japan and the United States.

The emerging industrial city was far from a nice place for most people to live in. It was polluted, over-crowded, full of slum-dwellings, sanitation was poor and there were few recreational areas. Most people did not come to cities because they liked them. They came because of work; they came because they had no choice.

The arrival of the car had the next greatest impact on the city, creating the suburb, as people could now work in the city and live in something approaching a rural environment.

How will the arrival of the Internet affect the city as we know it today? Ilan Salomon of the Hebrew University of Jerusalem, wrote in a paper entitled "Telecommunications and the 'Death of Distance': Some Implications for Transport and Urban Areas".[5]

In my view if distance is dead, we need to ask the question whether there is still a role for cities, and if there is a role for cities, what are its implications for transport?

The city is basically a transport-based phenomena. City structure and transport technology have been married together since the days of the walking city and certainly since the introduction of the automobile that brought dispersal to suburbia. Telecommunications, along the same line, may bring about further dispersal, into exurbia.

"Now that we have Internet communities, I wonder how much longer we'll need cities," Bob Metcalfe wrote for *InfoWorld* in 1997.[6] "Because they're unhappy so much of the time. Why must four out of five Americans continue cramming themselves into just 271 metropolitan areas?"

Over the next 30 to 50 years, we will see a much greater spread of human population and a relative decline of major cities. This is not in any sense to say that cities will die away, but that they will no longer be the magnet of old for people who wanted to get jobs and get on.

The simple fact is that quite a few people who live in big cities don't particularly like them. They don't like the pollution, crime, congestion, high property prices, lack of personal and family

space, traffic jams, etc. They live in cities because that's where
the jobs are. Given a choice, and the opportunity to retain their
jobs, they would move to the country.

The signs are already here, with the steady growth of teleworking (telecommuting). In 1998, the *Edupage*[7] e-mail newsletter reported that:

> The US Census Bureau says that previously published data
> from the 1990 census indicate that almost three and a half
> million people were then working at home – a jump of 56
> per cent over the previous census.

A 1997 survey for Telecommute America[8] found that the number
of telecommuters had grown to 11 million. In 1997 also,
Innovation,[9] an e-mail newsletter, stated that:

> There's a new term for the information workers who need
> only ideas and modern technology to conduct business
> from whatever locale they choose – 'Lone Eagles'.

According to the Center for the New West, which coined
the term, as many as 10 million Americans fit that profile today.

> "This is a technology-driven migration, and the technolo-
> gy is reducing the tyranny of distance," says the Center's
> President.

A general trend that is encouraging the acceptance of teleworking
from an employer's point of view is the fact that, in many Western
countries, it is becoming increasingly difficult to find new workers
for the information technology industry. According to a study
released by the Information Technology Association of America, at
least one in every ten technical jobs in the United States will go
unfilled. In 1998, 68 per cent of technology companies admitted
that not being able to fill vacancies could hamper their growth.

Reflecting how the whole nature of work and the workplace
is changing, a Pitney Bowes study, "Workplace Communications
in the 21st Century",[10] stated that:

> It is much more likely in today's workplace to have work
> groups dispersed in different physical locations and often
> in different time zones. Seventy-two per cent of workers

surveyed said that they regularly work with co-workers who are not in the office.

The Rural Life

An argument made against rural life is that it is isolated, sparsely populated and that there are very few modern amenities and opportunities around. Ilan Salomon writes about how people, "want the amenities of rural life styles, but they also want the opportunities offered by urban life, be it shopping, work opportunities or leisure activities".

This is indeed true today for many rural areas, which have been in decline for many years, with young people leaving to find work in towns or cities as soon as they finish school. After a while it became a vicious circle, as people chose to leave not simply to find work but because their peers and friends had also left.

If a rural area can reach a watershed of homecomings or new settlements, then a lot of these negative factors can be reversed. The Internet will help here in a number of ways.

1. It allows people to work in remote areas.

2. It allows people who live in remote areas to shop for a much wider range of goods.

3. It allows people to keep in touch with friends in a cheap and easy manner no matter how far away they live.

If the watershed of people returning/locating can be achieved, then isolation will no longer be such an issue. People will be able to go out locally and meet their peers. Businesses will be established to meet the varied needs of the new influx.

There are other implications should a large number choose teleworking and locate in rural areas. Imagine all the business that's done on the way to and from work and during lunch breaks. The papers and milk that are bought. Rushing out at lunchtime to lodge a cheque or buy some clothes. If people stopped travelling to work, then those who bring services into the home would have more opportunities, and those who expect people to come to them would begin to lose custom.

CYBERSPACE: THE SURFACE OF THE INTERNET

The only way I have been able to make sense of the Internet, and everything that happens on it, is to think of it as a 'space'. So, if

the Internet is a space, which we call 'cyberspace', then what are
the structures of cyberspace? What are its key foundational elements? How does it compare to and what can it learn from physical space? How should it evolve? What are its laws? How do
you do business within its borders? How should it be governed?
Should it be governed?

What is cyberspace made of? In a most basic way, cyberspace
is made of the same things the earth and humans are all made of:
atoms. After that, it begins to become fuzzy. Cyberspace is a digital realm. Everything in it is made up of bits and bytes. Every
letter, every word, every line of every code of software, every
part of every picture or sound is constructed with digital bits and
bytes.

If geography is the science of describing the earth's surface,
then what is the geography of cyberspace? What is the surface of
cyberspace made of? Again, in the most basic way it is made up
of digital bits and bytes, these currently being mainly represented by software, text and simple images, but increasingly in the
future by sound, video, complex animations and virtual reality
environments.

Just as the surface of the earth is diverse and multifarious, so
the surface of cyberspace will be diverse and multimedia.
Thinking of cyberspace today reminds me of the theory of the
'Big Bang'.

The Big Bang theory postulated that a very long time ago
what was to become the universe contracted into a tiny ball of
immensely dense matter, and that when it could contract no
more, it exploded outwards to form time, matter and the universe.

The Big Bang for cyberspace can probably be located with the
launch of the first World Wide Web browser in 1992. From there,
a massive explosion of websites and e-mails has occurred. After
the actual Big Bang, it took many, many years for the universe to
cool down and for the planets to form. This cooling and formation process is happening much quicker in cyberspace, though it
is by no means done.

We are still in the early years of cyberspace. Millions of websites, hundreds of millions of documents and hundreds of millions of e-mails have been put forth. Many of these have been
useful, many have not. What is true to say is that very little long-
term planning has occurred with regard to how cyberspace
should be structured.

Let us think for a moment of that path in time the Big Bang took. There was a tiny ball of matter. It exploded with a massive outwards force creating time and all matter. Slowly, things cooled, planets and minerals formed. Great diversity emerged. Over time, the universe became relatively settled and finally life forms emerged. Humans evolved, who would in time tame the 'wild' earth by cutting down trees, building roads and cities and eating hamburgers.

The growth of cyberspace has happened in reverse. It is human invention that has created cyberspace. First, there was a marriage of computers and telecommunications and cyberspace was born in the network that resulted. There then followed a stage where cyberspace was like some 'Garden of Eden'. There were very few people using it, and most of them were from an academic background. Cyberspace looked like a very manageable, civil, ideal place.

We are at the point in cyberspace's evolution where the commercial world and the mass public have begun to flood into cyberspace, bringing with them all their digital wares, habits and behaviours. That is why we now have millions of websites, hundreds of millions of documents and e-mail. That is why the search engines cannot cope, why there is information overload on a scale hardly imaginable.

It is humans who have caused the Big Bang this time and it is humans who are caught in the middle of it. By throwing on our documents and websites without proper planning, by communicating without proper thought for the response, it is like we are planting forests on our roads. It is like we are creating swamps, rather than draining them. Every day we congest cyberspace even more. Every unit of unplanned content we place in cyberspace adds to the overall confusion, contributes to the rapidly emerging chaos.

Living in Cyberspace

What will it be like living in cyberspace? How will it affect us? Because the Internet is so young, not a lot of solid research is available for the area. Common sense would indicate, though, that spending too much time sitting in front of a computer is not exactly the healthiest thing for a normal human being to do.

In 1998, the first results of a two-year study by researchers at Carnegie Mellon University[11] were released. The initial conclusions were that Internet use appears to cause a decline in your mental health.

"We are not talking here about the extremes," a spokesperson for the study stated. "These were normal adults and their families, and on average for those who used the Internet most things got worse...Our hypothesis is, there are more cases where you're building shallow relationships [on the Internet] leading to an overall decline in feeling of connection to other people."

However, a 1998 ActivMedia[12] study found that after a brief acclimation period, the majority of respondents considered the Internet a "valuable resource for expanding social networks and finding peers with common interests". The study went on to claim that, 54 per cent of respondents "reported that the Internet allows them to more openly express thoughts and feelings".

Interestingly, a number of reports during 1998 indicated that men felt to some degree liberated by e-mail, finding that it was a medium in which they felt more comfortable in expressing themselves in a more open way than in, for example, face to face encounters.

The Activmedia study also wrote about the "Internet's ability to reinforce long-term friendships and family relationships. In an era when the average US family moves every seven years, it is understandably difficult to maintain personal connections over time. Seven in eight FutureScapers (rising to nine in ten with greater online experience) report that the Internet provides a connective link to older, well-established relationships".

Also in 1998, Rutgers' Center for Research on the Information Society,[13] surveyed 2,500 Internet users. Their results found no evidence of social withdrawal. The research indicated that online participants are no less likely to join religious, leisure or community organisations than people who aren't online.

There is of course the situation of people with social or physical disabilities who can be liberated within cyberspace. "I've struck up an online friendship with a teenager afflicted with severe cerebral palsy," Internet pioneer Howard Rheingold is quoted as saying.[14] "This is a person with no other means of communicating with the outside world than punching out messages into a keyboard with a stick on his head, online has widened his world."

There are no simple summaries and descriptions for life in cyberspace. For some it will be a helpful or liberating experience, for others, it will be addictive and debilitating. But then, in life and the way we live it, what's new?

Cyberspace and Physical Space Compared

Physical Space	Cyberspace
Natural Structures	**Artificial Structures**
The Earth.	Cyberspace has no natural structures. Its 'earth' is the network – computers, telecommunications and the data that resides or is being transferred within this environment.
Natural resources.	No natural resources. Only digital bits and bytes.
Life forms.	The only life form is humans, unless we consider software and computers as an emergent life form.
Artificial Structures: Public Artificial Structures	**Public Artificial Structures**
Civil service, political and legal structures.	In many ways, cyberspace, although funded by government, was born and has evolved, at least to some degree, outside its control. (This will change, of course.)
Free public utilities: government and planning, policing and armed forces, certain education, health care, environmental protection, road networks, water, street lighting, public parks, etc.	Until 1996, the cyberspace/Internet infrastructure was almost totally funded by the US government. Many '.org' sites could be seen as free public utilities.
Fee-based public utilities: electricity, public transport, telecommunications, certain health care and educational services.	Governments in the West are currently employing a hands-off approach, allowing private industry (telecomms, Internet service providers, etc.) provide the fee-based public utilities.
Artificial Structures: Private Artificial Structures	**Private Artificial Structures**
Private industry and capitalism.	It is private industry and capitalism that has transformed cyberspace over the last couple of years and that is the driving force for much of its future direction.
Private companies have provided many free structures, often in the form of sponsorship (concerts, parks, directories, etc.).	Private free structures have flourished on the Internet. There are huge free information resources – Yahoo has built its business model around supplying free information.
Communal services and structures: local committees to promote tourism or employment in an area, people who help organise youth activities, people who visit old people, people who contribute to the building of a community centre, etc.	Many of the early community-focused activities on the Internet revolved around free/open source software and 'information wants to be free' philosophies.

The Need for Planning in Cyberspace

Civilisations did not occur by accident. They were the result of much thought and planning. The Roman Empire ruled vast areas not simply because its soldiers could fight. There were many that were more than willing and able to fight in those days. The Romans ruled because they planned and established better order than their enemies.

By 300 AD, the city of Rome covered almost four square miles and had upwards of one million people. To provide water alone for such a population required extraordinary ingenuity. Water was channelled from hills up to 45 miles away and was pumped to individual houses through an amazing network of lead pipes.

China is one of the great civilisations. It too built its empire and civilisation on planning and order, on channelling water. The Chinese have battled for thousands of years to control the great Yangtze River. Deadly floods are common, though it is extraordinary the success that has been achieved. Some 30,000 kilometres of levees, mazes of channels and canal and dikes, along with the world's biggest architectural project, the US$30 billion Three Gorges Dam, are designed to control the flow of the Yangtze, the "river in the sky" which often flows an amazing 10 full metres above underlying basins.

The 'empire' of cyberspace is growing, but it is very often growing without planning and without order. The significant danger exists that cyberspace might well collapse under its own weight if some sort of underlying order is not achieved.

Information is perhaps the *core* material of cyberspace. Information might be called the 'water of cyberspace'. It is everywhere and part of practically everything that exists in cyberspace. As we shall see in the next chapter, *The Three Properties of Information*, information is not information without structure. There is little real underlying structure and planning in cyberspace for information today. There are certainly no Three Gorges Dam projects. The channels and canals are in the form of Yahoo and AltaVista, but these search directories and engines are creaking under the weight of the increasing flow of new information.

We need a comprehensive information infrastructure, and that is a huge undertaking. But it must be undertaken, otherwise, much of the promise of cyberspace will be washed away in the coming information floods.

THE DOUBLING OF SPACE

When you think about it, the so-called 'death of distance' is a myth. Distance hasn't died. It's still there and business people are getting into cars and planes more than ever. What in fact has happened is that with cyberspace we have created two sets of spaces and two sets of distance.

One is the distance between Dublin and New York. The other is the 'distance' that I need to cover to find the information I am looking for. You see, information, in many ways, is the new geography – the new distance.

REFERENCES

1. J Johnson-Eilola, "Stories and Maps: Postmodernism and Professional Communication" Purdue University (1995)
http://tempest.english.purdue.edu/stories/distance.html

2. F Cairncross, *The Death of Distance: How the Communications Revolution will Change our Lives.* (Harvard Business School Press: 1997) (Originally published as an article in *The Economist* in 1995.)

3. *Ibid.*

4. Britannica Online, "City"
http://www.eb.com:180/cgi-bin/g?DocF=micro/129/49.html

5. I Salomon, "Telecommunications and the 'Death of Distance': Some Implications for Transport and Urban Areas" Hebrew University, Israel
http://www.bts.gov/tmip/papers/tmip/udes/salomon.htm

6. B Metcalfe, "Rethinking Big Cities in an Age of Small Towns and Virtual Communities" *InfoWorld* (1997)
http://www.idg.net/idg_frames/english/content.cgi?vc=docid_9-62576.html

7. *Edupage* is one of the best e-mail newsletters on the Internet
http://educause.unc.edu./edupage.html

8. Telecommute Americas, http://smart2.svi.org/telework/

9. *Innovation* Newsletter, http://www.newsscan.com/exec/summer1998/index.html

10. Pitney Bowes, "Workplace Communications in the 21st Century" (1998)
http://www.pitneybowes.com/

11. Carnegie Mellon University, http://www.cmu.edu/
http://www.news.com/News/Item/0,4,26074,00.html

12. Activmedia, FutureScapes Studys, http://www.activmedia.com/

13. Rutgers's Center for Research on the Information Society
    http://www.rutgers.edu/

14. "Study gives Web Users another Reason to be depressed" *New York Times*
    (January 1998), http://www.nytsyn.com/

© Fergal Lawler 1999

4
The Three Properties Of Information:
Content – Structure – Publication

THE DEFINING ROLE OF LANGUAGE

Language is the driver of civilisation and it has never had a more central role than on the present Internet. Because of bandwidth constraints, which means that images and visuals must be kept to a minimum, language has regained a level of importance that it had in many ways lost to visual mediums, such as television.

Information imbues our entire society from top to bottom. It can be delivered in a number of ways, such as by text, visual means and/or body language and mood. Social scientists R Boyd and PJ Richerson[1] have stated that, for example, culture is information transmitted from one generation to the next, by means of teaching and imitation, of knowledge, values and other factors that influence behaviour. However, for the purposes of this chapter, we are going to concentrate on information as written language, since this is what dominates on the current Internet.

Most of us take for granted the central role language has in our society and lives. In an age when everything is changing, including the language we use, it is important to understand more deeply this central position. In a paper entitled "The Great Mosaic Eye",[2] Robin Allott writes about the role of language in society.

> In society language plays a central role; it forms within the individual, within the group, a sense of the cohesion of the group. It creates within each individual images of the group, of the nation, and ultimately of humanity as a whole...Language, family love, social feeling, empathy, allowed the accumulation of experience, the transmission of successful techniques, the extension of the power of the group both in relation to the non-human world and to other human groups. The patterns of group-functioning over many generations, transmitted by spoken language, and later by written language, became established as the morality of the group, the practices that, over the very long-term, had proved successful for the survival and flourishing of the group, and so of the individuals forming the group.

For billions of years progress was extremely slow in the evolution of life on this planet. Single celled organisms dominated. In time, life forms with nervous systems, spines and brains evolved.

Ultimately, the human became the most advanced link in the evolutionary chain. For millions of years the human itself lived a basic and simple life, which was tribal and nomadic. Some 10,000 years ago, this all changed. Settlements grew larger. Modern civilisations and commercial structures emerged.

It has been widely postulated that the sudden development of civilisation was the result of a genetic evolutionary 'accident'. The shape of the throat changed with the result that a greater range of sounds could be produced.

Communication and language, and not the brain per se, is at the root of all civilisation and commerce. The more advanced the communication, the more advanced the civilisation. The size of the human brain had remained essentially the same for millions of years. It was language and the communication of that language that unleashed its creative potential.

In primitive times, humans drew on walls of caves with crude instruments to represent or symbolise things – to communicate. Initially, these symbols were pretty much an exact visual replication of what they were trying to represent (an animal, for example).

The animal, however, represented more than itself. To the human, it was the story of hunting, food, life. Thus, early symbols represented an entire concept or activity. In time, the quantity of symbols expanded, their visual relation to their subject matter loosened and they began to have much more precise meanings. In Western languages, symbols ultimately evolved into abstract alphabets of symbols that had no visual relationship to what they were attempting to describe. (Whereas, in modern Chinese, for example, which is still quite visually representative, there are more than 50,000 symbols in use.)

These abstract letters and the words they help create have become the tools we use to describe our world. They are at the core of how we make contact and make and sell things. They are the building blocks of language. As a general rule, you can measure the rate of change in a culture or society by counting the number of new words that enter its vocabulary in a given period.

Language is at the core of civilisation and community. Language is at the core of history. Language is at the core of science and invention. Language drives commerce. Language is the keeper of culture.

In *Power, Responsibility, Leadership and Learning: An Integrated Approach for the New Millennium*,[3] Dr Bruce Lloyd, Principal Lecturer in Strategy at South Bank University, writes how minds are as much changed by language as language is changed by minds.

> The dynamics of the language employees use to communicate with each other and with management is a key component in helping the company decide what knowledge is legitimate, and what is not as a base from which to see the future. The world both reflects the language we use and is changed by it.

Whenever our language starts filling up with new words, something big is happening. In the last number of years language has seen a lot of new words emerging. The Internet, World Wide Web, websites, webmaster, homepages, search engines, browsers, downsizing, globalisation, cyberspace, virtual companies, nerds, hackers, the list goes on. A frenzy of words attempting to describe, and somehow understand, a frenzy of activity, a frenzy of change.

Paolo Friere in the *Pedagogy of the Oppressed*,[4] emphasises the central importance of words and naming.

> The word is more than just an instrument, which makes dialogue possible...Within the word we find two dimensions: reflection and action...Thus, to speak a true word is to transform the world...To exist, humanly, is to name the world, to change it.

Words are firstly tools of compression. Our minds work as decompressers. When someone says 'door', you don't see the letters 'd-o-o-r'. Rather, you see, often subliminally, a large, wooden, rectangular object. Concepts are advanced compression tools.

In 1947, Max Horkeimer[5] made the following comments on concepts.

> Concepts have been reduced to summaries of the characteristics that several specimens have in common. By denoting similarity, concepts eliminate the bother of enumerating qualities and thus serve better to organise the material of knowledge. They are thought of as mere abbreviations of the items to which they refer. Any use transcending auxiliary, technical summarisation of factual data has been eliminated as a last trace of superstition. Concepts have become streamlined, rationalised, labour saving devices...thinking itself has been reduced to the level of industrial process...in short, made part and parcel of production.

Many of the words and concepts used to describe the Internet, and the digital age in general, have been created casually and have been used in a sweeping and general way. Concepts such as 'information wants to be free' and words such as 'website', 'homepage' or 'webmaster', have been bandied about without many people thinking very deeply about what they actually mean. For those wanting to run successful businesses in the digital age, it is vital that we understand what we are talking about.

We need to understand that these concepts and words were

the initial attempts to put some sort of handle on what was happening. Ask someone today, who works professionally in the area, what a 'webmaster' is and they are likely to respond that there are many functions, skill-sets and people required to keep a quality website up and running, and that there is no such thing as a 'webmaster' anymore.

It is, therefore, important to remember here not to accept any of these new concepts or words blindly. Every concept, every word, needs constant questioning and refinement. The whole area is still forming and these new words are often general and sometimes inaccurate describers. Some of them will fall by the wayside, some of them will develop new meanings. We need to be careful and cautious as we thread through this new, emerging language. (Don't believe everything you read, in a very real sense.)

What is essential though, is that business, and the world in general, actively engages with the new language that is emerging. Perhaps, ironically, as we step into the new millennium, the written word is regaining its old centrality. We who have grown up in a world where visual imagery was increasingly dominant need to significantly readjust our ways of thinking. In the digital age, the website – that great store of textual information – becomes a central place where an organisation is represented and defined.

We need to learn again how fundamentally important written words once were; how text and books drove forward learning, justice, commerce and civilisation. "In the beginning was the Word, and the Word was with God, and the Word was God." Thus, The Gospel according to John stresses the importance of language and naming. In the current Internet – this pre-visual environment – the 'Word' is something every organisation must treat with the greatest of care. For today, it is not enough to create or make something; that is only the job half-done. You must then go out and tell its story in the media and particularly on your website.

In this digital age, this virtual world and realm, it is our website, full of information, that substantiates us, that names us and brands us – that makes us real. If we do not supply a constant flow of comprehensive information to our websites, then we are making ourselves invisible. If we do that we drop off the digital age map. Not being on the map is a recipe for extinction.

WHAT IS INFORMATION?

We live in an 'information' society and economy and there is information everywhere. We need it to work. We need it when we buy things. More and more of what we create and what we buy is made up of information.

Information is indeed everywhere and if we want to play an active part in the digital age, we must become 'information literate'. This requires much more than reading and writing; it requires a deep understanding of what information is and how it behaves within the Internet environment.

So what is information? Many would see information as a type of commodity or resource, as something solid, something identifiable. If information is indeed a resource or commodity, then it certainly does not have the same characteristics as traditional resources and commodities. Resources tend to have a limited supply. Some are renewable, such as fish and forests, though they take time to renew and can be depleted if not properly managed. Some, such as oil and gold are not and are of finite quantity. Commodities have a definite cost attached to their creation, and to the creation of each new unit in any particular line. Information behaves differently.

- Information cannot be consumed; it can only be shared.

- Reproduction of information is generally cost-effective.

When information enters the digital realm, the above attributes are enhanced even further. The Internet allows information to be shared all over the world. While it is relatively expensive to create a physical copy of a book or article, there is an almost zero cost to copy a piece of digital information.

So if information is not really a commodity or a resource, what is it? Part of the answer can be found in exploring the very meaning of the word 'information'.

The *Merriam Webster Dictionary* defines 'information' as "the communication or reception of knowledge or intelligence". The root of 'information' is 'inform', which itself comes from 'form'. The word 'form' finds its origin in the Latin 'fōrma' which means, *'shape'*.

The *Merriam* defines 'inform' as "to give character or essence to: to be the characteristic quality of: to communicate knowledge to: to impart information or knowledge". It defines 'form' as "the shape and structure of something as distinguished from its material: the essential nature of a thing as distinguished from its matter".

Chambers Dictionary defines 'form' as a "shape: a mould: something that holds, shapes: a species: a pattern: a mode of being: a mode of arrangement: order: regularity: system, as of government: beauty". It defines 'inform' as "to give form to: to animate or give life to: to impart a quality to: to impart knowledge to". It defines 'information' as "intelligence given: knowledge".

The 1913 edition of *Webster's Dictionary*, defines 'form' as, "the shape and structure of anything, as distinguished from the material of which it is composed; particular disposition or arrangement of matter, giving it individuality or distinctive character; configuration; figure; external appearance". It defines 'inform' as "to give form or shape to; to give vital organising power to; to give life to; to imbue and actuate with vitality; to animate; to mould; to figure; to fashion". It defines 'information' as "the act of informing, or communicating knowledge or intelligence".

From the above discussion and definitions, we can isolate the primary characteristics that true information must exhibit. These are that it:

(a) is a process or activity, and not an object;

(b) communicates knowledge and intelligence;

(c) is made up of three essential properties: structure, content and the communication or publication of that structured content.

THE THREE PROPERTIES OF INFORMATION

The three properties of information are:

(a) content;

(b) structure;

(c) publication.

Content is the message. It's what you're trying to say. Content is the starting point of all information but it is *only* the starting point.

Structure is how content is put together – it is the 'form' in 'information'. Without structure, content has very little value as it cannot be easily communicated. Structure begins with how a sentence is fashioned. It moves to a paragraph, chapter, table of contents, index, etc. On a website, structure is how you organise and link your information. Lack of structure is behind much of the information overload on the Internet.

Publication is the final property of information. Information, as we have seen, is a verb, not a noun. It is a process, not an object, it is the "*act* of communicating knowledge or intelligence". Publishing is the act of making something public, of getting the structured content out there to your target market. If you don't publish your information, then it doesn't really matter how good the content is or how well it is structured, it will not reach your audience and, therefore, you will have wasted your time.

It is important to note here that creating a website is *not* necessarily an act of publication. The fact that you put a website on the World Wide Web is like opening a shop in your bedroom, or a store on the North Pole. Sitting deep among the millions of other websites, practically nobody will know that it exists unless you actively publicise it.

Measuring Information Value

Webster's Dictionary defines 'value' as, "a fair return or equivalent in goods, services or money for something exchanged". Therefore, we could say that information value can be defined as, "a fair return or equivalent in goods, services, or money for information exchanged". To measure the particular value of a piece of information, using the three properties of information, gives us the following formula.

Information Value = Content x Structure x Publication

Calculating 'information value' involves multiplication rather than addition. To illustrate the multiplier affect, let's say you have 30 hours available to create information value. If you spend fifteen hours on content, fifteen on structure and 0 on publication, what would be your information value? It would be 15 x 15 x 0 = 0. Not publishing your structured content would have been like printing up 100,000 magazines and leaving them in your office.

We should look at the above formula as indicative, but as a general rule it would be true to say that the level at which you will achieve maximum information value is when you are spending an equal amount of time on each property. So, in the original example, you spend ten hours working on the content, ten hours working on the structure and ten hours working on the publication. Thus, the formula would be: 10 x 10 x 10 = 1,000.

THE CHANGING ROLE OF INFORMATION

It has been widely stated that one of the prime reasons, that accentuated the 1998 Asian economic meltdown was the lack of proper information flows in Asian economies. The *New York Times* in October 1998 stated that a major report on the global economic crisis had, "called for the release of far more economic data by countries and companies alike, noting that the lack of such information 'exacerbated' the panic that began in Asia last year".

The *New York Times* also wrote about a World Bank report, which had noted that "information gaps had contributed to the Asian financial crisis. It found that the capital outflows and currency collapse experienced in Thailand, South Korea and Indonesia 'reflected the pervasive lack of information throughout the world about finance in the region'".

Whether we like it or not, we live in a world where the *flow* of information is becoming more and more important. It doesn't matter how well a company is actually performing, if it doesn't properly inform the market and the world, then its stocks will tumble.

Historically, it was not so much information that was seen as power, but actually the *control* of information. Power was wielded by the information you did not give, and many governments, businesses and religious institutions operated with this as their primary principle. Information was seen as gold, and hoarding and protecting it was a favourite activity.

It was also true to say that in an industrial age society, the vast majority of people did not require much ongoing information to do their jobs. Much work required either physical labour and skill (such 'information' being acquired by apprenticeship) or it was administratively repetitious.

Formal education, for the vast majority of people, was not, therefore, about learning knowledge but rather about learning the basics (reading, writing) and most importantly, 'knowing your place'.

In fact, for those in power, there was no incentive to allow information to flow throughout society because this was likely to raise people's awareness and expectations, throwing a light on their monotonous lives and poor living conditions, thus quite probably causing social unrest.

In the digital age, the function of information has changed as a result of:

- modern machinery and computers continuing to replace humans in the sphere of physical labour and skilled trades;

- the explosion in cheap, far-reaching information tools: printing, radio, television, Internet;

- the explosion in the need for information from a growing digital age knowledge workforce.

While in the industrial age information was like gold and hoarded, in the digital age it is like milk and needs to flow quickly to a hungry knowledge workforce, or to a consumer society hungry for news (and scandal). Today, a society that does not allow for the rapid diffusion of information at every level is quite simply not an information society, and is merely shoving its arm in the dyke of the modern media-saturated age.

So much about the digital age makes it difficult to hoard information. The very act of organising and storing information is becoming an increasingly difficult task. In this fluid, digital world, trying to keep such information 'safe' and out of the flow is equally time consuming. Companies are finding that with the Internet, and other networks, it is almost impossible to lock information away.

In many circumstances, the time spent keeping information safe would have been better spent acting upon the information, and, of course, you may find that no sooner have you organised and made the information 'safe' than it has lost its value – gone sour.

CHANGING INFORMATION CHANGES
STATE, BUSINESS, ETC.

The change from an industrial society to an information society has been a shock to the system to the historical centres of information: the Church, State and business. Many of the people

working in these institutions have failed to recognise the information shift that has occurred and have tried to play by the old
rules, often with disastrous results.

The Catholic Church, the State and the business sector in
Ireland, for example, has had a trying time in the last ten years,
as the floodgates of information have been opened up. Whereas,
historically, these institutions sat in stern silence, stonewalling,
or even intimidating, those who requested information (particularly with regard to wrongdoing within these institutions), today
this stonewalling has been washed away in the bright lights of
the new, questioning age.

These institutions are learning painful lessons about openness, transparency and accountability. They are realising that, in
an information society with a highly questioning populace, the
only strategy is to be as open as possible.

Commenting on how the role and function of information is
changing the very essence of how companies behave, digital age
pioneer Esther Dyson wrote in 1994 in "Intellectual Value"[6] that:

> ...companies will – must – become more visible. More of
> what any company sells will comprise information –
> whether it's plain bits over the Net or consulting services,
> design services, management development.
>
> As in the past, some companies will sell products to
> myriad customers; others will add value to only a few key
> ones. But in a knowledge world, the quality of those rela-
> tionships will matter more than the contractual conditions
> (as in a marriage). The best cement is a two-way flow of
> information, or visibility. Companies will try to find part-
> ners not by offering discounts but by sharing information
> about themselves and by exchanging their competitive
> wisdom. In order to make their wisdom credible, they will
> have to be self-revealing.

Dyson gave a strong warning to those companies that feel that
they can continue to behave as if they were still operating in the
industrial age.

> Whether or not a company chooses to be visible, it will
> happen. You can't hide. And the image you project – on
> your Web home page or elsewhere – will and should be
> true. It's not just outsiders peering in, it's your own

employees out in the electronic world: they are the company.

In a digital age environment, the product is increasingly the information. The product is also how you deliver that information and interact with your customers, employees, investors, media, etc.

In the industrial age, those who controlled industry controlled wealth. In the digital age, those who use information most effectively, control wealth. Again, we need to recall our earlier exploration of the word 'information' and remember that it is as much about a process and a structure as it is about content.

That is why Yahoo is one of the most valuable Internet companies. Although Yahoo is getting more into creating original content and content partnerships, it built its brand and reputation because it was a quality directory of the best sites on the Internet – because it was providing *structure* for the content on the Internet.

CHANGES IN HOW INFORMATION IS CREATED

In the industrial age, information leant more towards a commodity than a process. We had lots of information units in the form of books and reports, films and television shows. In such an age it was also relatively easy to decide who owned or created what information.

It was also true that the act of creation of information 'units' was a relatively solitary exercise quite simply because of the very tools available. It was difficult to share a pen and paper, difficult to create a co-operative information 'unit' in that solitary environment. The writer plied a lonely trade and, therefore, the results from such solitary activity were usually identifiable to one person.

With the Internet, and other networks, sharing and co-operation with regard to intellectual activities have become much easier. It is perhaps no surprise that in the academic and scientific environment – the very environments out of which the Internet has evolved – there has been a steady trend towards scientists and academics creating shared research and papers. Is this a general trend for how information will increasingly be created in the digital age? I believe so. Increasingly, we will see less individual authors and more co-operative efforts.

CREATING VALUE FROM INFORMATION

Getting value from information is not simply about getting paid for it in financial terms. Scientists and scholars, for example, often have different motivations with regard to information than commercial creators have. As Ann Okerson wrote in her *Scientific American* article, "Who Owns Digital Works?":[7]

> Most scientists and scholars are far more interested in the widest possible distribution of their work to their professional colleagues than in capturing every possible royalty dollar.

Why do we want to own things? Is it so that we can feel proud of owning things? Is it so that we can get value out of them? Think about it for a moment, and ask yourself this question: How much do I truly, absolutely own? Do you own your house and car or does the bank and leasing company own it? Do you own land?

My uncles own land in one of the most rural areas in Ireland. They have lived in a cottage all their lives, remote and without an inside toilet. Lately, they have decided to build a bathroom onto the cottage. They had started work when someone reminded them that they needed planning permission. Although they owned their land and there was nobody within miles of them, they had limited rights with regard to how they could use it.

The point I'm trying to illustrate here is that, when it boils down to it, 'ownership' is not really the issue for an individual or company when it comes down to gaining value. As with my uncles, you can own something and not be able to get the value you want from it. Use and value are what really matter. Who cares who owns what, once you can use something and get value from it?

COPYRIGHT: 'PROTECTING' INFORMATION

In industrial age economies, it was very important to protect what you had. Creators of information, and their publishers, protected themselves by use of copyright. *Chambers Dictionary* defines copyright as, "the sole right to reproduce a literary, dramatic, musical or artistic work – also to perform, translate, film or record such a work". According to *Copyright and Fair Use*, by Curtis R Cook:[8]

The copyright protects the tangible form in which the idea or concept is expressed and not the idea or concept itself. For example another author can write a book with a similar plot, but cannot copy the words of the original, give it a title and sell it.

A comprehensive approach to copyright law was not enacted until the early 18th century. However, issues of copyright date back much further, as Ann Okerson pointed out in her *Scientific American* article "Who Owns Digital Works?":

> One of the earliest copyright disputes, from 6th century Ireland, sets the tone. St Columba had copied out for himself a manuscript of the Latin Psalter, and the owner of the original, Finnian of Druim Finn, objected. The king ruled: 'As the calf belongs to the cow, so the copy belongs to its book.'

It is interesting to note how the American Constitution views copyright. Article I, section 8 states that:

> The Congress shall have Power to promote the Progress of Science and useful Arts, by securing for limited Times to Authors and Inventors the exclusive Right to their respective Writings and Discoveries.

It is clear that the emphasis of the Article is not so much on the rights of the author but rather focuses on the good of the public and the desire to "promote the Progress of Science and useful Arts". Authors are given limited rights so as to encourage them to create works that will be useful to the public.

Copyright has thus been a balancing act between protecting the rights of the creator and publisher and ensuring the general rights of society to 'fair use' and the 'free exchange of ideas'. That is why the granting of copyright, for example, is rarely permanent. Usually, it is for the life of the creator and some fixed period (50-70 years) after his or her death. As John Perry Barlow wrote in a *Wired* article:[9]

> When Jefferson and his fellow creatures of the Enlightenment designed the system that became American copyright law, their primary objective was assuring the widespread distribution of thought, not profit.

The principle of 'fair use' limits the rights of the copyright owner. This allows someone to copy a limited amount of the author's work without asking permission. Under what circumstances this can occur and what amount can be copied tends to vary from case to case, though generally, but not exclusively, criticism and comment, news reporting, research and scholarship, non-profit educational uses and parody, would fall under the fair use principle.

Copyright faces a number of challenges in the digital age, including the following.

- Things digital are extremely easy and cheap to copy and it is very difficult if not often impossible to monitor what is being copied. (See Chapter 10: *Things Digital*.)

- A digital creation may involve sound, images and text; copyright tends to have different rules depending on the medium. Figuring out the correct copyright approach for such a multimedia creation poses new challenges.

- With things digital, it is very easy to take slices or excerpts and to manipulate these to create something that may or may not be 'new'.

- Because of the ease of copying and manipulation, the lines between fair use and abuse are greyed even further.

It would be foolish for anyone to think that, because of these challenges, copyright will suddenly disappear in the digital age. Copyright has a very real function in ensuring that those who create something get a fair return on it. Publishers, who are also looking for their fair return, of course, will certainly not give up on copyright easily in the digital domain. Copyright will and is changing but it will not disappear.

What is evident though, is that copyright, and the general protection of intellectual property and information, must change in an environment that is radically changing. Information has very different functions today. It is created differently and value can be gained from it differently. We need new thinking here.

It also needs to be recognised that, while, undoubtedly, the Internet poses serious challenges to copyright and the protection of intellectual property, the medium itself, and other digital age technologies, may in certain circumstances make copyright protection easier.

- Crytographic technologies allow digital works to be protected by strong software codes which require special 'software
  keys' to open.

- In physical intellectual property, the original is where the central value lies, and the older the original often the more value
  it acquires. Certainly, in the case of software, the value of having the original is much less than having the 'latest version'. In
  fact, the older the original the less value it has. In many
  instances we are seeing a 'rent' of intellectual property (guaranteeing the latest version) rather than a straight-out purchase.

- Because duplication and copying is so easy in an Internet
  environment, it has started to cloud the whole environment
  with 'digital pollution'. Many people will prefer to stay with
  trusted sources where they are guaranteed a quality product,
  rather than venture out into the 'free zone' where it is hard to
  find what they want and where poor quality and viruses lay
  in wait.

- Because of the massive information overload now facing the
  Internet, people may be willing to pay for 'information
  guides' (perhaps authors and/or publishers) who will save
  them time and get them the right information, which might in
  itself be 'free'.

Making 'Free' Information Pay

If someone came to visit your office, you wouldn't charge them
for parking or using the lift, would you? You wouldn't charge
them for sitting down on the chair in your office? You wouldn't
charge them for the coffee or tea offered? When you bring a
client out to dinner, do you expect them to foot their half of the
bill?

In an offline business world, there are many things that we do
not charge for. Why don't we charge for them? Because we want
to create an appropriate context, within which to offer our product or service, and to do business. We are trying to establish a
sense of integrity, trust, partnership. A company, for example,
may spend a substantial amount of money on its buildings, in an
attempt to reflect its image; to provide context for its brand.

It is also true that a company provides actual information offline that is free, whether it is in the form of brochures, product
details or staff giving free advice. Therefore, providing free infor-

mation on the Internet is doing absolutely nothing new from a business practice point of view. In fact, online you need to provide substantially more information just to match the free value and symbols of integrity that you provide every day in a physical context.

On the Internet, information is your symbol of integrity, reliability – it is your trust builder. You can't build impressive, marble edifices online, but you can impress by the quality and consistency of your information. Providing some of it free is like offering a cup of coffee to potential clients. You make your free information pay by creating the impression with people that there's more where that came from and if you're willing to pay for it you'll get real value.

Giving away what was previously proprietary information on the Internet can also pay off in more direct ways.

> "Three years ago Rough Guides, a travel guidebook publisher based in London, took a bold, unprecedented step," *The Industry Standard* reported in 1998.[10] "The company placed the full text of several of its most popular travel guides on the Web. It was giving away the milk for free; but who would buy the cow?"

According to Jean Marie Kelly, Rough Guides' associate publisher, the cow was doing just fine, with *The Industry Standard* reporting that:

> Every year since Rough Guides launched its site, book sales have increased at least 20 per cent. In 1996, the company sold 825,000 books; in 1997, 1.1 million; this year, the company projects a jump to 1.5 million. Research shows that most people want to take travel guides with them on trips, and so it seems the online channel complements, rather than cannibalises, book sales.

The philosophy of making free information pay is not quite the same as Stewart Brand's phrase 'information wants to be free'. The implication here is that it will become increasingly difficult to gain economic return from information in the digital age. I don't believe that to be the case at all; quite the opposite, in fact. It may be that value is created at new points on the information value chain, but value nonetheless can be created.

Stating that, 'information wants to be free' is a bit like saying 'water wants to flow'. Water may want to flow, but sometimes it is kept in dams, with its flow regulated, while in our homes we regulate its flow with taps. Information is for us to use, to manipulate and to create value from.

Nua Internet Surveys

Since 1996, the Nua Internet Surveys website (www.nua.ie/surveys) has been a Nua implementation of the 'making free information pay' strategy. The Nua Internet Surveys site is based on a number of founding principles.

- That information is one of the key drivers in an information society.

- That it is better to cater for 'niche' information needs.

- That you should supply information that is relevant to your target market.

- That supplying information to the media is an essential function today.

- That you give away 'free' information, so as to get back brand recognition, trust and loyalty – and future business.

- That the Internet is the perfect environment within which to leverage already existing information and create new value from it.

- That in an age of information overload, those who save people time by supplying the right information will make money.

- That on the Internet it is vital to have a long-term vision and back up that vision with investment and commitment.

This site has become the world's premier resource for Internet trends and demographics. As of January 1999, between the website and the weekly e-mail, it reached over 150,000 people every week. It has been translated into Russian, German, Greek, Portuguese, Italian, Hebrew and Spanish.

The Nua Internet Surveys[11] website has two particular target audiences.

1. Journalists, consultants and Internet opinion leaders.

2. Managers who are creating business plans for Internet developments.

Journalists and consultants find Nua Internet Surveys a very valuable resource. It gives them quality, well-organised and searchable information. They pay by referencing Nua widely, thus building the Nua brand. There are few better ways to build a brand than to have respected third parties reference you.

As a result, the Nua Internet Surveys website has been quoted by such publications as *USA Today*, *ABC News*, CNN online, Yahoo, *ZDNet*, Mecklermedia, *Wall Street Journal*, *The Irish Times*, *The Australian*, the US Department of Commerce, etc.

Wired magazine has written a story about it, American Vice President Al Gore has quoted its figures, and it have been described by the *San Jose Mercury* (*the* newspaper of Silicon Valley) as "*the* place to go to when you're confused about the Internet". *The Guardian* newspaper voted Nua Internet Surveys as one of its top ten websites of 1998.

Managers, who seriously want to develop for the Internet, need to put together a business plan. Part of that plan invariably involves an analysis of Internet demographic and trend information. There is no better place on the Internet to get such information than at the Nua Internet Surveys website.

Thus, what happens is that Nua gets into the mind-space and becomes a trusted resource for the manager. This is a clear advantage for Nua over its competitors when the manager is looking a company to help them implement their plan. As a result, Nua has acquired clients such as Procter & Gamble, Lucent Technologies, Thomas Publishing and Gateway.

In creating the information for Nua Internet Surveys, Nua uses a technique, which we call 'information sampling'. Like music rappers sample classic riffs from old songs, so as to create new songs, Nua Internet Surveys samples/summarises quality information from reports and articles on Internet trends and demographics. The added value that Nua Internet Surveys delivers is that it brings together into one central resource, in a highly structured manner, all this information. The other information sources are happy to be 'sampled' by Nua, because if the person wants the 'full story' there is a direct link to the source.

The Nua Internet Surveys website also seeks to minimise the cost of production of information by maximising the database potential of the information. Let's say, for example, that we have come across a report on e-commerce in Europe. What happens is that when the article on this report is being put together, it is written in such a way that the first sentence can stand on its own as a summary of the rest of the article. It is then entered into the database and is categorised by date, geographic area and by subject matter (e-commerce, intranets, travel, etc.).

Then the database takes the heading, date, and first line of the article, and places it on the front page, with the full story behind it as a link. The same story can then also be accessed by choosing 'Europe' under the geographic categories, and/or by choosing 'e-commerce' under the subject matter categories.

Thus, the story has created four points of potential value. The first is as a heading and first line summary. The second is as an article by chronological context. The third is as an article within the context of other European stories. The fourth is as an article within the context of other e-commerce stories.

INFORMATION OVERLOAD

Industrial age societies often faced issues of scarcity; scarcity of oil, scarcity of fish, scarcity of timber. Many industrial age scarcity problems were as a result of careless management of resources. We have the same careless management of information and content today, only this time we are creating a *glut* of information, rather than a scarcity. One is as bad as the other.

Think about it for a moment, and ask yourself the following question: How well do I manage the space on my hard disk? I know what my answer is: "Not very well." Every day, drafts and drafts of digital documents are produced. Files are stored, not because of their value, but because it is easier to store them than to delete them. Things are published on the Internet because they *can* be published. E-mails are sent because it is easy to send them, not because of their communication value.

Information overload is the single greatest problem not simply facing the Internet but facing all of us in practically every aspect of life in the digital age.

Information overload can manifest itself in a variety of ways.

- Lack of planning with regard to how information is organised leads to an environment where it becomes increasingly difficult to find what you're looking for.

- Lack of 'weeding' of old and redundant information obstructs the paths to quality information.

- Lack of proper standards with regard to the publishing of information results in poor quality and error-prone content.

- The ease of copying and cheap storage encourages people to create masses of generally unnecessary copies.

- People can receive so much 'quality' information that they simply do not have time to take it all in.

- People, who have not been trained in information analysis and management, feel overwhelmed even when they have to deal with what should be average information demands.

- People can become 'addicted' to information, always wanting more information before they make a decision, so that they rarely make the decision on time.

The signs of information overload are all around us today. According to the *Encyclopaedia Britannica*:[12]

> The volume of books printed in 16th century Europe is estimated to have doubled approximately every seven years. Interestingly, the same growth rate has been calculated for global scientific and technical literature in the 20th century and for business documents in the United States in the 1980s.

This is the phenomenon called exponential growth. Think of it this way: If a lily doubles in size every day and it takes it 30 days to cover a pond, how many days does it take it to cover one eighth of the pond? Answer: 27 days. For all but the last couple of days the lily is hardly noticeable in the pond. Then in the last couple of days, following exponential growth, it explodes across the pond. Right now, information is exploding across the pond.

A 1998 study entitled "Workplace Communications in the 21st Century" conducted by the Institute of the Future, for Pitney Bowes,[13] had some interesting findings.

> The average worker across a broad range of positions, from administrative to senior executives, say they now send or receive approximately 190 messages on any given day. This volume of messaging, and the corresponding demands of managing the flow and responding in a timely and efficient manner, now shape how people in many different positions and industries actually structure their day.

A 1997 Reuters survey[14] of 1,000 business managers found that a growing number of them were addicted to information and the Internet. More than 50 per cent said that they didn't have the capacity to assimilate all the information they were getting. Ninety-seven per cent believed that their companies should provide courses in information management training.

In April 1998, NEC Research published a survey which claimed that there were already 320 million pages on the Internet and that this would grow by 1,000 per cent over the coming years.[15] The research claimed that even the most comprehensive search engine was only managing to categorise 34 per cent of all available pages.

> "Hundreds of pages are being added constantly," survey co-author Steve Lawrence told the *San Jose Mercury*. "There is no simple way to index it all. There could be any percentage of pages out there that nobody has actually accessed yet."

The impeachment of President Clinton broke a lot of records on the Internet. During the period that trial spent in the House of Representatives, House members were receiving an average of 1 million e-mails a day. When the trial moved to the Senate, the average daily number of e-mails moved from 70,000 to 500,000. Delivery delays ensued and systems crashed as the 100 senators were deluged with e-mails. A spokeswoman for a Senator claimed that e-mail had been, "rendered almost useless. We've been told not to rely on the e-mail system and not to use it to respond to constituents".

Searching for Information

Most of us don't spend our morning searching for a way to get to work. But we do increasingly spend our lives searching for information.

It is an irony of the digital age and the so-called 'leisure society' that knowledge workers and consumers are spending an increasing amount of their time searching. Surely, with all our advanced technology and software, the emphasis should be on 'finding', not 'searching'?

To some degree the reason why we have search directories and search engines is reflective of the early Internet and the pioneers that populated it. The early Internet was indeed a pioneering territory, full of individuals, full of adventure and the desire to explore. For this type of people to search for things was an interesting challenge.

As the Internet has matured, the vast majority of people who have started using it are not there as pioneers. The Internet to them is a tool rather than an end in itself. It is a thing to be used, not conquered. These people – the great majority of the population – see searching as something we do when we are lost. We don't like being lost. If we are looking for something we want to find it quickly.

But we have already seen that search engines are falling behind in their job of charting and organising the Internet. The Internet is simply growing too fast. At 1998 levels, it took AltaVista, one of the Internet's most useful search engines, almost two months to index what is out there. By the end of the process, vast quantities of new information had been entered onto the Internet, and much of the pre-existing information had been updated or changed. The popular search directory, Yahoo, links to less than 10 per cent of the sites available on the Internet.

ZDNet columnist, Jesse Berst,[16] made a stinging commentary on search engines and directories in 1998 by pointing out that they are:

- very poor at their core job;

- getting worse;

- doing it deliberately.

At a most basic level, search engines make advertising revenue by keeping you within their website. Yahoo's extraordinary market value is not because of its directory; it's because of its brand. Yahoo's strategy – and that of many of the other search sites – is to constantly leverage its brand, offering a stream of services from financial to free e-mail which keep people longer within the Yahoo environment. As these services expand there becomes less and less of an incentive for a search site to direct people outside its environment, particularly if what the person is searching for may be a service that the search site offers.

It's not all bad news about searching on the Internet. New search processes are using innovative ways of creating order and refining your search. Such approaches can involve prioritising search results in relation to how many previous times a page has been clicked on or that page has been linked to.

> "If you create a hyperlink page, you're suggesting to read-
> ers of one page that they should go out and read another
> page," inventor of the Web, Tim Berners-Lee, has stated.
> "Those suggestions are very powerful. It's the links which
> are actually creating order on the Web."

Two new search technologies, which indicate how future search
processes will be carried out, include Goggle by Direct Hit
Technologies and IBM's Clever.

> "The principle [of Clever] is to exploit the work of millions
> of participants on the Web, who are all over the world, cre-
> ating pages without any centrally directed motivation,"
> Prabhakar Raghavan, a researcher at IBM told *The Industry
> Standard*.[17]

> "You are important [or your website is important] if you
> are pointed to by important people," Larry Page, creator of
> Goggle stated.

This movement towards a new kind of search is positive because
it stops relying purely on raw processing power and starts feeding off the behaviour, likes and dislikes of people using the
Internet. The process is a bit like word of mouth and should,
therefore, have a strong chance of success, considering that the
Internet is the largest word of mouth environment in the world.

INTELLIGENT AGENTS

In some technology circles, intelligent agents were all the rage
around 1994/95. They didn't live up to expectations and have
since moved off the radar screen for many Internet commentators. I believe that their time will come, though it may take a
number of years before they become broadly popular.

Intelligent agents are pieces of software that learn our habits,
our likes and dislikes, our wants, our needs, and then go off into
cyberspace looking to fulfil those needs. For example, if we want
a cheap holiday in the sun, we inform our agent and then the
agent goes off, gets the best prices and options and brings them
back to us so that we can choose.

There are all sorts of types of intelligent agents but they are all based on the principle that a piece of software can help us find what we're looking for in an efficient manner. In some ways, these agents can be seen as advanced search engines. Others have compared them to the digital age equivalent of English butlers; endlessly obedient, never talking back.

While not a pure intelligent agent, priceline.com offers an intelligent agent-type service. Priceline.com informs us that:

> It's simple, yet powerful. Priceline is a buying service that lets you name your price...The first service available through priceline enables leisure travellers to name their own price for leisure airline tickets. You name the price you want to pay and priceline finds a major airline willing to release seats on flights where they have unsold space.

Essentially, priceline.com offers to find what you want for a fee. It becomes a type of search 'middleman'. Expect to see more such services in the future.

PERSONALISATION

The objective of personalisation is to allow you to customise the website to your particular needs. The payoff? As far as Adam Penenberg of Forbes[18] is concerned, personalisation results in, "user loyalty, which leads to greater retention, more page views and, ultimately, greater advertising revenue". According to Penenberg, the "trend toward personalisation is occurring across the commerce board – from financial services to online after-sales service to online record clubs to business to business selling".

A particular advantage of personalisation is that it establishes a profile for the user. By allowing a consumer to choose which areas within your website they like, you glean what sort of information needs they have. You can then track their behaviour patterns within your website.

There are problems with personalisation and they can probably be best illustrated by an experience I had with the Lycos search engine. When I type the website address 'www.lycos.com' into my browser and hit return, I don't go to lycos.com. Instead, I am sent to lycos.co.uk. The Lycos website is clever. It is able to recognise that I am located in Ireland and thinks to itself that it should send me to its UK directory, that being my neighbour. But I didn't want the UK directory and it took me quite a while to actually figure out how to get to the American site.

Personalisation should be left up to people themselves. It should also be easily reversible. Learning from people's habits or behaviour patterns can be a good idea, but you need to be very careful not to make the wrong assumptions or see patterns where there really are none.

FINDING IS A SKILL

Most of us have probably seen corny television advertising programmes that promote health and fitness equipment. A particular thing that strikes me about these programmes is the type of promise that many of them make. It is that you can get fit and keep in shape *without any real pain*. The models, who are working out, are all smiling and happy. 'Fun' is the big word – gain without the pain.

I think it is one of the great illusions of technology and the digital age that we can have it both ways. No matter how clever software and technology becomes, we will never escape a basic rule of life: 'no pain, no gain'. We may try to take short cuts, or be effusively promised them by digital age snake oil merchants, but in most cases we will end up walking the long way home.

There has been too much false promise and hype about the Internet. It's not easy to have an effective website and it's not easy to find what you're looking for. Finding is a skill. As with all skills, it requires learning and practice. Too many people assume that all they have to do is go to a search engine, type in a keyword, and that they should by some right find what they are looking for instantly.

Even if information was extremely well-organised, there is simply too much information to make finding exactly what you want a simple process. While in the early days, we all learned as we went along with regard to searching the Internet, more formal training procedures will have to be set in place in the future. Ideally, information management should become part of the core curriculum of schools and educational establishments.

THE NEED FOR INFORMATION INFRASTRUCTURE

New search technologies may, indeed, make it easier for people to find what they are looking for, but it is my firm belief that information overload is a more fundamental problem, which will not be solved by new search engines alone. Companies and countries and other entities that want to gain proper benefit from the Internet must plan for, and install, a comprehensive information infrastructure.

The key challenge today is to order what we have and not to create more information waste. A city that does not have an overall plan, covering housing, traffic, green spaces and amenities, etc., is one that invites long-term chaos and decline. Seriously developing for the Internet requires a comprehensive information plan. Otherwise, poor content and poor structures will choke off much of the useful information. Poor information will grow like weeds.

An organisation will require a sound information architecture foundation if it is to build anything that will have a long-term capacity to grow and remain useful. Organisations will require information planners, editors, archivists and 'librarians', whose job will be to put order on the information, to place the information in context, on its proper 'shelf'.

I don't know who described the Internet (circa 1995-1999) as like a library with all the books on the floor and with the lights turned out, but it was a fairly apt description. We need to turn the lights on and start putting the 'books' onto their proper shelves.

In 1998, it became generally recognised that information overload was reaching a crisis point. Inventor of the World Wide Web, Tim Berners-Lee told the *Los Angeles Times* that:[19]

> Whereas phase one of the Web put all the accessible information into one huge book, if you like, in phase two we will turn all the accessible data into one huge database. This will have a tremendous effect on e-commerce . . . You could say, 'find me a company selling a half-inch bulb to these specifications', and a program will go through all the catalogues – which may be presented in very different formats – and figure out which fields are equivalent and then build a database and do a comparison very quickly. Then it will just go ahead and order it. It would be a real mistake for anyone to think the Internet is done or the World Wide Web is done. We're just at the start of these technologies.

Indeed we are just at the start of a very long road. Creating a widely accepted, comprehensive information infrastructure on the Internet is a massive task that will take years to complete.

Some preliminary steps on this road have been taken. The 'Dublin Core' initiative and 'meta-tagging' being two examples. However, so much more is still to be done. A broadly accepted international standard, such as the Dewey system for libraries, which would deal with the organisation and categorisation of information, is badly needed.

At a basic level, this information infrastructure will have to categorise information *before* it is entered onto the Internet, not after as is the case with search engines and directories today.

Think of it this way: nobody publishes a book today without some sort of library categorisation information. On each book's back cover is a unique number, as well as a subject categorisation (business, philosophy, fiction, etc.) Nobody publishes a business book without a table of contents, and most business books have an index.

In the future, every picture or image, for example, stored in cyberspace will be asked a certain number of questions: When was this picture taken? Who is the copyright owner? Where was it taken? What geographic category does this picture fit into? What information category does this picture fit into? An equivalent set of questions will be asked of an article or other unit of text. Once these questions have been answered, it will be possible to build a proper map, which will allow people to find what they are looking for in the most efficient way.

THE INFORMATION VALUE CHAIN

From exploring information in a comprehensive manner throughout this chapter, it becomes evident that information links across a long chain of activities. Creating quality content is a huge area in itself. Those familiar with publishing will know that journalists go off and create quality content, but that it is then up to editors to put final shape and structure on that content. The distribution network is an entirely different area, requiring logistical and promotional skills.

Historically, information was packaged into specific units (newspapers, books, magazines) and then sold to the consumer. There was thus a very clear point at which the publisher 'cashed-in' their information value. On the Internet, things are not nearly as simple.

In 1994, Esther Dyson wrote about how on the Internet the value of intellectual property was shifting away from the unit or product itself and towards, "services, to the selection of content, to the presence of other people, and to the assurance of authenticity – reliable information about sources of bits and their future flows. In short, intellectual assets and property depreciate while intellectual processes and services appreciate".[20]

The important thing to note here is that there are more ways than one to gain value out of information. The value you achieve may be indirect, for example, in that people will think more highly of your organisation, rather than pay you for a piece of information, but value nonetheless it is.

Information is a complex entity that is radically changing its form and function in a digital age economy. It is, unfortunately, something many organisations have spent very little time focusing on and planning for.

In the media age of the 1960s onwards, Marshall McLuhan wrote about how "the medium is the message". In the digital age, it is increasingly the case that "information is the product".

REFERENCES

1.   R Boyd and P J Richerson, *Culture and the Evolutionary Process* (Chicago: University of Chicago Press) 1985

2.   R Allott, "The Great Mosaic Eye",
     http://www.percep.demon.co.uk/rolelang.htm

3.   B Lloyd, *Power, Responsibility, Leadership And Learning: An Integrated Approach for the New Millennium* (South Bank University)
     http://www.scenario-planning.com/art5.htm

4.   P Freire, *Pedagogy of the Oppressed* (New York: Continuum) 1971

5.   J Weizenbaum, *Computer Power and Human Reason: From Judgement to Calculation* (New York: WH Freeman and Company) 1976, page 249

6.   E Dyson, "Intellectual Value" *Wired* (July 1995)
     http://www.wired.com/wired/archive/3.07/dyson.html

7.   A Okerson, "Who Owns Digital Works?" *Scientific American* (July 1996)
     http://www.sciam.com/

8.   C R Cook, *Copyright and Fair Use* (Oregon State University)
     http://www.cs.orst.edu/~cook/copyr.html

9. J P Barlow, "The Economy of Ideas" *Wired* (March 1994)
    http://www.wired.com/wired/archive/2.03/economy.ideas.html?topic
    =&topic_set=

10. Shapiro, "Giving it all Away" *The Industry Standard* (26 October 1998)
    http://www.industrystandard.net/articles/display/0,1449,2175,00.html

11. Nua Internet Surveys, http://www.nua.ie/surveys/

12. Britannica Online, "Information Processing and Information Systems:
    Information Systems: Impact of Computer-based Information Systems on
    Society," http://www.eb.com:180/cgibin/g?DocF=macro/5003/15/38.html

13. "Workplace Communications in the 21st Century" Pitney Bowes (1998)
    http://www.pitneybowes.com/

14. Reuters, http://www.reuters.com/

15. S Lawrence C L Giles, "How big is the Web? How much of the Web do
    the Search Engines Index? How up to date are the Search Engines?" NEC
    Research Institute (April 1998)
    http://www.neci.nj.nec.com/homepages/lawrence/websize.html

16. J Berst, "Search Sites' Shocking Secret" *ZDNet AnchorDesk*
    (17 August 1998)
    http://www.zdnet.com/anchordesk/story/story_2432.html

17. M Frauenfelder, "The Future of Search Engines" *The Industry Standard*
    (25 September 1998)
    http://www.thestandard.net/articles/display/0,1449,1826-2,00.html

18. A L Penenberg, "Me, Myself, I" *Forbes DigitalTool* (22 May 1998)
    http://www.forbes.com/tool/html/98/may/0522/side1.htm

19. Tim Berners-Lee in an interview with the *Los Angeles Times* (1998)
    http://www.latimes.com

20. E Dyson, "Intellectual Value" *Wired* (July 1995)
    http://www.wired.com/wired/archive/3.07/dyson.html

5
Truths and Myths of
the Information Society

THE INFORMATION SOCIETY

"The traditional factors of production – land, labor and capital – are becoming restraints rather than driving forces," Peter Drucker, long one of the most influential thinkers on the role of information in an economy, told *Wired* in 1993.[1] "Knowledge has become the central, key resource that knows no geography. It underlies the most significant and unprecedented social phenomenon of this century. No class in history has ever risen as fast as the blue-collar worker and no class has ever fallen as fast. All within less than a century."

Drucker finished the above quotation with a severe sting in the tail. The information society, for all its benefits, is a very volatile place. In sport, they say that you're only as good as your last game. In the information society, you're only as good as your last piece of information.

(For the purposes of this book, I am treating 'knowledge' and 'information' as being essentially the same thing. As we learned in the previous chapter, information is defined as the "act of communicating intelligence or knowledge".)

> "A knowledge driven economy is one in which the generation and the exploitation of knowledge has come to play the predominant part in the creation of wealth," the British Department of Trade and Industry wrote in 1998.[2] "It is not simply about pushing back the frontiers of knowledge; it is also about the more effective use and exploitation of *all types of knowledge* in *all manner of economic activity.*"

The 1998 World Bank's World Development Report[3] stated that:

> For countries in the vanguard of the world economy, the balance between knowledge and resources has shifted so far towards the former that knowledge has become perhaps the most important factor determining the standard of living. Today's most technologically advanced economies are truly knowledge-based.

The *Foresight Project*,[4] an initiative led by New Zealand's Ministry of Research, Science and Technology, has stated that, in an information society:

> ...individuals who are well-educated, self-motivated, and linked into information networks, are the most likely to live prosperous and fulfilling lives. Enterprises that are attuned to their customers' requirements, employ educated workers, encourage innovation through their workplace organisation, and know more and learn faster than their competitors, are the most likely to succeed and grow. At the national level, societies that maximise opportunities for individuals and enterprises to develop knowledge-age skills and access knowledge-age services, and that enable people to share a common sense of national identity and belonging, are the most likely to be cohesive.

In the industrial age, education was not, except for an elite few, so much geared at creating learned people, but rather good citizens who knew their place and could join the ranks of factory and office workers, the current thinking goes. Stimulating the imagination of children who would spend their working lives in dull, monotonous jobs, did not make sense from the point of view of economic and social order. For the vast majority of people the essential things to be learned were to read, write, add and know your place.

We are increasingly living within a society driven by information, whether it is in the form of productive information or information as entertainment, we are endlessly told. For those who want a prosperous future, the issue in the digital age is not what you know but your ability to learn.

"It's an old-fashioned idea, but the most important thing to do is to learn how to learn," John Nasbitt, author of *Global Paradox: The Bigger the World Economy, the more Powerful its Smallest Players*, told *Wired*.[5]

Change involves movement, a shift in things. The shift as we move from the industrial age to the digital age is enormous. So much of the ground is moving and, therefore, so many of the ground rules are changing.

What we know and what we have learned is increasingly losing its relevance. The ability today is to know how to learn – how to be a life-long learner. Memorising and learning by rote may have got us through things in the past. However, for better or worse, the computer has become our memory in many situations. Its memory can store so much.

The issue for people today is not so much to remember, but to be able to evaluate and act upon information as never before. The old formulas don't work so well. Very little can be guaranteed, very little taken for granted.

And yet, so many jobs that are being created today are low-paid, low-knowledge service jobs. It could be said that the computer, instead of raising the general level of knowledge within society, is in fact dumbing down society. The skilled manufacturing jobs are being taken over by robots and automated processes. You either become an elite information worker or else you learn to serve the needs and lifestyle of this elite.

The information society, for all its life-long learning gloss, may not be all that it seems.

THE INFORMATION WORKER

The concept of information work and information workers is not new. Peter Drucker, for example, has been writing about the shift from manual labour to knowledge work since the 1950s.

In his 1993 interview with *Wired*, Drucker explained some of the fundamentals of knowledge work.

> In knowledge work, the first question is, 'What should you be doing?' Not how. There is very little joy in heaven or on earth over an engineering department that, with great zeal, great expertise, and great diligence, produces drawings for the wrong product. What you should do is the first question when you deal with the productivity of knowledge. It's a very difficult question, but an important one. Second, you have to make sure that people can concentrate on results. In manual work, you are concentrated by the task.

According to Johndan Johnson-Eilola of the Department of English, Purdue University,[6] there has emerged a new type of service worker – the 'symbolic analyst'.

> The primary job function of the symbolic analyst is to abstract information in symbolic form, and manipulate those symbols in ways that construct new, useful connections within markets of nearly any sort. Symbolic-analytic workers are essentially information brokers.

Johnson-Eilola goes on to explain that because computers are their primary tools, these new information workers are more likely to telecommute, they are highly paid, highly sought-after and highly mobile.

The information worker is flexible, adaptable, innovative, and exhibits a particular ability to network. Information is the *communication* of knowledge. Therefore, the information worker must have an excellent ability to communicate the information they acquire or create.

> "By its very nature knowledge work involves sensing many inputs, rearranging information and discovering or creating new knowledge," David J Skyrme wrote in *Update* in 1997.[7] "Generally the more creative the work, the greater numbers of inputs sensed and used. Management by walk-about and informal dialogue are ways of achieving this

sensing. 'Wandering and browsing around the (electronic) network' is another way that a knowledge worker does it. 'Networking' is the way of life for successful individuals. Real strides forward are often made in highly interactive group sessions where creative people bounce ideas around, and test against a variety of perspectives."

An inherent part of the information worker's life in the digital age economy is change. Change is what they know, change in what and who they work for. To deal with change, the information worker needs to be a good networker.

"With workers hopping from company to company – and even from industry to industry – several times over the course of their careers, making and maintaining contacts has emerged as a crucial career element," Steven Ginsberg wrote in a 1998 article for *The Washington Post*.[8]

Consequently, while the information worker is good at networking and working in teams, they tend to be mobile and independent-minded. Part of their week may be spent telecommuting and their loyalty will never be given blindly. They will judge the organisation that they work for as much from the point of view of how that organisation helps them learn more, as much as how that organisation financially rewards them. For the information worker knows that they are only as good as the knowledge they are acquiring.

In the digital age, it will increasingly be the worker who will differentiate the company. As silicon chips commoditise everything, technological advantage will become much rarer and short-lived. It will be the quality of the worker, and the quality of the relationship the worker has with the consumer, that will create advantage. Consumers will graduate towards companies with workers who care.

A 1998 Andersen Consulting study[9] of 200 major corporates indicated that they were beginning to recognise this fact.

"Many corporations are working to increase the skill levels and abilities of front-line employees, giving them the tools and power to enhance customer relationships," the authors stated.

A final point to note about the information worker is that the best of them are increasingly scarce. This is particularly true within the Internet industry. Those with a deep understanding of the Internet and an ability to communicate and act upon that understanding are few on the ground. This will remain the case for a number of years. Thus, in the digital age, we are faced with a scarcity of time and a scarcity of quality information workers.

In summary, the information worker exhibits the following characteristics.

- Highly adaptable and eager to learn new things.
- Good at searching for, evaluating and managing information.
- Computer literate.
- Self-motivated.
- Creative and innovative.
- Excellent communication skills.
- Good at working in teams.
- Good networking skills.
- Mobile and independent-minded.
- Scarce.

THE INFORMATION CONSUMER

When the information worker stops working, they become the information consumer. What this means is that the information consumer has all the same characteristics of the information worker – quite a customer.

This is a consumer the likes of which business has never had to deal with before. They are smart, they are sharp, they don't like being talked down to by billboard statements. They are used to working with information and they have come to expect that a proper flow of information should support many of their purchase decisions. With tools, such as the Internet, the information consumer is empowered as they have never been before.

The Internet empowers the consumer significantly more than it does the traditional company. It gives the consumer, the networking and organisational tools that were traditionally almost exclusively the domain of the company. What this means is that if consumers decide, they can come together to form a 'company' of their own that demands – with one strong voice – certain things from the traditional company.

"In the knowledge age, consumers have new rights and new opportunities," the New Zealand *Foresight Project*[10] states. "No longer are consumers bound by limited choice or at the mercy of limited distribution systems. Instead, individual choice is becoming the name of the game. In industries as diverse as fresh food to motor vehicles, the customer is now able to specify individual preferences, ranging from size, colour and delivery time. Manufacturing and distribution systems must adapt to this new focus on the customer. The value of consumer service is rising steadily."

Internet pioneer John Audette,[11] has often talked about how the consumer is even more empowered online.

"One of the major changes brought about by the new environment of the Internet is a shift in the balance of power between businesses and customers," he writes. "In order to be competitive, those doing business on the Internet must offer genuine value to customers. And here's the hard part – genuine value is defined by those pesky customers, not by the businesses."

"If I had to find a phrase to sum up the period we are beginning to live through, I would have to call it the age of the empowered consumer," Morris Tabaksblat, Chairman of Unilever, has stated.[12] "With this corollary: not only do these consumers have the power, thanks in part to the new technologies; they know they have the power. And they are quite prepared to use it. Not surprisingly, they feel it's their turn…Mass marketing is no more. We shouldn't be using the term any more, because the thought it expresses is no longer relevant…The consumer decides…The era of push selling is definitely over. We are now well and truly in the era of pull marketing…The balance has tipped towards the smart consumer, the empowered consumer. And I for one believe that to be inevitable in the ecology of business. I don't expect to see it tip back ever again. The forces that set it in motion are too enduring."

THE INFORMATION COMPANY

As the empowered consumer rises to prominence, the uncaring organisation climaxes.

"In the 1980s, years of cost-cutting and downsizing led to record corporate earnings and stock-price performance," Barry Patmore and Dale Renner of Andersen Consulting stated in an article entitled, "Closer to the Customer, Closer to the Goal".[13] "But by the early-1990s, some executives began to realise that this success was a house built on sand. As their gaze shifted from cutbacks to growth, many senior managers saw that in their zeal to run lean, they had lost touch with the customer. To complicate matters, those customers had grown, and continue to grow, more sophisticated and discerning."

There are some signs that companies are realising the importance of focusing on the customer again. Don Peppers in a 1998 article entitled "The Coming Customer Revolution"[14] stated that:

A dramatic transition is under way – one that will propel the world's major corporations to organise around customers as opposed to product lines or geographical business units.

However, business practices of the last twenty years have left a lot of legacy.

"Focusing on customer needs seems the most basic, fundamental tenet of business," Dale Renner of Andersen Consulting has written.[15] "Yet, major corporations are just now beginning to blend strategic thinking, management resources, front-line support and technology to better understand and serve more sophisticated buyers."

The very real problem is that the latter day industrial age organisation is particularly unsuited to getting closer to its customers. In the lean and mean 1980s and 1990s, customer and employee loyalty and care came under sustained attack. The results, as Frederick F Reichheld points out in his 1996 book *The Loyalty Effect*,[16] are that:

US corporations now lose half their customers in five years, half their employees in four, and half their investors in less than one.

It was rightly acknowledged that many companies had become overweight by the 1980s. It could also be pointed out that the downsized organisation, while having sliced away one type of fat, lived off the fat of that organisation's brand, reputation and loyalty.

In the outsourcing 1990s, one wonders if some companies have forgotten that they are actually supposed to *do* something. You see outsourcing your support and getting closer to your customers is an oxymoron. As the consumer fights back – or becomes more cynical – companies are finally realising that there is only so far you can take cost-cutting, downsizing and outsourcing.

In 1998, Andersen Consulting and the Economist Intelligence Unit (EIU)[17] carried out a major study on customer relationship management. The results clearly showed that the present-day industrial age organisation is not structured in a way that allows it to easily get closer to its customers.

> "Functional departments and geographic divisions fragment and compartmentalise the various activities that go into serving the customer," Barry Patmore and Dale Renner of Andersen Consulting wrote. "Ultimately, this fragmentation means that information about the customer rarely finds its way far enough into the organization to provide useful feedback. As a result, customized service is difficult, and organizations tend to take a one-size-fits-all approach to the market – a powerful impediment to building closer relationships with specific segments of customers."

The EIU/Andersen study went on to forecast that:

> Over the next five years, for example, the percentage of surveyed companies organised around customer segment is expected to increase more than 170 per cent...As one corporation president pointed out, '[Executives] are only beginning to understand that what used to be acceptable no longer works.' Those organisations that succeed in finding what does work in customer relationship management

will be on their way to sustained, profitable relationships with customers.

Customer relationship management is a supposed technological solution to a very human issue – relationships. It is the old information technology mind-set of, 'there must be a way we can model this'. It's all about the statistical analysis of customers and their habits and patterns. That's all well and good, but if there isn't some intent to genuinely engage with these customers to establish some form of positive relationship, then you might as well take the 'relationship' out of customer relationship management – at least that would be the honest approach.

For the marketer and company, having a positive relationship with your best customers should be like breathing. Unfortunately, the downsizing approach has become a mind-set of cost-cutting at all costs. Thus, many marketers and companies need to re-educate themselves in the basics again. They have become too dependent on the oxygen tank of mass media, while they fed of the fat of the brands and economies that had been built in the previous 40 years.

The information company is really not going to be doing anything fundamentally different than what quality companies have done down through the years – focus on the customer, care about the customer. As Denis Beausejour, Vice President, Advertising Worldwide for Procter & Gamble has stated:[18]

> If we stay focused on the consumer one thing will quickly become apparent. Any divergent interests any of us may have – as advertisers or technology companies or content providers, whoever – are subordinate to this one purpose that we all share: improving people's lives with products, information and services that we can create, package and deliver in ways that just weren't possible before.

As we have seen earlier, the information consumer and worker are one and the same. The information company must look after and respect their increasingly empowered information workers. Whereas traditional management was about managing output – the production of products – information age management is about managing processes – the production of information. In this day and age, we take for granted that the information worker has all the necessary tools. The company must thus provide them with much more. The company must create the right environment within which the information worker feels stimulated and motivated.

David J Skyrme gave an excellent summation of the characteristics of the information company in the June 1997 issue of *Update*.[19] These characteristics were:

1. Organisations today need a balance of the highly innovative and the tightly co-ordinated. The former needs a networked approach, the latter a structured approach (some bureaucracy). Many established organisations have too much of the latter and too little of the former.

2. More and more work will be knowledge work – processing information, not physical product. Where it is done is less important than how it is done, and how it is delivered to the client.

3. Knowledge does not exist in isolated compartments. Its capacity to grow is enhanced if expertise can be tapped from as wide an 'expert' base as possible – people with different perspectives, experiences, age, gender, knowledge and cultural traits. In other words, people worldwide provide the best base for enriching knowledge and creating worthwhile innovation.

4. Tasks and the interrelationships between various tasks are becoming more complex. Variety in the environment is increasing (partly aided by technology and communications). There is more choice. Simplistic solutions no longer suffice for many business and societal problems.

5. The role of managers is changing from a 'director' to a 'facilitator', 'coach', 'mentor', 'advisor' and indeed a peer in the exchange of knowledge and experience.

THE INFORMATION CHILD

For the first time in history, children are more comfortable, 'informationable' and literate than their parents about an innovation central to society. And it is through the use of digital media that the N-Generation [Internet generation] will develop and superimpose its culture on the rest of society.

So wrote Don Tapscott in the introduction to his 1997 book, *Growing Up Digital: The Rise of the Net Generation.*[20] Tapscott's book paints a picture of a young world full of vibrancy, confidence and the embrace of the new. Two things struck me about this book. Firstly, that it was created in a co-operative way using Internet-based interactive tools. Secondly, it continuously surprised me as I read the book at how 'mature' the children who are quoted throughout the book sounded. When asked about the latter point in an interview with *Internet News*, Tapscott replied that:

> Other adults we interviewed who work with N-Geners [members of the Internet generation] expressed the same observation without exception. That said, their clarity did surprise us at first, but that says more about us and our view of youth than it does the kids themselves. There's a general fear in North America among parents and teachers that educational standards are dropping, that our children are not as well educated as we were, that they have short attention spans and do not know how to communicate as well as we did as children. N-Geners definitely contradicted all those fears.

The digital age is in its early childhood. Like a child, it is growing very fast. It is hungry, inquisitive, changing, volatile, unpredictable. The digital age is like a normal world to a child who only knows new things and changing things.

When we grow up we're supposed to settle down. We think of houses and cars and marriage (and children), anchored by secure careers. The adult world is supposed to be a relatively predictable place. Unfortunately, our adult world finds itself in the middle of a digital age childhood world. To cope and learn about this new and rapidly evolving world, we need to regain a number of the playful and inquisitive characteristics we had as children.

> "Man is only completely human when he plays," Nobel prize winner Konrad Lorenz once wrote.[21] "Play releases the unpredictable, and often innovative, within us. Through play we often discover what the logical mind cannot. Because, if a discovery is very new, it may well be outside the bounds of our logical parameters."

Writing about play in his 1994 book *Being Digital*,[22] Nicholas Negroponte stated that:

Most adults fail to see how children learn with electronic games. The common assumption is that these mesmerising toys turn kids into twitchy addicts and have even fewer redeeming features than the boob tube. But there is no question that many electronic games teach kids strategies and demand planning skills that they will use in later life.

Seminal thinker on education, Seymour Papert, in a 1997 interview with Italian publication *Media Mente*,[23] predicted radical change for education in the years ahead. He gave the metaphor of an 18th century physician transported to a modern theatre and how that physician wouldn't have a clue what was going on. However, an 18th century teacher transported to most of today's classrooms would be able to pick up the chalk and carry on where he had left off, indicating how little technology has impacted on education.

In the interview, Papert went on to state that:

We are going to see mega-change in education. It is going to change as much as medicine or transportation or telecommunications has. And you are just bluffing yourself if you pretend that there will only be small changes.

Papert talked about the traditional classroom as a production line, where information was attached to children, like a door is attached to a car.

With modern information technology, they can learn much more by doing. They can learn by exploring themselves, by finding out for themselves. The teachers' role is not to hand out each piece of knowledge but to be a guide, to deal with the very difficult situations, to stimulate the child, perhaps, to be a counsellor.

Papert went on to talk about how we need a vision and long-term plan for education, so that we can change the nature of how we educate children in small but definite steps. He emphasised that education programmes need to create "situations within schools where children pursue with their own passion from their hearts. They pursue projects that they're really interested in, they find out by getting the information they need from the Internet. They work with one another. They do something difficult. The teacher acts as a counsellor, as a guide".

We all need to think afresh, we need to play, we need to be amazed, we need to be innocent, we need to think outside, not just the box, but the factory society that created the box and the factory classroom that made the people to fill the box. We need to never say, 'that can never happen' or 'that's impossible'.

We also need to take a very different view of the parent-child relationship. Because children are so fast in the uptake of technology, there is much that they can teach adults. There is a new sort of partnership that can be fashioned.

We should not get carried away though. I have two young children and it sometimes surprises me at how mature they can be. I have learned, though, that children have flashes of maturity, from which they very quickly lapse back into their natural state of childhood, imagination and innocence. Children have indeed a new and exciting role to play as educators and explorers in this new age. Working with their parents, teachers and other adults, a very productive and co-operative environment can be created.

This does not in any way mean that children will *subvert* adults, that children will end up running business or politics. Children are children, and children need to be allowed to be children. Children, who are expected to live up to their, sometimes, mature words and take on adult responsibilities, quickly become uneasy and unhappy.

We should not forget that an inherent part of childhood play is that there are rarely major consequences as a result of the play. This allows children to truly explore their environments, their social settings and their minds. We need to find the balance between engaging children more in the digital age and in allowing them their necessary time in the land of innocence.

The Internet and other multimedia tools are in themselves learning tools. The Internet is the most wonderful library the world has ever seen. It can be an extraordinary interactive resource where children can communicate with experts from all over the world. American Vice-President, Al Gore – a general champion of the digital age – has cited research that showed that children in classrooms equipped with computers outperform their peers in basic skills by 30 per cent.

"The Internet is not a luxury or a diversion, but an essential tool for learning," he has said. "I encourage you to think of more ways to provide kids with green spaces and safe havens on the Net where they can roam and thrive."

Not everyone is enamoured with the Internet as a tool of learning. Clifford Stoll, author of *Silicon Snake Oil*, told the *Dallas Morning News* in 1998 that:[24]

> ...for all the many, many hours that I've spent online and on computers, it seems to me that most of the important work that I've done has happened independent of the hours that I've spent online.
>
> When I think of the skills that I need as an astronomer, they're skills like knowing mathematics, understanding physics, being able to manipulate a telescope, being able to write a paper, being able to read analytically and understand what someone else has written. Being able to poke holes in arguments. To be able to stand up in front of a meeting and present my ideas.
>
> These days, the computers are loaded with programs to guide the kids through things. Do they spend more time playing and learning, rather than just doing the rote work as you were doing? The main thing the computer is teaching is that if you want to learn, you sit behind a screen for hours on end, that you'll accept what a machine says without arguing, that relationships that develop over e-mail, Web pages and chat rooms are transitory and shallow. That if you're ever frustrated, all you have to do is pull the plug and reboot the machine.

Of course, there is an even darker side to the Internet. The Internet of 1999 is largely an open space, a space without 'walls'. For those who want ultimate freedom, that is all well and good. However, the world and the Internet has its share of disturbed minds, ready to prey on the weak and the young.

- A March 1999 report published by the Simon Wiesenthal Center found that the number of 'hate' websites was growing rapidly.

- A 1998 report by Forrester Research estimated that there were over 60,000 porn websites in United States alone, and that the online porn industry has reported an annual growth rate of 40 per cent over the last number of years.

- A January 1999 report by CNN quoted experts as stating that the, "online revolution has made it easier for pedophiles to access illicit materials, but it also has made it easier for police to track them down".

The digital age will face a significant challenge in allowing children the vital room to 'roam' and experiment on the Internet, while at the same time protecting them from those who would seek to do them harm. Getting the balance right will not be easy.

THE 'LIBERATED' WOMAN

The industrial age was the age of brawn. The digital age is the age of brain.

The industrial age by its very nature rewarded physical power and championed the status quo. Things were solid, things were predictable. The world didn't change much, so people didn't change much. The industrial age depended on hard-shouldered working men and hard-nosed businessmen. There were clubs and there were networks. But they were closed shops. And women were rarely on the inside.

The digital age is of course all change. It is not driven by muscles but by minds. The world doesn't work like clockwork anymore. Out goes 9-to-5 and in comes 24-hour shopping and cash machines. Out goes the 'organisation man'. In comes 'hyperkinetic woman'.

In a review of Sally Helgesen's *Everyday Revolutionaries: Working Women and the Transformation of American Life*, Polly LaBarre writes about Helgesen's comparison of the organisational man of the 1950s with hyperkinetic woman of the 1990s.[25]

In almost every respect, the 1950s organisation man is a perfect foil for the 1990s hyperkinetic woman…He embodied an absolute faith in large organisations, an overriding homogeneity, a sense of leisure and unhurried ease. His paradigm – life as a progression through predictable stages – has no relevance in a community where only 18 per cent of households feature a dad at work and a mom at home with the children. Faced with increasing complexity and a squeeze on their time, the women of Naperville lead every trend of new-economy work – from entrepreneurialism to project work to careers punctuated by periods of education.

The Internet is an open network. Co-operation and networking make sense. The digital age and the Internet is an environment that takes away some of the impediments that women have historically faced in gaining an equal footing in society. As the 'Advancing Women'[26] organisation puts it:

> Women are no longer asking men if they can join the game. The Net has allowed them to route around men and start their own game.

Women are embracing the Internet. Consider the following.

- A January 1999 published study by Pew Research Center found women were accounting for 52 per cent of new users.[27]

- In January 1999, AsiaBizTech reported that women in Japan were "surging" online, comprising 39 per cent of new users; up from 8 per cent in 1993.[28]

- According to the respected Georgia Tech, annual Internet users survey, 1998 was the first year women outnumbered men in the new user category.[29]

- IDC predicted that by the end of 1999, there would be more women online in the United States than men; women comprised less than 20 per cent of the US online population in 1993.[30]

- The Marketing Corporation of America estimated that for the Christmas 1998 period, women spent more than men online, purchasing an average of US$495, compared to an average of US$260 for men.[31]

> "Women now make up more than 40 per cent of the work force in every G-8 country except Italy," Rana Dogar wrote in a 1998 *Newsweek* special entitled "It's a Woman's World".[32] "At the same time, the developed world is shifting from manufacturing industries fuelled by fossilised carbons to knowledge and information industries – computers, telecoms, health care and financial service – driven by silicon chips. These two mutually reinforcing trends are

transforming not just the workplace but some fundamental aspects of the way we live."

The *Newsweek* feature covered the concept of 'womenomics', stating that there was a "seismic shift taking place in the world economy". A number of trends and statistics they put forward to illustrate this shift included the following.

- Between 1991 and 1995, 846,000 German men saw their jobs cut, while only 428,000 women lost theirs. In Western Germany, women actually gained 210,000 jobs while men lost 440,000. In Germany, 1996 marked the first year more women than men entered college.

- In Britain, women are expected to gain 1 million of the 1.4 million new jobs that will be created in the next ten years.

- Across the European Union, 110 women have college degrees for every 100 men who do.

- In Japan, the number of female engineers and scientists increased nearly ten-fold between 1975 and 1995.

- In the United States, the number of women-owned businesses increased 78 per cent between 1987 and 1996.

- In 1979, women earned just 62.5 cents for every dollar earned by men. By 1993, women were earning 77.1 cents.

> "The new economy is transforming not just business practices, but family life, too – and breaking down the divisions between the two," Dogar wrote in her *Newsweek* feature. "Changes wrought by the feminisation of the economy and the information age offer millions of people a chance to have a richer and fuller life than ever before."

"What does the new woman want from life?" Polly LaBarre asked in her review of Sally Helgesen's book.[33] Helgesen's answer was "remarkable and unexpected", as far as LaBarre was concerned.

> "What they are looking for," she suggests, "are 'new vernaculars of work and life that seek to reconcile the demands of personal ambition with the need for embeddedness in family and community'. In other words, these revolutionaries part company with the women warriors of the last genera-

tion. Instead, their real kinship is with the bloomer girls, suffragettes, and immigrant women of the late 19th century. Their ultimate quest? To 'make the whole world homelike'."

If this is so, and I believe the general trend to be true, then women will be a strong engine for *The Caring Economy*. They will have increased purchasing power and influence and they will want to make the world more homelike, more caring.

THE 'NEW' MAN

On many levels, the industrial age has been very kind to the male of the species. Men have acquired most of the available wealth, and hold the vast majority of the positions of power, whether they be economic, social, political, religious or military. In a very basic way, men acquired their initial dominant position as a result of physical strength. They may have used their brains but they always backed up their thinking with brawn when necessary. (Of course, men who toiled in coal pits or spirit-draining factories had very little to cheer about.)

In the digital age, things aren't nearly as simple. Brawn is becoming redundant and while business is still driven by those with an absolute focus and will to win, the world is not as black and white anymore. Women have raised their voices and have backed up these voices with increasing purchasing power. Change brings with it uncertainty and many men feel that they are under attack.

In a 1996 interview with Peter Baker for *Body Politic*,[34] Susie Orbach, one of Britain's leading psychotherapists, stated that:

...men are brought up to be warriors and economic providers. These two characteristics are central to how men are related to as little boys from the very beginning, which kind of values they have to ingest and the kind of psychology which is created. Other important male characteristics, such as sexual prowess and being in control, are, I think, derivatives of the imperative to be a warrior.

The battles and wars are not so obvious or common anymore. The enemy is not so visible or definable. In an economy supported by caring, men are at a disadvantage.

"I think men's socialisation is appalling," Orbach stated. "I think it's very limiting. It gives them certain skills which are important but their lack of emotional literacy and their lack of relational skills is a serious matter."

In some ways, the sexual saga of President Clinton reflects the radical change in the environment for men. Historically, powerful men had as much sex on the side as they desired and nobody batted an eyelid, let alone condemned them in history for it. But times have changed, and powerful men must be more measured and careful today. The eye of the media is everywhere, the Internet is a worldwide memory and store of information. It's a difficult time for many men.

In the United States there is an organisation called the 'National Coalition of Free Men'.[35] On its website it has a heading entitled *Some Common Untruths about Gender in the USA*. The untruths it claims are that:

- men have all the power;
- only wives are abused by husbands;
- all men are in a conscious conspiracy to keep all women in fear of rape;
- women are a special 'oppressed' class in need of special compensation because of past discrimination.

The website may often be overstating the point, but there is no doubt that many men are victims of one situation or another. As with everything else about life, social structures and relationships are hugely complex. The male in the digital age has to deal with massive uncertainty and is being forced to face emotions that otherwise he would have hidden. The clearly defined roles of men are no longer so clear. Men were the breadwinners but now there are *two* breadwinners. Men never cried, but that wasn't they didn't feel hurt, but rather because men were supposed to be tough soldiers.

The film *Good Will Hunting* explored a number of the issues that digital age man must address. Will Hunting had a very difficult childhood, which explained much of his withdrawal symptoms. However, there are more Will Hunting's in the world than many of us might expect. Consider the following statistics.

- In Britain, "between 1980 and 1990 the suicide rate for men aged 25-44 increased by approximately a third and in men aged 15-24 it increased by 85 per cent. For women the rates for all ages have fallen with the greatest falls taking place in those aged 45 and over. It is the first time since 1911 that male and female suicide trends have moved in opposite directions". (The Mental Health Foundation).[36]

- In Ireland, since 1990 the increase in the rate of suicide of men between the ages of 15 and 34 was over 300 per cent.[37]

- Averaged across all age groups, Australian males kill themselves at four times the rate of women. (Certified Male).[38]

- The American suicide rate for boys jumps from two male suicides for one female suicide in the 10-14 age group to four male suicides for one female suicide in the 15-19 age group. The male suicide rate continues to increase while the female suicide rate decreases as they get older. (US Bureau of Health and Human Services).[39]

These are shocking statistics. For all the bravado, it would seem that men are finding it much more difficult than women to adapt to all the change brought about by the digital age. What implications this has for commerce, I don't know, but it is clear that the death of the old certainties has impacted severely on the male population.

THE CHANGING FAMILY

From Los Angeles to Ho Chi Minh, the family is changing. The extended family of aunts, uncles and cousins is certainly in decline. The traditional family, with several children, the mother at home and the father at work is also in decline. Does this mean that the family as an institution is in decline?

Change is not necessarily decline. We should consider the fact that the family as we know it today is a relatively modern idea. Before the 19th century, the family was a very open entity in most Western societies and the vast majority of children were out working as soon as they were able. The 'traditional' family of the 19th and early 20th centuries is thus a relatively recent phenomenon.

In his 1988 book, *Disturbing the Nest: Family Change and Decline in Modern Societies*,[40] David Popenoe argued that families were in decline for a number of reasons.

1. They were less directed towards common goals.

2. They carry out less of the defined social functions for society, from procreation to control of children.

3. Institutions, such as the state and school, have taken away power and control from them.

4. They are smaller and not as stable.

5. There is a general weakening of the commitment to the family.

We could add to these reasons the fact that far more women are working today. Also, older people, instead of often being the glue that held families together, are now more than likely to find themselves in old folk's homes.

We should pause before idealising the traditional family. In these traditional families, many marriages were 'arranged'. The husband worked 14-hour days in factories, mines or out in the fields. The women had little or no rights. Children were often treated with great cruelty. In the upper echelons of society, there was one standard of sexual morality for husbands and a whole other one for women. Divorce was also a rich man's tool.

As with every new age, the digital age has the potential to both strengthen and weaken families and communities. University of Guelph family studies professor, Kerry Daly, in his book, *Families and Time: Keeping Pace in a Hurried Culture,*[41] wrote about how, "our lives are so tightly scheduled that we do not have breathing space. Families have to constantly wrestle with gaining control over time".

On the other hand, a 1998 study by Roper Starch Worldwide[42] found 90 per cent of respondents said they used the Internet primarily "to communicate with family and friends". Perhaps the Internet can be a type of social glue that keeps families – which are geographically spread – closer together?

If we look to the United States as the country that lives in the forefront of the digital age, then the signs for strong and vibrant families do not look great. As of 1998, the US has the highest level of divorce in the world, the highest level of teen pregnancy, while almost half of American divorced fathers lose regular contact with their children within a few years.

THE SENIOR CITIZEN

The digital age may well be full of shiny, new technology, but in the 'advanced' world, its population will be getting increasingly older. If for this fact alone, the digital age will have to be a caring economy.

At the end of the 19th century, the average American could expect to live for some 50 years, with only 4 per cent of the population reaching 65. By 1999, life expectancy had reached 76 years and 12 per cent of the population was 65 or over.

"By 2025," A USA Today report stated in March 1999, "one in 5 Americans – 62 million people, most of them baby boomers – will be 65 or older. Progress is so rapid that life expectancy could reach 80 or more in the next decade. Eighty-year-olds are already the fastest growing age group." [43]

This ageing trend is not just to be found in America. It is even more pronounced in Japan, where one in three of the population will be 65 or older by 2025. The median age has risen in Europe from a little under 30 in 1950, to a little under 40 in 1998. In Asia, it has risen from a little over 20 to almost 40 in the same period. In South America, it has risen from 20 to 23, while in Africa it has dipped slightly, staying under 20.

The great irony is that as the advanced world gets older, respect for old people has diminished. Pension funds will be severely stretched and it is likely that unless something radical is done, the working population will become increasingly unable to support through taxes, this rapidly growing population. This is a 'age-bomb' that the digital age must address.

Many older people suffer from isolation today. The extended family has been in decline – certainly in the West – for the last 30 years. Older people have been struggling to find a role in a technological world so in love with change and new things. In the information technology industry, in particular, being old – over 40 – is regarded by many as being past it. (I doubt, for example, Silicon Valley has too many old-age pensioners.)

Historically, older people just didn't buy computers. They had missed the boat. Many of them didn't know how to type and the whole computer interface felt alien to them. Of course, until very recently, computers were notoriously difficult to use, no matter what the 'plug 'n' play' marketers told us.

In the early years, very few older people joined the Internet. 1998 witnessed a small but important reversal of this trend. Older people, particularly in the United States, were realising that the Internet was not about computers, but rather about communication and interaction. Irish mothers could send e-mails to their daughters in Chicago. New York retirees could keep in

touch with their office friends. The Internet was allowing older
people get in touch, keep in touch and be kept in touch with.

Some of the specific indications that senior citizens have found
in the Internet a tool by which they can enthusiastically embrace
the Digital Age, include the following.

- In 1998, Microsoft set up one of its largest corporate exhibits
  at the annual American Association of Retired Persons con-
  vention.[44]

- Internet research company, Activmedia, in 1998 reported that
  senior citizens were one of the fastest-growing segments of
  the online population.[45]

- In a 1998 Roper Starch Worldwide study, 56 per cent of over
  50's said that they felt the Internet was narrowing the generation gap.[46]

- According to a 1998 study by SeniorNet and Charles Schwab
  Inc., over 13 million US adults over the age of 50 had Internet
  access, with the number growing rapidly.[47]

The latter part of the industrial age has seen older people as a
liability. But this was not the case, for example, in the agricultural age. In that age, an old person was respected for their wisdom. They held and passed on the knowledge of their society,
with the young acting as knowledge apprentices. They taught
their sons how to till the land and they taught their daughters
how to make clothes. When the grandchildren came along, they
too were taught values and respect. Older people were a vital
chain that connected one generation's knowledge base with the
next.

As I have written already, there is much we can learn from
how people lived in the agricultural age with regard to making
the very best out of the digital age. We can learn how to change
the view of older people from being a liability on the state, to
being a vital and productive asset.

Nicholas Negroponte, in his 1994 book *Being Digital*, wrote
about how older people are a tremendous latent resource of
information and experience and the Internet could help them
connect up with children so as to pass on experience and information vital to creating stable and long-lasting communities.

Indeed, at one end we have children who while learning lots
about how technological things work, are not learning nearly as

much about how society works, because both parents are usually out working long hours and don't have the time to pass on vital social skills. At the other end, we have older people with lots of time on their hands who want to be useful and contribute in a positive manner to society.

Why not use the Internet as a vehicle that connects up an old person with a young child, creating an old-young 'pen-pal' environment? Certainly there are obstacles, and proper monitoring needs to be in place, but think of the productive social potential. We could even go a step further by getting whiz kid children to adopt an old person in the neighbourhood, showing them how to use a computer and get connected to the Internet.

The old learning from the young. The young learning from the old. With the Internet, it's not an impossible dream.

THE POLITICS OF INFORMATION

Politics may be the art or science of government, but it has often been described as the 'art of the possible'. At the 1998 'Cyberspace and the American Dream' conference, Internet evangelist John Perry Barlow talked about how the Internet was "creating the first truly universal (political) forum", which will result in the "renegotiation of every significant power relationship on this planet".

Lofty words, which were backed up by Ed Black, president of the Computer and Communications Industry Association, who talked about how the Internet would ultimately require, "a revision of almost every law". Bill Burrington, America Online Inc.'s Director of Law and Global Policy made the point that:

> The Internet is fundamentally about empowering people within the political process.

A central question asked at the conference was: is the digital and the political mutually exclusive? "The conclusion was that the two are inextricably bound," ZDNN's Maria Seminerio reported.

In a 1998 post to the Online Europe[48] e-mail discussion group, Jordan Ayan commented that:

> My sister was living in Indonesia for the past year, and left two weeks before Suharto's resignation. She had many friends there, and as events were unfolding, she was get-

ting a large volume of e-mail from her friends providing extensive details about what was happening as it was happening. She forwarded many of these to me, and it was an amazing experience. It is one thing to watch CNN and hear detached dispatches on some remote place. It is quite another to receive as it happens news copy from people you have some connection to.

A 1998 article by *Cox News*, made the following point.

> "Voters have long been accustomed to the glossy political pamphlets that arrive in the mail before elections and the barrage of television advertising on the evening news. But tax-exempt groups such as *Putting Children First* are now experimenting with the power of the Internet to distribute political issue advertising, recruit supporters and wage on-line lobbying campaigns in Congress."
> "The potential for online advocacy is really fantastic," Oron Strauss of Net.Capitol, Inc., told *Cox News*. "The speed with which you can react and mobilise large numbers of constituents or members is really powerful."

Lynn Reed, who ran the Web page for the Clinton-Gore 1996 election campaign, made the point to *Cox News* that e-mail offered the potential for more "sophisticated" communication between voters and politicians. He noted that "politicians could e-mail a 12,000-word issue paper to voters for a fraction of the cost of mailing it". But he conceded that political dialogue in the United States has been a "steady drive in the other direction".

The Internet, of course, starred in one of *the* political events of the 1990s. The Monica Lewinsky story was first broken on the Internet. The 'Starr Report' was published in full on the Internet. The Internet became a hub of discussion and comment with regard to the affair. However, there were signs in 1998 that all this discussion and comment had its downsides.

> "The reaction to Monicagate might represent an implicit rebuke to the way the computer is changing our lives," Jonathan Alter wrote in *Newsweek* in 1998.[49] "Cyberspace is dedicated to the idea that more information is better. But many of us are experiencing info-remorse. Did we need to know all of this? In the name of 'disclosure' and 'openness'

– bywords of the baby boomers – we got these document dumps full of gratuitous detail. Do they help us understand anything important? I'm not sure that my kids will grow up thinking that the truth – and nothing but the truth – will truly set them free. But it might make a funny skit."

Daily, we are flooded with more information. If we're interested in a story we can get multiple versions and opinions. This can have great value but in the flow comes large chunks of largely irrelevant, titillating news, lies and scandal.

"The newspapers which used to be full of politics and economics are thick with stars and sport," *The Economist* lamented in 1998.

"Americans are increasingly savvy about sorting through various media, and we know how to take a joke," Jonathan Alter wrote in *Newsweek* in 1999. "But as Neal Gabler argues in his new book, *Life: The Movie*, we do pay a price when 'politics becomes show business for ugly people'. If everything's for entertainment, everything shrinks in significance, and we risk losing ourselves in the new American wilderness of noise."

However, like it or not, the Internet and information technology is having a profound impact on political institutions.
Foreign policy expert, Dr Francis Fukuyama, in a discussion with the Merrill Lynch Forum[50] in 1998 stated that:

...the one area where information technology is probably going to have a vast effect is in citizens' relationships with the state. There are a lot of trans-national, non-state actors today that didn't exist in the past – environmental groups, for example...One of my former colleagues at Brown did a study of this phenomenon in Mexico during the Chiapas rebellion. The Mexican government was going to respond to the rebellion in the way that it usually has, which is to send troops into the area and suppress it militarily.

However, international human rights organisations were able to mobilise very quickly, using faxes, e-mail and other communications technology. These organisations were able to put the Chiapas Indians on television to tell

their side of the story. The Mexican government decided
that they needed to attempt negotiations with the Indians
because of the widespread publicity. I think you're probably going to see more of this in the future.

All the above accounts point towards the fact that the digital age
is changing the relationship between the citizen and the state.
The digital age citizen is more educated, demanded of and
demanding. Increasingly cheaper communication costs, allied
with more flexible communication and information devices, such
as the Internet, mobile phones, faxes, etc., empower not simply
the individual, but the group, making it a lot easier to establish
'pressure groups'.

We are entering into a period of high interaction and perhaps
equally high friction between citizen and state. Citizens will
want answers not bland assurances. Very little will be allowed to
be brushed under the carpet.

While the great opening up of society is to be generally wel-
comed, the rapid and constant change is putting a significant
stress on legislative structures. Today, states are increasingly
falling behind in their ability to legislate for the digital age. The
Internet alone throws up legislative problems of gargantuan pro-
portions. Many issues need resolving, such as: liability definition,
jurisdiction identification, taxation and customs duties, intellectual property protection, data privacy protection, security and
authentication, consumer protection, Internet governance and
illegal and harmful content.

A central problem in all this is that a large percentage of legislators do not belong in the digital age. They were fashioned in the
thinking and politics of the industrial age. Many of them have neither the desire nor ability to understand this new age sufficiently to
legislate properly for it. Without legislators truly understanding
what they are legislating for, legislation will be inherently flawed.

If measures are not taken to improve the awareness and
understanding of legislators throughout the world and to engage
them as much as possible in the process, then two things are likely to happen.

1. Some legislators will take a laissez-faire approach, and there
    will be little or no planning and legislation.

2. Some legislators will overreact and we will get reactive legis-
    lation, which will stifle appropriate progress.

The above two points are likely to create a vicious circle. Those legislators who foolishly think they can stamp out or at least rigidly control the Internet will constantly be scouting for cases of abuse from countries where laissez-faire attitudes are the norm.

Even if legislators are willing to educate themselves it is a difficult task for them to achieve a sufficient knowledge or understanding of all of the areas for which they need to plan and legislate. Add to this more demanding citizens who are using e-mail to establish pressure groups to flood politicians' offices with questions and demands, and you leave politicians in an unwelcome position. Something will have to give. The pace of change will have to slow or else we will end up implementing badly thought-out laws or no laws at all – which is worse.

I must slightly digress here for a moment so as to defend politicians. I know it is a modern sport to hunt and revile them, but I feel that in many cases it is a pathetic sport, as reflective of a contempt for ourselves as the politicians. As a result of extensive research over a long period of time, I made a starling discovery: *we* elect our politicians.

Perhaps hunting politicians is not in fact a sport of our making, but rather that of the media. The media, that wonderful institution that wields immense power without any direct accountability, except to its shareholders, of course. The media, that protector of the public good who watches politicians and their ilk for us – but who watches the media?

Certainly the Clinton saga was much more driven by a media feeding frenzy than a public outcry. The media is a strange beast, containing some of the very best and some of the very worst of humanity. Just like politics. The major difference is that we have some say in who our politicians are. Not alone is the media not accountable but it is increasingly falling under the control of fewer and fewer moguls, who seem only interested in power and profit, not truth and justice.

Let's be very clear here: without politics, without long-term planning, without effective legislation, the future of the world is in serious, serious trouble. But how to plan effectively for this future with information overload raining down on us?

I believe the answer is to be found – as many of the answers are to be found – in thinking network. The Internet, in particular, ushers in the ability to create a truly effective co-operative society, where complex problems can be addressed through the co-operation of many minds.

THE CO-OPERATIVE SOCIETY?

The more people, the more complex.

Society is a truly complex place and for every statistic or fact that you find to prove your case, there is another statistic or fact that will disprove it. There are inherent ironies and contradictions at the heart of everything we do. Whether we like it or not there are always forces pulling against the force that is pulling us forward.

If we accept that the invention of the computer in the 1940s signalled the birth of the digital age, then there is much to indicate that the digital age signals the rise of individualism and the decline of communities.

However, if we stand back and look at the larger picture, it should become clear that individualism can't triumph completely over community. That, in fact, what we are seeing is an age-old tug-of-war between the rights of the individual and the rights of the community: neither side wishes to lose but, equally, neither side can afford, totally, to win.

The community without individual energy and creativity is a dying community. The individual who has no community is a hermit. Hermits generally don't make good consumers or good business people.

Let me make something clear: human civilisation exists because of the principles of co-operation. The origin of the word 'commerce' is "together with merchandise". A company is a company of people. An organisation organises people. A market of one is no market.

As everything comes into question in this war of change we live through today, it is important to keep the above in mind. All the technology and gadgets that are piled on top of us should never cloud the core mission. We are people living in societies of people. We co-operate, we communicate, we trade, we interact; that is what humans do.

Knowledge and information – and by extension influence and power – in the digital age are not things we can hoard. We need to refresh them on an ongoing basis. Some of the best ways to do this is through interaction and co-operation with other people. It is through networking, through connecting into the web of human information and understanding.

Of course, there is absolutely nothing new about co-operation. It is an inherent part of nature. In a paper entitled "The Great Mosaic Eye"[51] Robin Allott writes about how "the mosaic eye of the dragonfly has 28,000 ommatidia, 28,000 micro-eyes". He goes on to explain how humanity, through communication, information sharing and community infrastructures, manages to look out on the world with millions of eyes.

> "The multi-faceted eye of humanity, present, past and future, constitutes a great mosaic eye," Allott writes. "Collectively, humanity has opened its eye on all time and all space; the explorers in the past revealed the shape of the earth, the distribution of land and sea, the mountains, rivers, natural phenomena; the zoologists and botanists listed the animals and plants; the physicists and chemists, the doctors, revealed and integrated the patterns of living and non-living material, the historians, dramatists, investigated and recorded the succession of human lives, of human communities; the poets, philosophers, composers, psychologists, explored the human mind, human emotions, language, thought, consciousness.
>
> "These explorations, geographical, historical, intellectual, social, emotional, by thousands of millions of humans being over the centuries have been brought together through language, the power of words, spoken and written, through the multifarious devices now available for recording life from moment to moment, for communicating more and more rapidly and fully between individuals across the world and across time. We (the collective human eye) can look to the remotest past, imagine the remotest future, explore the distances and the minuteness of the universe. All this information, all this perception, all this imagination and thought, no longer held within any single small brain but spread, reflected, multiplied, through massive quantities of neural matter, human brains behind human eyes."

The Internet is the 'great mosaic eye'. The roots of a tree have a tremendous capacity to hold up that tree. The roots are a network and their power lies in how firmly they spread themselves and embed themselves in the earth – the network of life. If a tree has only one root, it is weak, no matter how thick or strong that particular root may be.

Let's imagine for a moment the Internet as the earth and people and organisations as trees. Our health and the health of the organisations that we work for are dependent on how many roots we can put down in the Internet. In the network, it is not sufficient for the organisation to have one strong leader and visionary (one root). Rather, leadership and vision must be distributed downwards just as a tree distributes its many roots downwards.

With every day that passes, we know less and less of the total sum of information that is in the world. In the industrial age, it was possible for people to have a great command of their area, and thus to have potential to wield great power. Many industrial age leaders had great memories and a tremendous capacity for work.

Today, we are fools if we think we can learn all the things that we need to know on our own. Intelligence in the digital age will not be measured by the memory and processing power of the brain (the computer increasingly carries out those functions). It will rather be measured by our ability to have visions and ideas and to co-operate with others in order that they are achieved.

Only by joining with others do we have any chance of understanding a world that is frantically exploding with information. Such joining means knowing how to get the best out of ourselves in group situations and also knowing how to get the best out of others in these same situations.

Individualism is to be cherished and encouraged. Independent thinking – thinking outside the box – is essential in the digital age, where things are changing so quickly and where new innovations are required all the time. But today it must be like a glove that fits on the co-operative hand.

The Massively Parallel Society

The Internet as we know it was not the invention of one organisation. It is an amazing example of what co-operation can achieve. The best way to succeed on the Internet is to observe and apply the things that made the Internet itself a success. Co-operation and networking are two of those things.

The Internet offers up many new co-operative possibilities. For example, most problems can be broken down into a number of distinct parts. This is the principle upon which the 'massively parallel' computer was designed. Instead of having one processor, as most computers do, a massively parallel computer has a large number, perhaps 50 or more.

Let's say that a problem can be broken down into 50 parts. Using a normal computer, the processor would solve part one of the problem and then move on to part two and so on. With a massively parallel computer, each part of the problem can be fed to an individual processor, thus greatly speeding up the time to solve the overall problem.

The Internet thus opens up the opportunity for a 'massively parallel society'. At a basic level, the Internet is a network of computers, but really the Internet is a network of people, probably the greatest network of people the world has ever seen. By feeding out the problem to the Internet there is the possibility of getting many minds to focus on it, or on particular parts of it. There is also the possibility of getting very different perspectives on the problem, as the Internet allows us to potentially tap into people and ways of thinking that we would not have traditionally had access to.

Each age has a loss and each age has a gain. The industrial age brought with it much machinery and many products. Humans became less dependent on nature and their own physical strength, as invention and clever thinking created a much more mechanised society.

In previous times, people depended on each other much more. There was far more collectivism and co-operation. When we look at the pyramids and the giant icons on Easter Island, we see monuments to the collective effort of people working in co-operation. Even with all of our machines and computers, we would find it difficult to build structures such as the pyramids today.

I remember once watching a documentary about Easter Island. The producers had estimated that it would have taken hundreds of people to pull the giant stones. They found a similar size stone, tied ropes to it, put tree trunks under it and assembled a similar number of people who would attempt to pull that stone.

It was very difficult to move the stone. People had forgotten how to work together in such large numbers. Their ancestors were able to work as a very large team – a co-operative brain and body. A worker knew when to pull, at what angle to pull and at what intensity to pull, in direct relation to the person in front and the person behind.

Some of the greatest rewards that will be achieved in the digital age will be by those individuals and organisations that use the Internet as a network to connect and extend their potential by reaching within and without. If we equate a processor with a mind for the moment, then the Internet can facilitate a massively parallel society, whereby many minds join together to solve our complex problems.

It could be said that the Internet as a whole is the first 'invention' of the massively parallel society. On a specific level, e-mail discussion lists are practical applications of the massively parallel society principle. People who have been part of such lists that were run in a professional manner, will testify to the value and learning that can be achieved through them. I can certainly say that I learned more about Internet marketing and business principles by participating in such lists than I ever learned from books or university courses. (As we shall see in the Chapter 10: *Things Digital*, the open source community is an active example of the massively parallel society principle.)

THE LEISURE SOCIETY OR THE PRESSURE SOCIETY?

The information society will be a better, easier place to live. We'll have more time, won't we? Consider the following.

- The median number of hours worked per week in the United States rose from 40.6 in 1973 to 50.8 in 1997, according to a Harris Poll.[52]

- 11 per cent of all full-time paid Canadian workers put in 50 hours or more a week in 1990, up from only 8 per cent fifteen years previously, a Statistics Canada study stated.[53]

- In 1991, Japanese workers spent an average of twelve hours per day either working or commuting to work, Rengo, a labour organisation in Japan, reported.[54]

- From 1972 to 1994, the total amount of time that the average American couple worked increased by seven hours a week, according to research by Marin Clarkberg of Cornell University.[55]

"Do you remember the debate about the leisure society?" the Statistics Canada study asked. "And do you remember the concern that everyone would have to find more and more activities to fill their time as the length of the work week diminished? Well, for an increasing proportion of Canadians, the opposite has occurred."

So much for the leisure society, more like the 'pressure society'. As a Yankelovich Group[56] study put it:

> Untethered workers are reported to work longer hours under even more deadline pressure; nothing has to wait until you get to the office; everything has to be done where you are.

Ned Ludd was an English textile worker who destroyed textile machinery in the vain hope of halting the progress of the industrial age. When I saw Ned being talked about favourably in a computer magazine, I knew something strange was happening.

> "After nearly seventeen years in the IT industry, I am beginning to gain a certain amount of respect for old Ludd," Peter Hind wrote in a *Macworld*[57] opinion piece. "I see technology intruding on our lives to the detriment of not only our lifestyles but also to the quality of work we generate. While technology is increasingly sold and promoted as a way of saving time, in reality it is consuming more and more of our leisure time.
>
> "As a baby boomer I find this especially galling. The 70s prophets told us that we would inherit the leisure society. Technology would free us from the drudgery of work and significantly reduce our working week."

Hind is not the only one to feel let-down and short-changed.

> "When the Leisure Society was first mooted fifteen or twenty years ago, it was assumed, in an idealistic frenzy, that everybody would be able to benefit from the fruits of new technology – the gadgetry, the computer games, the travel – irrespective of their wealth or position," Labour peer, Richard Rogers told *The Guardian* in 1997. "That has turned out to be a sham."

In a piece entitled, "Where has all the Leisure Gone?"[58] Richard R Danielson and Karen F Danielson asked some very pertinent questions.

> Have modern day industrial societies lost their leisure? Why cannot modern musicians create as much music as

the classical composers? In pre-industrial societies people had the time to decorate their possessions with painstaking effort, play with their children, meditate by a stream, help a stranger and dance. Even one hundred years ago our ancestors could take time over dinner, play an instrument and write letters.

A special issue of *Demos Quarterly*[59] entitled "The End of Unemployment–Bringing Work to Life", made the point that we have jumped headlong into frantic work without questioning whether all this work is in fact making us more productive.

> "Contrary to forecasts of a leisure society, work has taken on an ever more central role in our culture," *Demos* wrote. "But the institutions of work remain chronically underde- veloped: not just childcare and adult learning, but also lack of equivalents to the Consumers' Association to inform people about the quality of work. Job stress is thought to cost the UK up to 10 per cent of GDP [Gross Domestic Product] annually, through sickness, poor productivity, staff turnover and premature death. We lose more days to illness than all but one of the EU countries, while working longer average hours than any other."

Have we become slaves to the machine? Why are we all working so hard and what is all this hard work for? Bigger houses, better televisions, the latest computer and software in every room?

Personally, I find it all quite thrilling. I know, though, that I cannot keep up this pace forever, and that one day I will tire men- tally and physically. I am pretty certain as well that the vast majority of people are not madly in love with rapid change. Life- long learning is all well and good but sometimes we need to stop and ask: what are we learning and what are we learning it for?

JACKS OF ALL TRADES?

On a Friday night, as we sat back to relax, the video got stuck in our video player. The casing informed us that only a profession- al should open it. The next day, we rang a repair service. Then we rang up the video shop to inform them and that's when the fun started. None of the staff knew anything. The manager wasn't there and nobody knew whether we would get a credit if it was the video cassette's fault, whether we would have to pay rental until we got the cassette out, etc.

That same weekend, I couldn't get Microsoft Powerpoint to work. It kept coming up with an error screen, which said that I should shut it down and start it again. I spent half an hour messing around and then gave up. The idea of ringing up 'support' crossed my mind but was chased away by experience. The last time I had rung such 'support' I was left waiting for ages and then got stock answers with the final one being, "I'd advise you to re-install the software."

It struck me forcibly that weekend that if we are all such great life-long learners, then why does society sometimes feel so dumb and helpless?

The first summer job I had was in a hardware store. An oldish man took me under his wing. He had been in the store for 30 years, he proudly told me, and he knew everything about hardware. It was great to watch him deal with customers. It left a lasting impression on me, not simply the depth of information and understanding he had but the pride and dedication he brought to his job.

I know that today life-long learning is the in thing, life-time job security has gone out the window, and we are all supposed to be singing the 'change is good' mantra. However, I feel that we may be in danger of turning our society into a place full of jacks of all trades and masters of none.

When I got that summer job in the late-1970s, the idea of giving 30 or 40 years dedicated service was seen as something a young person should aspire to. Now, it seems almost ridiculous. Today, if you're not changing jobs every three years and finding new skills as you race down the road of life-long learning, you're out of step.

I wonder how many apprentices there are today in comparison to twenty years ago? Or, how many trades you can now apprentice at?

My brother-in-law is a mechanic and has a small garage beside his home. A couple of months ago we were having a chat and he joked that I'd probably know more about cars these days than he does. He smiled rather sadly as he informed me that engines are increasingly being controlled by computers. I told him that I knew probably more about fixing a car than fixing a computer. We both laughed.

I cannot escape from the uncomfortable feeling that the more intelligent our machines get, the more dumb we become. Just what are we life-long learning? What sort of real skills are we acquiring? In twenty years when our glorious digital world gets broken – as everything breaks at some point – will we as people have the remotest clue how to fix it?

Let's not long for a misty past, but let's not just skip blindly into the digital future without asking a few hard questions. When nobody knows how to fix anything anymore, worse, when nobody wants to fix anything anymore, where will we turn to for support?

A TALE OF TWO WORLDS

Is the digital age not just a fast-forward replay of a very old story: a tale of two cities, a tale of two classes, a tale of two economies, a tale of two worlds?

There are those who believe that the Internet and digital age in general is a major window of opportunity for people in poorer, less developed countries. These are important figures such as Nicholas Negroponte, Newt Gingrich and Al Gore. Negroponte believes that the new technologies can help jump-start emerging economies into the fast lane. Gingrich talked about giving laptops to the poor.

In 1994, vice-president Al Gore stated that:

> We now have at our hand the technological breakthroughs and economic means to bring all the communities in the world together. We now can at last create a planetary information network that transmits messages and images with the speed of light from the largest city to the smallest village on every continent.

It is true that for emerging economies there is certain potential. However, for very poor countries, the Internet and all the other opportunities are very likely to pass them by, because, you see, a glass of water costs a lot less than a computer. In a documentary I saw a while back on AIDS in Africa, a researcher made the point that if curing AIDS was as simple as giving every victim a clean glass of water, that simple act could not even be achieved.

Telecommunications is wonderful, but it is not for all.

- Four billion (out of six billion) people around the world are without a telephone.

- Half the people on the planet have never made a telephone call.

- There are more telephones in Tokyo than in sub-Saharan Africa, with fewer than one in 300 people having a phone line in that region.

- There are 44 million people in Zaire (Congo). There are 30,000 phones. About one-third of them work.

- To purchase a computer would cost the average Bangladeshi more than five years' income.

- Of the 150 million people using the Internet worldwide in 1998, only a million of them were in Africa, 800,000 of whom were in South Africa!

For all the wonders of computers and the Internet, we need to recognise the fact that there are large parts of the world that suffer on a daily basis from hunger and famine. There are large parts of the world that are still living in the agricultural age. There are parts that are just entering the industrial age. And there are parts that are somewhere in-between.

Some commentators put forward the view that because many countries have little or no telecommunications infrastructure that that is an advantage. The logic is that there is no infrastructure to pull up in order to put the new one in. That's all well and good, but maybe the reason there is none is because none could be afforded in the first place, and that the new-fangled one cannot be afforded either.

To live and prosper in the digital age you don't simply need technology. You need a *technological culture and attitude*. You need a culture that is familiar and comfortable with using technology. Because you can't talk about wonderful opportunities brought about by teleworking to someone who has never used a phone. The digital age is in many ways a stage on from the industrial age. Much of what we learned in an industrial age society allows us the opportunity to be players in a digital age economy.

We say that the Internet is a global network and that it creates a 'global village'. In theory that is true but in practical reality it is not. True or false? Every nation has a road network. True, of course. Every nation has a road network, it's just that some nations' roads are of tarmac and others are of dirt.

Internet bandwidth is like a road network. In some countries, such as the United States, Internet bandwidth is relatively plentiful. In other countries, such as India, it is scarce. What this means is that we will have essentially different Internets in different countries as the digital age progresses. The overall Internet will be one in theory but multiple in reality. Just like the world we live in today.

Earlier in this chapter we read about Seymour Papert's metaphor of an 18th century physician transported to a modern hospital theatre, and how they would feel totally impotent, while an 18th century teacher transported to most modern classrooms would be able to pick up some chalk and carry on. In some ways isn't it comforting that a teacher can teach with such simple tools, for that means they can reach a very large segment of the population?

Time for a reality check. Some schools in poorer countries cannot afford the *chalk*.

"In our enthusiasm for the information superhighway, we must not forget the villages and slums without telephones, electricity or safe water, the primary schools without pencils, papers or books," James Wolfensohn, President of the World Bank, stated in his 1998-1999 World Bank Development Report.[60] "For the poor, the promise of the new information age – information for all – can seem as remote as a distant star."

THE INFORMATION ECONOMY
AND THE SERVICE ECONOMY

In 1998, Stanley Fischer, First Deputy Managing Director of the International Monetary Fund,[61] stated that there was increasing evidence that inequality of income was rising in every part of the world, and not simply in the traditional weak economies such as Latin America and sub-Saharan Africa. He pointed out that the phenomenon has taken on a regional dimension with average incomes in urban areas significantly higher than in rural areas.

In most 'advanced' countries, two distinct economies are emerging as the digital age gathers pace: the information economy and the service economy, or more particularly, the low-paid service economy. "America: Who Stole the Dream?"[62] is a major 1996 report by *The Philadelphia Inquirer* writers Donald L Barlett and James B Steele, it examined the 1996-97 edition of the US Department of Labor's *Occupational Outlook Handbook*. The top ten occupations expected to have the highest job growth over the following ten years were:

1. cashiers;

2. janitors and cleaners;

3. retail sales clerks;

4. waiters and waitresses;

5. registered nurses;

6. general managers and top executives;

7. systems analysts;

8. home-health aides;

9. guards;

10. nursing aides, orderlies and attendants.

So, these are the job opportunities for the life-long learners in the information society?

Barlett and Steele wrote passionately about a divided American society. According to the report, many of America's best-paying manufacturing jobs were being exported as a result of technology and globalisation and were being replaced by low-paying service jobs.

Reading the report reminded me of a cartoon I saw some years back. The President of the United States was making a speech proclaiming the fact that millions of new jobs were being created. As he was talking, a waiter near his table was saying to himself, "And I have three of them."

As Morgan Stanley's Stephen S Roach puts it in his 1997 paper, "The Boom for Whom: Revisiting America's Technology Paradox":[63]

> This is the dark side of America's technology para-dox...more than fifteen years of virtual stagnation in aggregate real wages, an unprecedented widening in the inequalities of the income distribution, and a dramatic shift in the work-leisure trade-off that is putting increasing stress on family and personal priorities.

Of course, many have done extremely well out of the last fifteen years.

"There can be no mistaking the windfalls that have accrued to a small slice of the US population," Roach writes, "mainly those managers, executives, and investors who have been fortunate enough to have benefited from the corporate earnings and stock market bonanza of the 1990s."[64]

I wrote earlier about the opportunity for women. Well, it is by no means all good news on this front.

"Except for those in the professional class, most women now must resort to service jobs: the clerking, cleaning, table-waiting and cashiering jobs that provide little money, few or no benefits, and part time or irregular hours," Barlett and Steele wrote in their report.[65]

In this context, it is worth considering the following.

• In the United States and Britain, only 2 per cent of employers offer workplace nurseries.

• Women everywhere hold the vast majority of part-time jobs, with that estimate being as high 81.5 per cent for the European Union.

• Women holding political office are scarce on the ground: Canada – 18 per cent; Japan – 4.6 per cent; US – 11.7 per cent; UK – 9.5 per cent.

• By 1996, women made up 13 per cent of the computer industry.

• Women's salaries still lag behind men's: Canada – 63 per cent; Japan – 51 per cent; US – 79 per cent; UK – 79 per cent.

• Among the *Fortune 500* companies, there are only two female CEOs; among the next 500, there are only five.

• *Financial World's* annual list of the top 100 earners includes no women.

• In 1994, more than 15 million children lived below the poverty line in America. That was up from 13 million a decade earlier.[66]

THE INFORMATION POOR CONSUMER

Much of the media attention is now on the information consumer, but the previous sections indicate that in vast parts of the developing world, and in significant areas of Western rural and urban society, we will find increasing numbers of information 'poor' consumers.

What need has the cashier, janitor, cleaner, retail sales clerk, waiter, waitress, home-health aid, guard, nursing aid, orderly and attendant, for life-long learning? Many of these jobs are mind numbingly boring. In the industrial age, at least, the people who must take up these jobs, had the opportunity to apprentice to a trade. But the computer has got rid of most of the trades. Maybe, there is good reason why there are "59 channels and nothing on", as Bruce Springsteen sang.

It thus looks like two very distinct marketplaces are emerging.

1. The information consumer marketplace, where the consumer is smarter and more demanding than ever, and where saving time and convenience is top of the agenda.

2. The information poor consumer marketplace, where the brand is expected to deliver a dream or illusion of escape, as much as the product or service it offers, and where price is top of the agenda

WHY WE SHOULD CARE

The digital age brings with it the opportunity that comes with change. For those that are on the right side of learning, it is an exciting time, full of promise. For those not so lucky, globalisation will likely shift their job to a lower-wage economy or the computer will automate it. Most of the 'opportunities' left for these unfortunate people will be to serve for low wages.

We live in a world of multiple presents and futures. In the West, we are constantly ahead of ourselves from the perspective of goods and services and life styles. In the developing world, for many it is a daily battle just to survive.

Along comes the Internet, this 'global' network, which many hope will connect up the world in some harmonious whole. I doubt it. The Internet and the digital age will most likely see a widening of the gap between rich and poor. The information 'haves' are already racing ahead and embracing and making the future happen. The information 'have nots' are at the moment not worried about the information they don't have, they are more concerned with the food they don't have.

So, why should anyone reading this book care? After all, you are probably either on or entering the fast lane of the information superhighway. Morals are all well and good, but at the end of the day, most of us fight for our own piece of the cake for ourselves or for our family. And I'm not talking about scaling some of that rocky and precarious high moral ground, that is a dangerous and hypocritical activity at the best of times, as I have invariably found that those who profess to stand at its peek have the muddiest feet of clay.

No, what I'd like to propose is that we should care about the general welfare of the world for a very different reason; for a reason very close to the heart of self-interest.

There is a theory that everything in this whole universe is connected. That nothing happens that does not impact on everything else in some small way. We have all heard about the butterfly flapping its wings in Brazil causing a storm in Chicago. Well, the Internet and the computer may turn out to be hotbed for such butterflies.

The world and the universe is, and has always been, a network, that everything is indeed connected. Today that has never been more the case. Globalisation may not be as real as some would like to think, but there is no denying the fact that countries are exporting and importing at far greater levels than they were 50 years ago.

More and more people are travelling internationally today, whether on holiday or for business. The goods of the digital age – silicon chips – are incredibly portable and flexible. Advances in telecommunications mean that before long we will be communicating anywhere in the world for the price of a local call. The Internet is just another example of the world becoming more networked.

If the world becomes more networked and that world becomes even more divided between rich and poor, then we are surely sowing the seeds for future conflict and perhaps grand disaster.

Today's ordinary PC has more processing power than what was used to land people on the moon. Think of nuclear and biological weapons and nanotechnology and computer viruses for a moment. What will the ordinary PC of ten years time be like? What will it be able to concoct and develop? All it will take will be one cheap PC and a fanatic. Or perhaps not even a fanatic is needed. Perhaps it will be someone or some group who looks at a divided world, three-quarter of which is hungry and exploited, the other quarter rolling in it. That person may righteously think that they have a duty to teach the rich a lesson.

The computer is a wonderful tool. But we should not forget that the computer was born out of a military need. That the Internet was born out of a military need. That the Internet is networking the world and that the computer is getting more powerful, and that as we can reach across the Internet, so can we be reached across too.

Doing our part to create a just and fair a world will not stop every fanatic, but it should reduce the pool of resentments that they feed on.

As intelligent beings, we are constantly faced with a choice between the short-term focus, the short-term need and the long-term vision. Short-term is about maximising what we have now. Long-term is about leaving behind a world that is sustainable and liveable. Long-term is for our children, their children and their children. Long-term is also for all the other living things that share this truly beautiful earth with us.

It's very easy to be short-term today. It takes a lot of effort to be long-term. Sometimes, I am surprised at how much of a long-term view humanity has managed to achieve, despite the pressing short-term needs that gather all around us. It is so much easier to look after ourselves and not think about how our present day actions will affect our world in 50 or 100 years.

I believe that so much short-term flux demands that we strive for a long-term vision more than ever. In this age of frantic change, when the pressure is to be short-term, the long-term thinker is needed more than ever. If we aspire to be life-long learners, shouldn't we learn to respect life, learn to think in the long-term?

REFERENCE

1. P Schwartz, "Post-Capitalist (Interview with Peter Drucker)" *Wired* (July 1993) http://www.wired.com/wired/archive/1.03/drucker.html

2. British Department of Trade, http://www.dti.gov.uk/

3. World Bank, 1998 World Development Report http://www.worldbank.org/

4. The Foresight Project, New Zealand Ministry of Research, Science and Technology, http://www.morst.govt.nz/foresight/front.html

5. K Kelly, "Mr Big Trend" *Wired* (October 1994)
    http://www.wired.com/wired/archive/2.10/naisbitt.html

6. J Johnson-Eilola, "Stories and Maps: Postmodernism and Professional
    Communication" Purdue University (1995)
    http://tempest.english.purdue.edu/stories/distance.html

7. D J Skyrme, "Virtual Teaming and Virtual Organizations: 25 Principles of
    Proven Practice" *Update* (Issue No. 11 June 1997)
    http://www.skyrme.com/updates/u11.htm

8. S Ginsberg, *The Washington Post*, http://www.washingtonpost.com/

9. A B Patmore and D H Renner, "Closer to the Customer, Closer to the
    Goal" Andersen Consulting (1998)
    http://www.ac.com:80/overview/Outlook/over_2nov97.html

10. The Foresight Project, New Zealand Ministry of Research, Science and
    Technology, http://www.morst.govt.nz/foresight/front.html

11. J Audette, Multimedia Marketing Group, http://www.mmgco.com

12. M Tabaksblat, Chairman of Unilever NV, *Smart Routes to the Smart
    Consumer*, http://www.unilever.com

13. A B Patmore and D H Renner, "Closer to the Customer, Closer to the
    Goal" Andersen Consulting (1998)
    http://www.ac.com:80/overview/Outlook/over_2nov97.html

14. D Peppers, Peppers And Rogers Group, http://www.1to1.com/

15. A B Patmore and D H Renner, "Closer to the Customer, Closer to the
    Goal" Andersen Consulting (1998)
    http://www.ac.com:80/overview/Outlook/over_2nov97.html

16. F F Reichheld, *The Loyalty Effect: The Hidden Force Behind Growth, Profits
    and Lasting Value* (Harvard Business School Press: 1996)

17. Economist Intelligence Unit and Andersen Consulting, "Managing
    Customer Relationships: Lessons from the Leaders" (July 1998)
    http://www.eiu.com/samples/N281des.html

18. D Beausejour, "The Promise of Interactive Advertising" Procter & Gamble
    Worldwide (1998), http://www.4interactivemarketing.com/digitrends
    /dtonline/features/promise.html

19. D J Skyrme, "Virtual Teaming and Virtual Organizations: 25 Principles of
    Proven Practice" *Update* (Issue No. 11 June 1997)
    http://www.skyrme.com/updates/u11.htm

20. D Tapscott, *Growing Up Digital: The Rise of the Net Generation* (McGraw-Hill 1997)

21. K Lorenz, *The Waning of Humanness* (Unwin Hyman 1983)

22. N Negroponte, *Being Digital*, (Knopf) 1995

23. "Schools in the Next Millennium (Interview with Seymour Papert)" *Media Mente* (1998) http://www.mediamente.rai.it/english/bibliote/intervis/p/papert02.htm

24. *Dallas Morning News* (24 August 98)

25. P LaBarre, "The Starbucks Sisterhood" *FastCompany* (February 1998) http://www.fastcompany.com/online/13/sisterhood.html

26. Advancing Women, http://www.advancingwomen.com/

27. Pew Research Center, http://www.people-press.org/

28. AsiaBizTech, http://www.asiabiztech.com/

29. GVU's WWW User Surveys, http://www.cc.gatech.edu/gvu/user_surveys/

30. International Data Corporation (IDC), http://www.idc.com/

31. Marketing Corporation of America, http://www.interpublic.com/

32. R Dogar, "It's a Woman's World" *Newsweek* (1998)

33. P LaBarre, "The Starbucks Sisterhood" *FastCompany* (February 1998) http://www.fastcompany.com/online/13/sisterhood.html

34. P Baker, "An interview with Susie Orbach" *Body Politic* (1996) http://www.body.arc.co.uk/body3/orbach.html#1

35. National Coalition For Free Men, http://www.ncfm.org/hist.htm

36. Mental Health Foundation, http://www.mentalhealth.org.uk

37. *The Irish Times*, http://www.irish-times.com

38. Certified Male, http://www.pnc.com.au/~pvogel/cm/contents.htm

39. US Bureau of Health and Human Services, National Center for Health Statistics, http://www.cdc.gov/nchswww/default.htm

40. D Popenoe, *Disturbing the Nest: Family Change and Decline in Modern*

Societies (Walter De Gruyter: 1988)

41. K J Daly, *Families & Time: Keeping Pace in a Hurried Culture (Understanding Families* (Sage Publications: 1996)

42. Roper Starch Research, http://www.roper.inter.net/75years/re.html

43. *USA Today*, (16 March 1999) http://www.usatoday.com/

44. American Association of Retired Persons, http://www.aarp.org/

45. Activmedia, http://www.activmedia.com

46. Roper Starch Research, http://www.roper.inter.net/75years/re.html

47. SeniorNet, http://www.seniornet.org/

48. Online Europe, http://www.isys.hu/online-europe

49. J Alter, "The Lewinsky Legacy" *Newsweek* (19 October 1998) http://www.newsweek.com/

50. "Economic Globalization and Culture: A Discussion with Dr Francis Fukuyama" *The Merrill Lynch Forum* (1998) http://www.ml.com/woml/forum/global.htm

51. R Allott, "The Great Mosaic Eye", http://www.percep.demon.co.uk /rolelang.htm

52. Harris Poll, http://www.harrispollonline.com/

53. Statistics Canada, http://www.statcan.ca:80/english/Pgdb/

54. Rengo, http://www.jtuc-rengo.or.jp/english/index.html

55. M Clarkberg, Cornell University, http://www.cornell.edu/

56. Yankelovich Partners, http://www.yankelovich.com/

57. *MacWorld*, http://macworld.zdnet.com/

58. R R Danielson and K F Danielson, "Where Has All The Leisure Gone? The Industrialization of Lifestyle" (1997)

59. "Agenda for Ending Unemployment" (Adapted extracts from "The End of Unemployment - Bringing Work to Life" special issue of '*Demos Quarterly*' (9 Bridewell Place, London, EC4V 6AP), http://www.globalideasbank.org/reinv/RIS-51.HTML

60. 1998-1999 World Bank Development Report, http://www.worldbank.org/

61. International Monetary Fund (IMF), http://www.imf.org/

62. D L Barlett and J B Steele, "America: Who stole the dream?" *The Philadelphia Inquirer* (1996), http://www.phillynews.com/packages/america96/free/NOFRAMES/A_ch_1.html

63. S S Roach, "The Boom for Whom: Revisiting America's Technology Paradox" Morgan Stanley (1997), http://www.ms.com/

64. *Ibid.*

65. D L Barlett and J B Steele, "America: Who stole the Dream?" *The Philadelphia Inquirer* (1996) http://www.phillynews.com/packages/america96/free/NOFRAMES/A_ch_1.html

66. R Dogar, "It's a Woman's World" (*Newsweek* 1998) http://www.newsweek.com

© Fergal Lawler 1999

6
Community Feeds Commerce

COMMUNITY FEEDS COMMERCE

Amazon.com is not in the 'business' of selling books. Microsoft is not in the business of making software. Yahoo is not in the directory business. America Online is not an online service provider. To one degree or another, all the above companies are in the business of creating and servicing communities.

A major trend in the digital age will be companies who will create an offering around customer sets and communities, rather than around product sets. This sort of strategy is exactly what Amazon, Microsoft, Yahoo, America Online – basically some of the most successful online and offline businesses in the world – are doing.

They are establishing communities to which they can then offer a wide range of products and services. Take Amazon.com, for example. Amazon.com is not in the business of selling books. It *is* in the business of building up a community of satisfied consumers who trust Amazon and will be willing to purchase a wide range of products and services from it. Amazon is about creating a community space and taking a share of the revenue from the transactions that occur within that space. That's why Amazon's stock price is so high. (You didn't think it was because it was a bookseller?)

In March 1999, Amazon.com launched an auction section to its website. In introducing the auction section, founder and CEO, Jeff Bezos, wrote about, "our community of 8 million shoppers". References to community can be found all over its website: "Our community rules are firm to keep your bidding and selling worry free...The strongest communities are ones where neighbors know and help each other." In fact, customers are even described as "Amazonians".

Also in March 1999, Microsoft president Steve Ballmer announced a reorganisation of Microsoft calling it, "part of the reinvention of Microsoft". Ballmer stressed the fact that Microsoft was redirecting its primary focus away from products and technology to the customer. The new groups proposed were: Business and Enterprise (software for information technology customers); Consumer Windows Division; Business Productivity Group (developing products for "knowledge workers"); Developer Group (focused on assisting software developers); and Consumer and Commerce Group (focusing on bringing consumers and businesses together online).

Amazon, Yahoo and Microsoft are seeking to supply very broad customer community bases. A central part of their strategy is leveraging their organisation's size, financial strength and massive economies of scale. However, there will be thousands of groups and communities that will and are being established at the opposite end of this spectrum. What we are talking about here are 'niche communities' or 'communities of interest'. Examples of these include the following: gay communities, U2 fans, vintage car enthusiasts, James Joyce fans, people who like organic food, etc.

Historically, those who had specialist interests and leanings often felt isolated, as it was hard to find people in the locality who had similar tastes. The Internet offers the first effective and efficient environment within which such people can gather together and share their interests. Those companies who are truly specialists and can supply the needs of these communities of interest in a professional and passionate manner, will find the Internet to be a wonderful facilitator in the process.

So, 'community' is not that corny a word after all. In fact, when you step back for a moment, it becomes clear that community feeds commerce. Nobody would think of establishing a shopping mall in the Sahara Desert or building an exclusive hotel on the North Pole. Well, there a lot of desert and a lot of ice on the Internet, and millions of websites are waiting vainly for the traffic to come. While many are waiting, Yahoo has been building 'New York', while Amazon was building 'Los Angeles'- places where millions of people congregate and do business.

Sustainable commerce needs community. Sustainable community needs commerce. That is how it has always been; and how it will always be. Commerce pays the wages, community buys the products. Yes, it is individuals who actually buy products, but if we look at world marketplaces we see that the vast majority of individuals reside within communities. Communities give structure, form, context and long-term sustainability.

But what is a community? And how can a commercial organisation benefit from community-related strategies? Read on.

WHAT IS A COMMUNITY?

It is interesting to note that the Latin root of words such as 'community', 'common', 'communication', 'commerce', 'commune' and 'communism' is the same. 'Com' in Latin is used to mean "together, in combination or union, altogether, completely", according to *The Concise Oxford Dictionary of English Etymology*. Thus, a word such as 'commerce' means "together with merchandise".

The *Webster Dictionary* defines community as:

> ...people with common interests living in a particular area; interacting population of various kinds of individuals (as species) in a common location; a group of people with common characteristics or interests living together within a larger society; a body of persons or nations having a history or social, economic and political interests in common.

Thomas Bender in his book *Community and Social Change in America*[1] defines community as follows.

> A community involves a limited number of people in a somewhat restricted social space or network held together by shared understandings and a sense of obligation. Relationships are close, often intimate, and usually face to face. Individuals are bound together by affective or emotional ties rather than by a perception of individual self-interest. There is a 'we-ness' in a community; one is a member.

The Foundation for Community Encouragement (FCE)[2] defines community as follows.

> "A community is a group of two or more people who have been able to accept and transcend their differences regardless of the diversity of their backgrounds (social, spiritual, educational, ethnic, economic, political, etc.). This enables them to communicate effectively and openly and to work together toward goals identified as being for their common good.
>
> "The word 'community' is used in many different ways," the FCE continues. "It can refer to a specific group of people (a geographical community, a church congregation) or it can describe a quality of relationship based on certain values and principles. For example, many people are familiar with a unique phenomenon that frequently

emerges between individuals during a crisis like a hurri-
cane or flood. In such situations, people tend to drop their
pretences, overcome obstacles and reach out to help or
emotionally support one another and, in the process, find
surprising strength, tolerance and acceptance. The FCE
calls this phenomenon or collective spirit, that emerges
during a crisis, community."

In an article for *The Irish Times*[3] in 1998, Fintan O'Toole, gave a
description of a community environment.

That world was one in which the generations mixed freely,
the young and the old eyed each other with both affection
and disdain, and people shared memories, jokes and feuds.
It is what most Irish people probably still think of when they
hear the word 'community', a kind of mutual social space in
which, however mercilessly they mock each other's foibles,
people retain some sense of obligation to each other.

I grew up in what might be described as the hidden, hidden
Ireland. It was as rural as rural can be. The first vehicle I learned
to 'drive' was an ass and cart. From my youngest days I had a
very keen awareness of community, for the simple reason that I
was not really part of one. Because of certain circumstances, I
was half-in, half-out, and I cannot express here properly how
much as a child I yearned to be fully in, to be fully accepted.
Fintan O'Toole's description rings true for me, the observer that
I was. For there is a paradox at the heart of communities, like
there is a paradox at the heart of everything.

Sou Yang,[4] an American 12th grader defines community in a
way that would be typical of many youngsters.

"What is a community?" Sou asks. "A community has several meanings depending on the question(s) or how we
view a community. A community plays an important part
in everyone's daily life. Without quality communications,
a community cannot have an understanding of one another. My definition of a community is a population of people
in a certain part of a country. It is where we live and grow.

"Living within a community we try to find the best way
to improve our environment and our surroundings. People,
places, or things around us are our community. Community

could also mean what or who we are. The uniqueness of our
society is the foundation of our community. The diversity of
our culture defines the community we live in."

Sou Yang writes about his community in an idealistic way. He
writes about the "uniqueness of our society" on the one hand
and then about how the "diversity of our culture defines the
community". There is a certain paradox here. A unique society
tends to drive towards a homogeneous culture. Later, in his
description, Sou Yang states that: "What makes my community
is my ethnicity."

It is interesting to note that how communities see themselves,
or more particularly, how they wish others to see them, is often not
how they are, how they live and behave on a day to day basis.

Ireland is famous for its communities. The Irish community in
America has made a significant and proud contribution.
However, it is also true to say that the conflict in Northern
Ireland, in which thousands have died, while having its roots in
imperialism, illustrates the raw edge where two strong and
proud communities rub against each other. It is not always the
case, though it is certainly not uncommon, that the stronger a
community is and the deeper its traditions run, the less hos-
pitable it is to outsiders, particularly if they are judged to be
threatening valued traditions.

There are many who will say that this is not what communities are *really* about. However, communities are complex, difficult entities. Commerce needs communities, but those businesses wishing to engage with or help develop communities on the
Internet need to be aware of the paradoxes and contradictions
that lie at their heart. Communities do not fit neatly into business
plans; nor should they. Working with a community to establish a
viable marketplace is an endless task with great rewards and
great difficulties. So it should be.

TRADITIONAL COMMUNITIES

There are two basic types of community:

- **traditional communities**: communities into which you are
  born or settle;

- **chosen/online communities**: communities that you choose to
  join. (For the purpose of this book, the type of chosen community that we will focus on will be online in nature.)

Traditional communities are very much to do with place. Frances Moore Lappé and Paul Martin Du Bois, in an article entitled, "Me to We: From Devolved Community to Involved Community",[5] describe them as "devolved communities". They write that:

> We become who we are through relationships with others. Far from autonomous egos, human beings are creations of community. Devolved community comprises those relationships, often ground in family and place, that human beings have always assumed. They are givens. Many we do not choose.
>
> These communities were predictable, governed by inherited codes of conduct. Within the devolved community, dynamics of power, self-interest and related conflict — which exist in all relationships — were implicit, not explicit. Indeed, they were largely denied. If thought about at all, they were typically believed to be alien to community.

It is a natural impulse for many to look back on the 'good old days' and bemoan the fact that 'things aren't like they used to be'. There is little doubt, however, that traditional communities have declined in the Western world particularly during the latter half of this century.

In Ireland, where community is regarded as very strong, a 1998 survey on religious activity in Ireland, which also dealt with broader issues, found that people were most concerned about, "community, education, spirituality, the family and youth", according to an article in *The Irish Times*.

> "Concern and dissatisfaction were expressed at the disintegration of the community," *The Irish Times* article went on. "Previously the parish was a meeting place; today, fearing crime, people are cocooned in their homes. Before, people attended mass together and spoke to one another afterwards."

In and excellent article on communities entitled "(How) does the Internet Affect Community? Some Speculations in Search of Evidence",[6] William A Galston commented on how Daniel Yankelovich has written about how the 'affluence effect' emerged in America particularly after the Second World War.

"People came to feel that questions of how to live and with whom to live were a matter of individual choice not to be governed by restrictive norms," Yankelovich wrote. "As a nation, we came to experience the bonds to marriage, family, children, job, community and country as constraints that were no longer necessary."

Galston neatly summarises the dilemma communities face within the modern world.

"The problem is that as individual choice expands, the bonds linking us to others tend to weaken," he writes. "To the extent that the desire for satisfying human connections is a permanent feature of the human condition, the expansion of choice was bound to trigger an acute sense of loss, now expressed as a longing for community. But few Americans are willing to surrender the expansive individual liberty they now enjoy, even in the name of stronger marriages, neighbourhoods, or citizenship. This tension constitutes what many Americans experience as the central dilemma of our age: as Wolfe puts it, 'how to be an autonomous person and tied together with others at the same time'."

Kathryn Holmquist, writing in *The Irish Times*[7] in 1998 stated that:

We are becoming disembodied in our relationships and within communities. As work takes over our time and our lifestyles, our emotional lives are being squeezed into boxes. We have moved from a life based on community to one driven by individualism – but that 'freedom' may be deceptive.

Holmquist quoted Ruth Barror, the Chief Executive of the Marriage and Relationships Counselling Service in Dublin as saying that:

Everybody needs contact with older and younger people, otherwise you have a splintering of energy and the community becomes very fragmented. I'm concerned that by the time we start talking about the importance of community, the patient will already be dead. In cases where there is no extended family, how do people cope? We have the

State trying to buttress the family, but the State cannot replace a sense of community.

While communities have certainly been in decline over the last 40 years, there are some signs of a rebirth. A 1996 American survey of Civic Involvement with 1,500 respondents, as reported in a William A Galston article, found that, "only 15 per cent of respondents failed to offer any example of what they considered to be a community".

Francis Moore Lappé and Paul Martin Du Bois, co-founders of the Center for Living Democracy write in support of renewed community involvement in America.[8]

In one-third of all the nation's school districts, parents and other community members are assuming roles beyond bake-sale organisers and field-trip chaperones. As part of what's called school-based management, parents and teachers are being entrusted with school-development questions once left to top administrators. In law enforcement, it is increasingly recognised that ordinary citizens are key to create safe neighbourhoods. As part of 'community policing', now in 40 per cent of our major cities, in some places neighbours who have never spoken to each other before are working together as members of citizen patrols.

Influential technology journalist John C Dvorak wrote in *PC Magazine* in 1998 that:[9]

The community movement on the Web is part of a bigger societal change. The Web and the kinds of communications we are seeing are actually an exaggeration of a new kind of togetherness movement unlike anything that we've ever seen in the past. Exactly where it is headed and how far it will go is impossible to predict. But it can't be overlooked.

Characteristics of Traditional Communities

To establish a better understanding of what needs to be done to create successful online communities, I will now examine the key characteristics of traditional communities, since these are concrete models from which to build. These characteristics draw extensively from the writings by and on various communities about which I have found material.

There is one characteristic of all communities that I have not specifically mentioned below because it so infiltrates all the other characteristics. It is in fact a self-evident one. *Communities are about people.* Of course, it is the theme of this book that the economy is about people, that the Internet is about people, and certainly that communities *are* about people.

If an enterprise is seeking to build an online community it would do well to measure it against these characteristics so as to see how many of them it has in place. If there are very few of these characteristics in place, then serious questions should be asked. These characteristics are as follows.

- Common vision.

- Connected.

- Participation.

- Diverse.

- Contained.

- Free spaces.

- Family focused.

- Adaptability.

- Spiritual.

- Leadership.

- Membership.

- Stable and secure.

- Sustainable.

Common Vision

For any sort of community to exist, its members must have things in common and must share a common, generally agreed vision for their community. It may be that in many circumstances the vision for a community is unstated; that doesn't mean that it isn't there. "Community connects us all to a common vision, shared goals, caring neighbours and friends," the Racine County Community Principles[10] state. The Four Worlds Community Principles[11] echo this thinking when stating that, "A vision of who we can become is like a magnet drawing us to our potential. Where there is no vision, there can be no development."

A vision for a community is often something that is divined from the history of that community. Thus, most communities place emphasis on their history and the traditions that have resulted from that history.

> "Every community has a history, and events planned around it are both educational and cultural. These activities provide local character and strengthen community ties," the Sustainable Communities Network Principles[12] state.

> "We preserve and build upon the strong traditions that make Coronado unique," state the Coronado Community Principles.

> "Healing and development must be rooted in the wisdom, knowledge and living processes of our cultures," the Four Worlds Community Principles state.

Civil rights legend, Rosa Parks believes that children are central to community and encourages older people to "pull out a map and help them chart a history tour of their own town or region; Interview an older member of your neighbourhood and learn history through his or her eyes".

A common vision while drawing strength and character from the community's history must also be a map for the community's future. Communities, in this sense, are always working to a long-term agenda. As the Coronado Community Principles state:

> We value our future and, therefore, place emphasis on the development and well-being of our children and youth.

Connected

Communities are about creating a holistic entity, a togetherness, a connectedness. As the Four Worlds Community Principles state:

> Because everything is connected to everything else, any aspect of our healing and development is related to all the others (personal, social, cultural, political, economic, etc.).

The Hannover Principles[13] emphasise that we should, "respect relationships between spirit and matter. Consider all aspects of human settlement including community, dwelling, industry and trade in terms of existing and evolving connections between spiritual and material consciousness".

At the core of all communities are relationships between people, as far as the Racine County Community Principles are concerned.

> "Building community," they write, "requires our understanding that individuals – children, youth, adults, families – can only flourish in relationships involving others. Those relationships are themselves communities...We will support collaborations between parents and children, teachers and students, learners and other learners, employers and workers, business and schools, necessary to assure the knowledge and skills required in a community of excellence and innovation."

Here we see a weave of connections – both social and commercial – come together to make a community. However, while a community must have strong internal connections and networks, it must not forget that it is part of a larger network and set of connections. A community thus needs to work to create the appropriate external connections. As the Coronado Community Principles state:

> We seek positive relationships with regional agencies with whom we need to work co-operatively to achieve our goals.

Communication is a seed for community – it is the tool that allows us to connect. As Internet pioneer Howard Rheingold[14] has stated:

> Would the Internet have become the most rapidly growing communication medium in history if it was not for electronic mail, mailing lists, BBSs, MUDs, IRC, chat, all the ways that people communicate with each other socially.

Participation

Connections are no good unless they are used. Communities flourish when the widest possible participation is achieved. The Four Worlds Community Principles stress this point very elegantly when they state that:

> People have to be actively engaged in the process of their

own healing and development. Without participation, there can be no development.

The vast majority of participation within communities tends to be voluntary. People give generously, not for a short-term gain, but to move forward the common vision, to secure the future of the community. Voluntary work does not show up on a country's balance sheet, but without it a nation would be spiritually, socially and economically much poorer. (America Online has 12,000 workers and 10,000 volunteers)

In an article in *The Irish Times* in 1998, Kathryn Holmquist wrote about James O'Gorman, a voluntary community worker, who has been "unemployed" since 1986. James is, "secretary of the parents' council at his local Gael Scoil, a member of Nenagh Community Network (part of the area development management initiative), a soccer coach of 5 to 17 year-olds and organiser of a summer camp for children with special needs". James states his belief that, "Community is the backbone of our society, and if you don't get it right at the local level, you can forget about it nationally."

The Coronado Community Principles recognise the value of voluntary work and the necessity for as many citizens as possible to be involved in helping the community grow.

> We foster a positive community spirit in all who live, work and visit in Coronado and value the volunteers who demonstrate the true depth of the spirit...Building community requires the persistent, patient effort of every citizen.

> "Be active in your local school or scouts, even if you don't have kids," Rosa Parks urges.

> "By walking the path, we make the path visible," the Four Worlds Community Principles summarise.

A strong community tends to have an extensive range of customs and rituals, which allow for the widest possible participation of community members. In Ireland, Sunday mass was a place where everyone gathered – the congregation outside the church itself was as important as the one inside.

Diverse
"Diverse communities are healthy communities," *Britannica Online* states in an article on biological commu-

nities entitled, "Biodiversity and the Stability of Communities".[15] "Long-term ecological studies have shown that species-rich communities are able to recover faster from disturbances than species-poor communities."

Most of the community principles I came across were very much into championing diversity.

"A community should contain a diversity of housing types to enable citizens from a wide range of economic levels and age groups to live within its boundaries," the Awahnee Principles states.

"Communities with the greatest and most diverse citizen participation are often resilient and strong," the Sustainable Communities Network Principles states.

"Diversity recognizes that every one of us is different from every other and that a real community includes us all equally and with respect," the Racine County Community Principles state.

It is interesting to note that within biological communities diversity is a positive factor. I also found it intriguing that all of the sets of community principles I came across champion diversity. However, there is no getting away from the fact that inherent tensions are at play as diversity and common vision seek to create common ground. It is also true that diversity runs counter to the principle of chosen communities, where groups of like-minded people come together.

Contained

Communities need to be contained – they need to define their boundaries. For all their need for diversity, something has got to be on the inside and something has got to be on the outside. "What is left in, left out, who is *let* in, let out?" These are questions that unfortunately often bring out the very worst in people, as narrow-mindedness and racism can come into play. However, we must accept that if a community is not stable, if it accepts everything that comes along, then it ceases to be a community. A community needs to be contained.

A community needs to have borders. It needs to know where it begins and where it ends.

"Each community or cluster of communities should have a well-defined edge, such as agricultural greenbelts or wildlife corridors, permanently protected from development," the Awahnee Principles state.[16]

These principles go on to state that:

Community size should be designed so that housing, jobs, daily needs and other activities are within easy walking distance of each other. The community should have a centre focus that combines commercial, civic, cultural and recreational uses.

Free Spaces

Some people question the use of 'free information' on the Internet as if the approach of having free things was a totally unusual thing in normal society. The Internet is the space in which the 'information society' lives and it is no more unusual for it to have free information for its citizens than it is to have free parks in normal society.

Communities need free and open spaces (not to mention voluntary activities, which is 'free work'). As the Awahnee Principles state:

The community should contain an ample supply of specialised open space in the form of squares, greens and parks whose frequent use is encouraged through placement and design.

Family Focused

A strong characteristic of communities – and one that differentiates them from clubs and associations – is that their members generally range in age from babies to old people.

"Family and youth are the basic elements of every community. Our adults and young people will engage in learning and tasks that bring the generations together for shared purposes," the Racine County Community Principles state.

What is important to emphasise from the above quotation is that communities "bring the generations together". Rosa Parks believes fundamentally that the strength of a community can be measured by the way it looks after its children.

Children help a community rekindle itself. A community is not a static thing. It is organic. Either it is growing or dying. Children and families allow communities to go through a cycle of change that is challenging, though at the same time familiar. Even in 'winter', you know that there is a 'spring'.

Adaptability

A problem with many traditional communities is their inability to change and adapt as the world around them changes. This is easier said than done when you consider that the very objective of a community is to establish a sense of stability and tradition.

However, modern communities must have a capacity to adapt. As the Racine County Community Principles point out, "lifelong learning is the key to excellence at home, at work, in the community, in public life". The Coronado Community Principles emphasise this point when stating that:

> We are committed to a vigorous program of continuing learning and personal development.

Spiritual

> "The sacred is a special dimension of life, private as well as public. It energises and guides many of us in ways and along paths that can strengthen our community," the Racine County Community Principles state.

> "Spirituality is at the centre of healing and development. Connection with the Creator brings life, unity, love and purpose to the process, and is expressed through a heart-centred approach to all that we do," the Four Worlds Community Principles emphasise.

There are a number of community characteristics that do not sit easily with business, and spirituality is one of them. However, practically every community I have researched has had at least some sort of spiritual element, with many of them having it as a central driving force.

Leadership

Communities need good leadership, particularly in times of change. However, communities tend to be subtle entities. Their traditions and rules are generally unwritten. A member tends to live community rather than think about it and define it. Leaders walk a thin line between helping the community achieve its objectives and being accused of self-interest.

Because so many communities never write down what they are about and what their rules are, they often face severe problems when disputes arise. The unwritten rules can be interpreted in different ways, depending on the viewpoint and agenda.

Communities that want to survive long-term need to address dispute resolution processes, with the last resort being the use of the legal system. The Sustainable Communities Network Principles propose that:

> Alternative dispute resolution is a tool for resolving conflicts within a community, and mediation is used in the workplace and in institutions to help individuals find common ground and peaceful solutions to problems.

Francis Moore Lappé and Paul Martin Du Bois[17] state that:

> In every example of effective community problem solving we know about, power is consciously acknowledged. Community based on conscious choices to work toward a larger purpose also requires us to acknowledge self-interest. This, too, is painful for many, because too often self-interest is equated with narrow selfishness.

Membership
One is a 'member' of a community. However, the question is: How does one become a member? The process of becoming a member of a community is rarely defined. At a core level, we achieve membership by being born into communities.

Simply moving into a particular community does not grant us automatic membership in the eyes of other community members. We often have to live within and contribute to the community for many years, to be seen as a member. In Ireland, someone who is living in an area for more than 30 years can still be described as a 'blow-in' by the locals.

Stable and Secure
Most members look to communities for a sense of security and stability. If they can let their children out to play without constant supervision then it's a good community.

Ed Schwartz of the Institute for the Study of Civic Values, Philadelphia,[18] has posed a number of questions as a measure of the security within a neighbourhood.

> To what extent do residents feel secure – in their homes and in the streets? Are their property values secure – for homeowners and for renters? Are public services, in general, reliable and sufficient to maintain the neighbourhood at a minimally acceptable level of safety and comfort?

Stability is a very important characteristic that people look for in communities. As David Popenoe wrote in *Disturbing the Nest: Family Change and Decline in Modern Societies*:[19]

> Community cohesion is highest in those communities where people have lived the longest.

Sustainable

If a community cannot sustain itself then it has no long-term future. Irish communities, for example, have been historically weakened as a result of emigration. Young people were forced to leave the countryside because agriculture could no longer provide them with a living.

The Sustainable Communities Network is an organisation which seeks to link "citizens to resources and to one another as they work to create healthy, vital, sustainable communities".

As the Racine County Community Principles puts it:

> The economy provides work, income, and the resources to support our common institutions. Our businesses must be helped to flourish and they, too, must see themselves as good citizens responsive to our common needs.

Communities cannot sustain themselves without commercial activity. Communities need commerce. The equilibrium between community and commerce is the central axis upon which civilisation is built. One of the great challenges of the digital age, for governments, communities and businesses, is to achieve that equilibrium on the Internet.

ONLINE COMMUNITIES

Communities based on geography are wonderful places for those who 'fit in'. For those who don't fit in, they can be a very different story. The modern age, offering greater mobility and now the Internet, allows, in theory anyway, people to choose the communities with which they want to become involved.

Frances Moore Lappé and Paul Martin Du Bois[20] describe this type of community as an "involved community". They write that:

> Based on our involvement in roles we choose, it offers not predictability, and comfort but challenge and deeper sense of purpose. If devolved community provides us status based on our place in the order of things, involved community offers us the chance to find meaning based in our unique contributions to purposes larger than our immediate families and ourselves. Thus, compared to earlier understandings of community, today's emerging possibilities for involved community meet different but equally deep human needs. Social scientists are learning that the need, for example, to contribute to a purpose larger than ourselves is vital, not only to our mental health but also to our physical being.

William A Galston labels this sort of community as "voluntary". He writes that:[21]

> This conception of social ties compatible with autonomy has three defining conditions: low barriers to entry; low barriers to exit; and interpersonal relations shaped by mutual adjustment rather than hierarchical authority or coercion. Part of the excitement surrounding the Internet is what some see as the possibility it offers of facilitating the formation of voluntary communities, so understood. Others doubt that the kinds of social ties likely to develop on the Internet can be adequate substitutes – practically or emotionally – for the traditional ties they purport to replace.

Internet pioneer and community builder, Howard Rheingold,[22] has defined online communities as "social aggregations that emerge from the Net when enough people carry on…public discussions long enough, with sufficient human feeling, to form webs of personal relationships…Communities can't be manufactured, but you can design the conditions under which they are most likely to emerge, and encourage their growth when they do".

In his sociology masters thesis at UCLA, graduate student Marc Smith studied the Well, perhaps the best known and longest existing online community. He defined an online community as a "set of ongoing social relations bound together by a common interest or shared circumstance".[23]

Amy Jo Kim, who runs a company called Naima,[24] which specialises in strategic consulting for community spaces, defines online communities as "a group of people who gather together around a shared purpose, activity, or interest".

Commerce and Online Communities

In 1997, a cover article in *Business Week* stated that "people of like minds and interests are establishing Internet communities faster than any construction company in the brick-and-mortar world".[25] Writing for *CIO* magazine, Scott Kirsner introduced an article on online communities by stating that "battered and bleached by over-use, the word 'community' deserves its Buzz-Concept-of-the-Year status for 1997".[26]

Certainly, the word 'community' has been used with vigour in relation to the Internet.

Realising it's not enough to be the doorway to the Web, the major portals are turning to community services – bulletin boards, chat rooms, groupware services and personal home pages, among other things – as a way to keep users, and their all-important ad-perusing eyeballs, hanging around their sites," wrote Connie Guglielmo and Kimberly Weisul in *Inter@ctive Week* in 1998.[27]

"In the furious competition among a shrinking number of Web wannabes, one thing will separate the victors from the vanquished: community", according to Lycos Inc. CEO Bob Davis.

"Community newspapers have the most to win online," Eric K Meyer, a journalism professor at the University of

Illinois in Champaign stated in 1998.[28] "They have the most loyal audiences and the news that you can't get else-where. A local newspaper won't get scooped by CNN."

What seems certainly true is that community sites do draw a lot of repeat visitors and that this is a basic foundation of commer-cial activity. For example, in June 1998, Media Metrix ranked GeoCities, Tripod and Angelfire among the top ten most popular websites. It is also true that other portal sites, such as Yahoo and Lycos, have focused on communities, and that America Online, perhaps the most successful online enterprise, has increased its already strong community focus.

In his 1998 article for *CIO* magazine,[29] Scott Kirsner wrote that many companies are investigating a community orientation because "traffic to corporate sites is abysmal – people may visit once in response to an advertising campaign or a URL on a busi-ness card, but they're unlikely to deploy a bookmark". Kirsner then stated that:

Community has become a catch-all for the last-ditch efforts of websites to communicate in a new way with customers.

Kirsner gave the example of Barnes & Noble as a company with major online community strategies. Barnes & Noble has created a community website "where readers can come to chat with their favourite authors, get book recommendations from a community-formulated database and converse with other visitors about literature," he writes.

He quotes Susan Boster, the director of marketing at Barnes & Noble's site as stating that:

Our bricks-and-mortar stores have become centres of real-world communities. We offer events and readings and encourage people to hang out. We wanted to take what goes on in our stores and bring it online.
The return?
You're building a very, very loyal customer. They come back all the time because it becomes their home.

Barnes & Noble is an example of a company that an online com-munity should work for. (A major problem is that competitor Amazon.com has stolen a march on them in building that community.) The reason is that they already have an existing offline community and their product offering – books – is oriented towards bringing people together.

Technology and management guru Don Tapscott believes that our present business world is a transitional structure.[30] He believes that what will replace it is "e-business communities", which he defines as "networks of suppliers, distributors, commerce providers and customers that carry out a lot of communications and transactions through the Internet and other electronic media. Rather than building internal information systems, companies should embrace the Internet as a new infra-structure in the creation of wealth and the evolution of the business structure".

Tapscott believes that e-business communities can help an organisation:

- transform value propositions;

- enable one to one marketing;

- engage customers in value creation;

- motivate performance and agility among suppliers and chan-nel partners;

- add capabilities or dramatically reduce costs without com-mitting capital;

- facilitate a focus on core competencies;

- share risks and rewards.

What about companies that make light bulbs? Companies that make telephones? Companies that make washing-up liquid? While community-oriented websites will work well for certain product and services offerings, it is fairly obvious that they will be less effective for others.

The Historical Business Link

You load sixteen tons, and what do you get?
Another day older and deeper in debt
St Peter don't you call me, 'cause I can't go
I owe my soul to the company store.

Tennessee Ernie Ford 'Sixteen Tons'

The 'company town' has long been an inherent part of industrial age society, as Editorial Media & Marketing International explain in "Death of the Company Town?"[31]

> While Americans might like to believe that this country was built on the pioneering spirit and the resolute independence of rugged individualists blazing their own trails, the reality is that the sweat that greased the wheels for the development of the greatest industrial power in the world dripped from the brows of working men who, as Tennessee Ernie Ford pointed out, 'owed their souls to the company store'.

It is clear on investigation that large companies have been central in the establishment and evolution of community life in many of our cities and towns. Johnson & Johnson in New Brunswick, Corning in Corning, Procter & Gamble in Cincinnati, Kellogg in Battle Creek, the list of company towns is long.

These companies paid the wages of a significant number of community members in a particular area and thus often exerted a major influence on how the area evolved. Once the community and company's objectives were the same, everything was fine. When those objectives diverged, such as when the community wanted the company to introduce better environmental controls, problems and conflicts inevitably arose.

In an article entitled, "Industrial and Organizational Relations: Worker, Manager and Society: Responsibility to the Community",[32] *Britannica Online* outlines the shifting relationship between commercial organisations and communities over the last hundred years or so. It explains how the 'company town' or paternalistic approach diminished as a result of unionisation.

> As the plants became part of large corporate organisations with headquarters in distant cities, company executives found themselves increasingly estranged from the local people.
>
> A common reaction to this estrangement was the development of public relations and community service programmes. The plant manager's role was redefined to include the function of representing the company in the community, and this meant participating in community activities along with locally based business and profession-

al persons. Thus, it became common to find the manager
and other plant executives playing prominent roles in community fund drives and other service programmes.

The article goes on to explain that:

In the 1960s managers began to recognise that the community service orientation was not adequate for coping with
the problems of cities that were erupting in violence...It
became evident that the acute and chronic problems affect-
ing society as a whole and industry in particular were not
going to be solved simply by having a 'good' management
relating to its union and indulging in 'good' relations with
the communities.

The 1980s, which was often a period of 'corporate restructuring',
resulting in many job losses, found community leaders arguing
that "employers should provide their workers and communities
with advance notice and should work with employee and community leaders either to avoid the closing and job loss or to ease
the process of worker and community adjustment," the
Britannica Online article states.

Of course, the 1980s and 1990s found organisations setting up
plants in low-wage countries to which management had little or
no understanding of local cultures or communities, with the distance between the company and community continuing to widen.

The digital age sees companies, and particularly the larger
corporations, becoming rootless, almost nomadic in nature.
"Death of a Company Town?" deals extensively with Microsoft,
a model for the new global village corporation.

"Microsoft dominates the small Washington community of
Redmond but has from its inception taken almost no interest in the community's affairs," the article states. "When
asked what Microsoft has done for Redmond, most local
residents point to traffic congestion as the most visible
manifestation of the company's presence. Mayor Rosemary
Ives complains that while she has met with Bill and Hillary
Clinton, she has never been granted an audience with
Microsoft chairman Bill Gates."

Although Microsoft has little interest in the town beside which it
is located, it seems keen to establish its own 'company town', with
the objective of creating a Microsoft community for its workers.

"Microsoft employs close to 10,000 people in the Redmond area, almost 8,000 of them at its corporate headquarters," "Death of a Company Town?" explains. "About one in every five of the city's residents are employed by the giant software company. But the way Microsoft designed its campus, with two million square feet of office space spread out in 26 separate buildings, interaction between the company and the town is kept to a minimum. The campus has its own restaurants, its own stores."

Companies used to stand for something. They used to have identities and cultures. They used to reflect the national characteristics of the countries from which they originated. Often these cultures and identities grew in a natural way over time and were shared with the physical community within which they were located, as their employees were also members of that community.

Today, with globalisation and the like, companies are increasingly being forced to ask themselves: Who are we? What do we stand for? What makes us different? Why should someone be loyal to us? Why should someone stay working for us rather than move to a competitor? If a company does not have at least some sort of identity and community spirit then it will have created a very fickle and fluid environment where it is liable to lose people (and customers) at an increasing rate.

The Company as a Community
In 1998 a study of America's *Fortune* 25 companies by Hally Enterprises found that employees are the biggest audience for the corporate website, but that companies rarely recognise that fact.

"While naturally targeting customers, the media and investors with their websites, corporations may be missing a huge productivity bonus by not recognising what they can do with the source of their real market power – the company staff," Mike Reilly, President of Hally stated.[33]

Community starts at home and from a company's point of view, this means its staff. When you think about it for a moment, if a company has any real community potential then it resides first within its workforce. If a company cannot establish a sense of loyalty and belonging among its workers then it has little hope of creating a community atmosphere among its customers or a wider audience.

The reason is very clear: it is a company's staff who will be responsible for the establishment of any community atmosphere with customers. If they do not feel loyal to the company, then the likelihood of them fostering loyalty or building communities with customers is minimal.

A 1998 study, published by human resource consulting firm Towers Perrin,[34] found that there is a solid link between customer loyalty and staff loyalty. A spokesperson for Towers stated that:

> Companies that have practices that create or maintain a highly loyal workforce have superior customer retention.

According to Britton Manasco in an article for *1to1 Marketing*: [35]

> The research suggests that companies with employee turnover rates of 10 per cent or less have as much as a 10 percentage point customer retention advantage over companies with employee turnover rates exceeding 15 per cent.
>
> While the study focused on the insurance industry, Towers contended that the same correlation likely exists in all businesses. The implications are huge. Increasing customer retention just two percentage points can add 6 per cent, or $60 million of value to a typical insurance agency with $1 billion in revenues, according to the study. A five-point improvement can add $140 million in value.

A 1996 book by Frederick F Reichheld entitled *The Loyalty Effect*,[36] found that American companies were losing half of their customers in five years, half of their staff in four and half of their investors in less than one. This is incredible churn and Reichheld pointed out that the long-term effects of this massive drain will result in low growth and weak profits.

Reichheld's analysis showed that even small improvements in customer loyalty could add up to a doubling of profits. He states that companies that pursue loyalty, such as State Farm, Toyota/Lexus, MBNA, and John Deere, have achieved market-leading positions and strong profitability. Reichheld noted that traditional accounting systems did not show the "loyalty effect".

At a chief executives' summit in New York in 1997, Xerox Chairman and Chief Executive, Paul Allaire, said:

> The bottom line is this: people who have a say in how work gets done have a greater sense of control over their lives. Workers with this sense of empowerment are more efficient, productive and satisfied on the job. A 'family-friendly culture' is just one of the approaches we use at Xerox to unleash the full creativity of our employees.

As a result of extensive research and analysis both in the United States and Europe, Pierre DuBois & Associates Inc.[37] have established a set of key management factors responsible for organisational commitment, or what we are describing here as company internal community building.

Presented in decreasing order of importance, the factors are:

1. Perception that the employee is treated with respect and consideration by the organisation.

2. Perception that the organisation is highly concerned with quality and customer service.

3. Clearly defined job and responsibilities.

4. A stimulating job.

5. Quality of information given to employees on the company's plans and activities.

6. Perception of administrative effectiveness.

Alternative 'Company' Communities

Companies need to realise that the Internet is the world's greatest grapevine, the world's greatest word of mouth channel. News can spread fast on the Internet, and as we know, bad news or gossip can spread even faster.

Those who were on the Internet in late-1994 will surely remember coming across Intel Pentium joke websites, which mushroomed as a result of the famous calculation bug in the Pentium. You might think that a company the size of Intel would be able to ignore such joke websites, but Intel found out very quickly that the Internet grapevine can be a dangerous weapon which can spread rumour at an incredible speed if not addressed in a logical and comprehensive manner. What I found also in researching the Pentium Bug story was the negative legacy that it imbedded within the network. When I searched AltaVista for the year 1994, with the keyword 'Pentium', for example, the first ten responses were all to do with the Pentium Bug. (For more on the Pentium Bug story, see Chapter 9 *Think Network - 'Intel and the Price of doing Nothing'*.)

The Internet is a tremendously cheap and flexible networking tool. Such a tool can be the glue that holds together all sorts of groups and communities. I know that within my own company there are e-mail mailing lists that the staff have established and that management are not welcome onto. In an industrial age environment, management would react quickly and crush such dissent, perhaps firing the organisers. If you accept the principles of a network – openness, co-operation, transparency and accountability – that cannot be the case.

From talking to other companies, I was made aware that these 'underground' networks were not uncommon. I talked to a former member of Quarterdeck, who pointed me to a website where former staff were carrying out animated conversations. Some of these conversations were with respect to helping people find work. Others included rumours and gossip about the company.

When I logged into this website on Sunday 20 September 1998, I came across the following conversation.

Poster 1:   "I just heard from someone on the inside, that the Dublin site was outsourced today. More cuts..."

Poster 2:   "I tried e-mailing folks and oh – how they bounced. Thus, yes – tech support and customer service in Dublin has been outsourced and the 'redundant' employees were let go. And I thought we stopped the bleeding... Sick of it all."

Living in Dublin myself, I know that Quarterdeck had not shut down at that date. However, nobody from the company was replying. The damage was being done, and at least some of this damage in rumour and innuendo, staff and former staff dissatisfaction, was surely contributing to the very poor stock price for Quarterdeck.

(Interestingly, when I wrote about this episode in my New Thinking column, within 24 hours I had several people from this discussion group communicating to me – the power of Internet word of mouth.)

Gary Heil, author of the book *One Size Fits One*,[38] has talked about how companies are increasingly losing their ability to control how they are perceived in the marketplace. Heil referred to one customer who felt he had been mistreated by United Airlines. He launched a website. He was not the first, nor will he be the last.

There are lessons to be learned here. When former staff or former customers can create a community or grouping that has a worldwide network of the Internet, then it is time for companies to sit up and take notice. If companies do not work at informing their staff and satisfying their customers and trying to establish loyalty, then staff and customer dissatisfaction will begin to fill the vacuum. If companies do not work as fostering positive communities, then alternative communities will fill the vacuum.

Characteristics of Online Communities

How do you help build an online community? Well, that's a very difficult question, because communities are living things, full of the life of people. You can join a community and contribute to how it evolves, but you should not set out with some masterplan, because it won't work.

However, whether you help facilitate an already existing community move online, or whether you help build a brand new community online, the Internet environment is certain to impact on the nature of a community over time. The following are a number of characteristics that need to be considered when building or getting involved in online communities. Not surprisingly, they echo some of the central characteristics of traditional communities and include the following.

- Purpose and objectives (common vision).
- Connect with the 'real' world.
- Membership.
- Leadership.
- Rituals and planned activities.
- Rules and regulations.
- Managing change and evolution.
- Commercial transparency.
- Long-term commitment.

Purpose and Objectives (Common Vision)

> "Communities that survive have a purpose," Amy Jo Kim
> from Naima informed *Microsoft Internet Magazine* in 1997.
> "This is the single most important issue and one that's
> often forgotten, particularly by large corporations."

It is, indeed, amazing the number of website developments,
whether they be community-focused or not, that have no clear
purpose or objectives. It is amazing the number of websites that
are failures.

It is vital that when a purpose is articulated, it is followed
through with consistency. Many nascent online communities
start off with a particular set of objectives, only to diverge into
chaos soon after formation. In summarising the results of the
CIO.com survey on online communities it was stated that:

> Many people thought the worst thing about online commu-
> nities was information overload. A frequent complaint from
> the comments section was that e-mail discussion groups
> often change their focus from the original intention, and at
> times become an opinion free-for-all or fail completely.

Connect with the 'Real' World

One of the best ways is not to help build a community at all, but
rather facilitate an *already existing community* to spend some of its
time online. In pursuing such an objective, you need to see how
the characteristics of traditional communities, which I have
already described, can find best expression within an online context.

Even if it is appropriate to build an online community, it is
difficult to see how such a community can sustain itself on a
long-term basis, if all its interactions are virtual. We are, after all,
flesh and blood people and some sort of physical contact is necessary for strong and lasting relationships to develop.

There is a danger in general about the Internet that through
convenience and expediency it begins to replace social face to
face communication in areas where such face to face interaction
is vital for establishing and reinforcing company and community spirit and cohesion. There are things than should never be
said by e-mail.

A CIO.com 1998 online community survey[39] found that 86 per cent of respondents felt the best thing about online communities "was the extension of the real world, and the ability to interact with a broader range of people". The survey went on to state that online communities "are best to extend either existing relationships or further the relationship circle".

Internet consultant, Marc Rettig, in offering some tips on how to avoid ghost town syndrome stated that a online community should be "tied to real-world activities". In establishing 'Local Ireland',[40] an online community, with which Nua is involved, we set out not so much create an online community, but rather facilitate an already existing community to spend some of their time in an organised, well-structured manner online. It is estimated that the Irish Diaspora is 70 million worldwide. With 'Local Ireland' we are trying to create a global online structure and space that establishes a cohesive environment and marketplace for that community.

Membership
"Focus relentlessly on the needs of members," Joseph Cothrel, Research Director of Arthur Andersen's Next Generation Research Group[41] stated when discussing a 1998 study the group had carried out on online communities within large commercial organisations. To understand member needs, those who create successful online communities need to ask the right questions at the outset:

> Are members isolated from one another? Do members share information among themselves already? Do the people who lead or influence the members of the group support the idea of online collaboration? Is the subject matter something that people can be passionate about?

According to Jo Kim:[42]

> Part of being in a community is knowing the difference between being a member and not being a member. A lot of sites ask you to register, but it's not clear what you get for signing up. I encourage clients to make membership a ritual, to offer a newsletter, a unique member name, a unique portrait that allows you to express yourself and your interests. You should also receive access to different levels of service depending on your membership level.

If you want to create a strong online community, then there has to be some sort of 'price' attached to becoming a full member. While visitors should be actively encouraged to get involved, they should realise that full membership is not achieved until they have spent a certain period within the community, shown a strong commitment to the community, and/or have been accepted by other members. Remember, 'easy to join, easy to leave'.

Leadership/Moderation

As with traditional communities, online communities require charismatic leadership that is based on principles of co-operation. Howard Rheingold, in a conversation with Jennifer Fleming of *Anchor* magazine, emphasised the importance of a quality host (leader), stating that a host should be:

- an authority, or enforcer of rules;

- an exemplar, or one who models behaviours;

- a cybrarian, or guide to community information;

- a character/participant;

- a member of a community of hosts.

The Andersen study outlined a number of key functions of a host:

- **Member development**: Discovering core community members, recruiting others to join and participate.

- **Value management**: Managing the human, structural, and knowledge capital created by (and for) the community.

- **Moderation/Facilitation**: Finding ways to promote value-creating interactions.

In my experience, a good moderator, particularly in relation to discussion and debate, should:

- channel the discussion and activity without dictating it;

- make sure that things don't get out of control without seeming to impose control;

- seed new topics into the debate when there are signs that the debate might be waning;

- know when a topic has been fully explored and know how to put it to bed and move on to a fresh topic.

"What a good host does is welcome newcomers and make them comfortable," Jo Kim states. "A host will keep topics on track; ask interesting questions during lulls; acknowledge interesting posts; keep bad behaviour under control; and throw out disrupters. A good host makes all the difference in making people want to come back."

Not all hosts/moderators and other people who help out with an online community have to get paid, though this voluntary effort does need to be rewarded in other ways. (The Well, the oldest online community, used voluntary moderation very effectively.) One reward is that their efforts are recognised and praised. Another, is that they are given more say in how the community is run. The Andersen study stated that online communities need to "seek out and support members who take on informal roles". It claims that successful online communities have "a high degree of role differentiation. Many of these roles are informal and voluntary – and may not work otherwise".

Rituals and Planned Activities

As with all communities, rituals and other planned activities are an essential glue which will keep an online community together and give it a unique sense of identity. As Amy Jo Kim states:

Habits are built around daily, weekly monthly and yearly rhythms. Stopping to meet friends for a beer after work can be a daily thing. Watching your favourite television show has a weekly rhythm. Professional organisations have monthly meetings. Family reunions are yearly events. These rhythms are strong community builders, and you want to build these cycles into your online community. They give people something to plan for and help people to build habits around your site.

Rules and Regulations

An online community will not last very long without rules and regulations. From the purpose and objectives, people should be very clear what the community stands for. However, on a day to day basis, there needs to be a clear set of guidelines with regard to what sort of behaviour is accepted and what is not.

There needs to be a clearly articulated disputes resolution mechanism. It needs to be fair and transparent, but it needs to have the authority to judge what material should be removed and which members should be expelled. There is no point in shirking from these duties, because otherwise the community will fall into chaos and disappear.

"The way in which you handle disputes will shape your culture," Amy Jo Kim states. She also points out that: "There also must be a system for handling outside attacks."

While an online community does need rules, overt control of that community is another matter. There will be those who will expect that the online community will be a direct reflection of what the organisation, which helps build it, stands for. There will be those who will want to turn the community into a company PR vehicle. Forget about it.

The Andersen study stated that an organisation must "resist the temptation to control". It went on to point out that:

> Control can eliminate the creative space that fosters innovation, and that ultimately, control can kill or send online communities underground.

If the community is going to be worth its salt, it will have its own unique purpose and identity. This identity should be broadly complementary to that of the organisation that is helping build it, but it *will* be different. At times, the community may criticise the organisation. It will have to respond to that criticism in a balanced and positive manner.

Rules and regulations are absolutely necessary but, where possible, they must be agreed by the organisation in close co-operation with the community members. Communities are about partnership, and if there's no partnership, there's no community.

Managing Change and Evolution
It is vital to understand that it is in the medium to long-term that communities deliver their best worth. Building a community is never a short-term strategy.

A twenty person online community is very different from a 200 person one, which is very different from a 2,000 person one. Because the Internet is growing and changing so fast, online communities tend to be volatile – growing fast or dying fast. Managing change properly is critical in the long-term success of a community. As a community grows, older members may get resentful, newer members may feel excluded. Getting the balance right is critical.

There are many other balancing acts that need to be achieved. While an organisation needs to avoid control, it does need to provide active support, certainly in the early days.

> "Don't assume the community will be self-sustaining," the Andersen study on online communities states. "Some believe once the dynamic is created the community takes care of itself. In most cases online communities require a significant investment of time and effort to maintain. This is almost always greater than that required to launch the community."

Often what happens is that communities are started with a flurry of energy and idealism, then the hard, daily grind of keeping them going sets in. Marc Rettig, in a conversation with Jennifer Fleming of *Anchor*, talked about the need to avoid of the 'ghost town syndrome'.

Fleming explained that:[43]

> Sites with ghost town syndrome are marked by forums with little or no activity. Why are they ghost towns? Because building a conversation space doesn't mean people will come – and what's more people don't build communities. They join them. These behaviours extend to the Web, and Web communities that rise up around existing communities are likely to have a better chance of thriving.

In his interview with Jennifer Fleming, Howard Rheingold isolated three broad phases in the evolution of online communities. These are: structure, involvement and independence.

> "A host first plans conditions and provides rules (structure), laying the groundwork for a Web community," Fleming wrote. "As the community evolves, the host still needs to provide attention and intervention when needed (involvement).
>
> "Howard points out that, eventually, each community will want the tools and opportunity to make their own rules. This can be facilitated by means of a process handbook for democratic decision making, and access to people who have experienced the process themselves. This final

step allows for growth, self-government and collaborative work (independence)."

There are very challenging issues to address here from a commercial perspective. If an organisation gets heavily involved in helping build and support the formation and early development of a community, is it willing to give the community 'wings' when it is fully matured? And if so, how does it get its overall return from the investment?

In summarising the benefits and impacts of online communities within commercial organisations, the Andersen study found that they can:

- be a powerful tool for leveraging discretionary energy;
- ultimately empowering for individuals;
- create dynamics that may change the nature of business organisations.

The final point is very interesting, in that a successful online community – certainly one that is internally focused – may, in the long-term, change the very nature of the organisation itself. Management needs to be aware of this potential and be prepared for change that flows both ways.

Commercial Transparency
No organisation invests a large sum of money or effort for the fun of it. And very few people expect them to. An organisation needs to define clearly what it expects commercially from its investment in a community. It needs to then articulate that to the community so that everyone knows exactly what the commercial equation is. Thinking that people won't ask questions and demand answers in this area shows a complete lack of understanding of how the Internet environment operates. Be up front.

Long-term Commitment
One thing to remember before you get started: online community building is hard work. It's also stressful work. It's work that requires a lot of human skills. More than anything, it requires a long-term commitment, as the benefits may not become visible for several years.

When helping build an online community, you should think of the iceberg principle; it looks like a small job on the surface, but the more you dig the more that's involved. The Andersen study found that organisations significantly underestimated the costs of running online communities.

Online Community Strategies

Start your Own

The central advantage of starting your own community is that you have more of a say in establishing the purpose and objectives of that community. You will be able to direct its focus and subject matter more. However, as we covered earlier, control is a delicate issue. Inversely, the stronger the community grows the less control you will have over it.

Starting and evolving a community requires a set of social skills that many organisations simply do not have. Really, industrial age companies were not made to build communities but rather to build and sell products. A company may be required to sow the seeds of a community that will buy and support its products, but once that seed is rooted it should step aside and become a partner with the community rather than a ruler of it. (Of course, there is a different objective if it is an internal company community that is being built.)

Partner with a Community

Unless you're specifically in the business of community-building, or there is a genuine gap and need for a particular type of community, the best approach is to partner or join with a community that already exists. For communities to be sustainable they need a good mix of the commercial and the communal. By partnering with a community, by sponsoring and supporting its activities, you contribute in a positive manner to the long-term sustainability of that community. The community, in return, will give you its loyalty, will be a source of quality information and might even buy a few of your products.

Benefits of Online Communities

There are three broad benefits that online communities can deliver to an organisation. These are:

- company culture;
- sharing information (market research);
- selling products and building brand loyalty.

Company Culture

Companies today are increasingly facing the challenge to define what they do, who they are and what they stand for. At the same time, many are also facing the challenge of finding, keeping and engaging with the information worker. It is no longer feasible to decide 'at the top' what the company culture will be. And if you want to get and keep your information workers, you need, among other things, to listen to them, and involve them in decision processes.

An internal online community can be a great way of creating and maintaining a cohesive company culture and sense of purpose. A company may already have this sort of community, and therefore the Internet can be a way of extending and deepening it.

Sharing Information (Market Research)

"The goal is to share information or knowledge," the Andersen study states when explaining why an organisation should get involved in establishing an online community. A central problem that many companies face today is the wall that technology has established between them and their customers. Historically, companies were very close to their customers. There was constant interaction as people came into banks and talked to tellers, as sales reps got out on the road, as the support person helped out with a problem, as customers and companies chatted at social gatherings.

The wonders of the ATM machine has meant that people don't walk into banks anymore. Banks are delighted because they see their operational costs go down. The wonders of telecommunications mean that more and more companies are outsourcing their support functions. Managers are delighted as they see their operational costs go down. Do none of them stop to think about what they are losing? Am I the only one who believes that outsourcing of such client-facing functions is a type of involuntary suicide?

Companies wonder why they have such customer churn these days, why they are spending so much on getting new customers. There is such customer churn because with all these new 'virtual' channels to market, the face to face channels are continuing to weaken. Companies are doing more 'official' market research and getting consultants to tell them about their customers.

A well-nurtured online community can be an excellent vehicle for market research, for the to and fro of information, for regular feedback on what the customer feels and wants.

"Online communities provide a full circle of communication," Robert Levitan of iVillage, an online community for women, told CIO.com.[44] "You can get your marketing message out, get instantaneous reaction to it, and get research and data about your product, which helps you market new products in the future."

"When you do an e-mail or Web-based survey, you're less intrusive with a respondent," John Gilbert, marketing research manager at United Parcel Service, told the American Marketing Association's[45] 19th Annual Marketing Research Conference in Chicago in 1998. "On the Internet, they can respond at their own leisure. They can do it after hours if necessary. They can give it much more thought."

The problem is getting them to answer that questionnaire, as there are so many other ones out there. If people feel a loyalty to a company then they are more likely to do so.

Other advantages of using an online community as a market research environment include faster turnaround time and more direct and honest answers, particularly for open-ended questions. Beth Landa, a product research manager at Avon Products Inc. believes that on the Internet people are more forthright.

"They just barrage you with what they're thinking," she states. "They're not talking to a person and they really don't feel the need to be polite all of the time. They tell it like it is, and that's what I need in order to make progress".[46]

A Quaker Oats study found similar results. *The Industry Standard*, reporting on an online marketing research workshop, hosted by the Advertising Research Foundation in January 1999, stated that a "Quaker Oats study presented by researcher MARC Online found that Internet respondents may be more honest on sensitive topics than survey subjects intercepted in shopping malls. For example, online respondents' answers about how many snack foods they eat per week were more in line with Quaker Oats' internal data than answers the firm received from people in shopping malls. This was attributed to the fact that respondents may be reluctant confess to a human interviewer about how many snacks they really eat every week".[47]

The Industry Standard summarised the conclusions from the

workshop by stating that, "The unanimous result was that online and offline findings resulted in consistent business direction." Harris Black International,[48] for example, reported that they were able to accurately predict 21 out of 22 results in the November 1998 American elections by using online methods.

Of course, we're talking about a two-way flow of information here. If an organisation wants quality information from the community, it too must deliver quality information and be honest. It's a network; it's a transparent, accountable environment.

Selling Products and Building Brand Loyalty

At the beginning of this chapter, I wrote about how Amazon.com is using community strategies to sell more and more products ranges. I also wrote about communities of interest, and how the Internet is a perfect environment for niche marketing. Used effectively, community-oriented strategies help build up a very loyal and stable customer base.

In 1998, Donna Hoffman and Thomas Novak, of Vanderbilt University, wrote, in an article entitled "Trustbuilders vs. Trustbusters",[49] that "most consumers currently avoid engaging in relationship exchanges online". Why would that be? "The real reason consumers aren't yet shopping online in large numbers – or giving websites information in exchange for access to information – has to do with a fundamental lack of faith between most businesses and consumers on the Web today. In essence, consumers do not trust most Web providers enough to shop online."

We need to recognise that the Internet is essentially a sterile environment. There is nothing very solid about it, nothing that is touchable and real, very little that feeds the senses with familiar queues. People may visit a website but they don't often know if it is for real or not. (That is why established brands have a lot of potential if they are migrated successfully online. More on branding later.) You don't meet or greet anyone on a website.

Based on analysis of various Web surveys Hoffman and Novak stated that:

> Web consumers want an exchange based on an explicit social contract built on trust. They say they would share demographic information if the sites would only explain how the information collected is to be used.

Online communities can, if effectively nurtured, help establish genuine trust and loyalty for a company with its customer base and wider audiences. Internet analyst Esther Dyson has pointed out that America Online – one of the world's most successful online brands – "evaluates its offerings by whether they contribute to retaining subscribers, not their independent profitability".[50]

Writing for *CIO* magazine in 1998, Scott Kirsner stated that:

> Providing a forum for community can also help companies service and retain customers – as Oldsmobile discovered when it sponsored a nightly celebrity chat series and accompanying message board on America Online. Not only did the celebrity vibe help Oldsmobile revitalise a stodgy brand, but users actually went to the message board to talk about the cars. When Olds marketing managers in Detroit checked in to answer questions, they found that other customers had beaten them to the punch. Members of the die-hard Olds community were promoting the car to sceptics and addressing the needs of dissatisfied Olds buyers.

Now, what could be better than that!?

The Problem with Online Communities

The problem with chosen or online communities is that they are indeed 'chosen'. The traditions and customs that can be seen as restrictive in traditional communities are often the cement that give these communities their stability and long-lasting quality.

Cyberspace is presently a very flexible world. As William A Galston points out:[52]

> Considerable evidence suggests that the Internet facilitates the invention of online personalities at odds with offline realities and that the ability to simulate identities is one of its most attractive features for many users (gender-bending is said to be especially popular). But the playful exercise of the imagination, whatever its intrinsic merits and charms, is not readily compatible with the development of meaningful affective ties.

Online communities tend to be easy to enter and easy to leave. Membership in what we have known as communities up until now has nearly always required some degree of sacrifice for the 'common good'. Squaring the circle of individual choice and free speech with the need to belong and feel part of something is what chosen communities essentially claim to do.

William A Galston uses irony to examine what is possibly a debilitating flaw in many online communities.

"In today's cultural climate, anything less than voluntary community will trap individuals in webs of oppressive relations," he writes. "And what could be worse than that? My answer: learning to make the best of circumstances one has not chosen is part of what it means to be a good citizen and mature human being. We should not organise our lives around the fantasy that entrance and exit can always be cost-free. Online groups can fulfil important emotional and utilitarian needs. But they must not be taken as comprehensive models of a future society."

The CIO.com survey[53] found that "70 per cent of respondents replied that although a virtual community felt like a legitimate community, it was not the same as a real-world community (barring obvious physical differences). Most respondents also stated that at least some face to face communication was necessary for complex relationships to form (partly due to trust issues)".

It may be that the word 'community' is very often being confused in an online context with what we know offline to be clubs or associations. A club or association has a rather limited and defined objective and sphere of interaction. People join these organisations for defined reasons, looking for defined returns. For example, somebody joins a chess club primarily to play chess. They may also want social interaction but chess will generally remain the central objective.

It may be that the Internet is a fertile environment within which business can help establish or support clubs, associations and loyalty programmes with defined rewards for both the members and the sponsoring company.

Whether it is clubs or communities, or some hybrid of the two, the Internet has established a new type of interactive environment. How it all pans out in the future, nobody exactly knows, but I am certain that organisations – particularly larger ones – will ignore the phenomenon of online communities at their peril.

REFERENCES

1. T Bender, *Community and Social Change in America* (Johns Hopkins University: 1982)

2. Foundation for Community Encouragement, http://www.fce-community.org

3. *The Irish Times,* http://www.irish-times.com/

4. Sou Yang, http://csucub.csuchico.edu/PubFld/96Mag/Science%2FCom/souyang1.html

5. F Moore Lappé and P M Du Bois, "Me to We: From Devolved Community to Involved Community" The Johnson Foundation (1995) http://www.johnsonfdn.org/library/annreps/rep9596/metowe.html

6. W A Galston, "(How) does the Internet affect Community? Some Speculations in search of Evidence" John F Kennedy School of Government Harvard University (1996) http://www.ksg.harvard.edu/visions/galston.htm

7. Kathryn Holmuist, *The Irish Times* (1998)

8. F Moore Lappé and P M Du Bois, "Me to We: From Devolved Community to Involved Community" The Johnson Foundation (1995) http://www.johnsonfdn.org/library/annreps/rep9596/metowe.html

9. J C Dvorak, "I could get fired for this" *PC Magazine* (31 August 1998) http://www.zdnet.com/pcmag/insites/dvorak/jd980831.htm

10. Racine County, http://www.racinecounty.com/

11. Four Worlds, http://home.uleth.ca/~4worlds/

12. Sustainable Communities Network, http://www.chebucto.ns.ca/

13. The Hannover Principles, http://minerva.acc.virginia.edu/~arch/pub/hannover_list.html

14. Internet News interview with Howard Rheingold (1998) http://www.techweb.com/wire/Internet /profile/hrheingold/interview

15. "The Biosphere and Concepts of Ecology: Community Ecology: Patterns of Community Structure: Biodiversity and the Stability of Communities" *Britannica Online,* http://www.eb.com:180/cgibin/g?DocF=macro /5000/74/39.html

16. Awahnee Principles, http://www.geog.utah.edu/urbpl527/ traditional/ahwahnee.html

17. F Moore Lappé and P M Du Bois, "Me to We: From Devolved Community
    to Involved Community" The Johnson Foundation (1995)
    http://www.johnsonfdn.org/library/annreps/rep9596/metowe.html

18. Institute for the Study of Civic Values, http://www.libertynet.org/edcivic/
    iscvhome.html

19. D Popenoe, *Disturbing the Nest: Family Change and Decline in Modern
    Societies*, (Walter De Gruyter: 1988)

20. F Moore Lappé and P M Du Bois, "Me to We: From Devolved Community
    to Involved Community" The Johnson Foundation (1995)
    http://www.johnsonfdn.org/library/annreps/rep9596/metowe.html

21. W A Galston, "(How) Does the Internet affect Community? Some
    Speculations In search of evidence" John F Kennedy School of
    Government Harvard University (1996)
    http://www.ksg.harvard.edu/visions/galston.htm

22. Howard Rheingold, "*The Virtual Community: Searching for Connection in a
    Computerized World* (1993), http://edge.stud.u-szeged.hu/cyber/ xan-
    ner/1-vircom.html

23. J Michalski, "What is Virtual Community?" *New Perspectives Quarterly* (1995)

24. Amy Jo Kim, Naima, http://www.naima.com/

25. R D Hof, S Browder and P Elstrom, "Internet Communities: Forget
    Surfers. A New Class of Netizen is Settling Right in" *Business Week*
    (May 5 1997), http://www.businessweek.com/1997/18/b35251.htm

26. S Kirsner, "Community Theater" *CIO Magazine* (December 1997)
    http://www.cio.com/archive/webbusiness/120197_main.html

27. C Guglielmo and K Weisul, "Portals are getting into the community spir-
    it" *Inter@ctive Week* (17 August 1998)
    http://www.zdnet.com/intweek/print/980817/345091.html

28. C Bermant, "Welcome to Hometown.com" *The Industry Standard*
    (9 August 1998), http://www.thestandard.net/articles/article_print
    /0,1454,1320,00.html

29. S Kirsner, "Community Theater" *CIO Magazine* (December 1997)
    http://www.cio.com/archive/webbusiness/120197_main.html

30. D Tapscott, "Wealth Creation in the 21st Century" *Intellectual Capital*
    (11 June 1998), http://www.intellectualcapital.com/issues/98/0611
    /icbusiness2.asp

31. "Death of The Company Town?" Editorial Media,
    http://www.prcentral.com/rmso95cotown.htm

32. "Industrial and Organizational Relations: Worker, Manager, and Society:
    Responsibility to the community" *Britannica Online*
    http://www.eb.com:180/cgi-bin/g?DocF=macro/5007/45/3.html

33. Hally Enterprises, http://hallyenterprises.com/

34. Towers Perrin, http://www.towers.com/

35. B Manasco, *1to1 Marketing*, http://www.1to1.com/

36. F F Reichheld, *The Loyalty Effect: The Hidden Force Behind Growth, Profits,
    and Lasting Value* (Harvard Business School Press: 1996)

37. Pierre DuBois & Associates, http://www.pierre-dubois.com/

38. G Heil, T Parker, D C Stephens, *One Size Fits One: Building Relationships
    One Customer and One Employee at a Time* (John Wiley & Sons: 1996)

39. "Virtual World Communities Survey" *CIO.com* (1998)
    http://www.cio.com/forums/behavior/survey4.html

40. Local Ireland, http://www.local.ie

41. Next Generation Research Group, Arthur Andersen,
    http://www.ngrg.com/

42. Amy Jo Kim, Naima, http://www.naima.com/

43. J Fleming, "Web '98 Conference Coverage" *Anchor* (September 1998)
    http://www.ahref.com/features/web98/jenniferfleming.html

44. S Kirsner, "Community Theater" *CIO Magazine*, (December 1997)
    http://www.cio.com/archive/webbusiness/120197_main.html

45. "Market Surveys Hit The Net" Reuters (September 1998)
    http://www.pcworld.com/pcwtoday/article/0,1510,8136,00.html

46. *Ibid.*

47. M J Thompson, "Market Researchers Embrace the Web" *The Industry
    Standard* (26 January, 1999), http://www.thestandard.net/articles/dis-
    play/0,1449,3274,00.html

48. Harris Black International, http://www.harrisblackintl.com/

49. D Hoffman and T Novak, "Trustbuilders vs. Trustbusters" *The Industry*

Standard (11 May 1998), http://www.idg.net/idg_frames/english/content.cgi?vc=docid_9-60444.html

50. J Michalski, "Community, Part I" *Release 1.0* (June 1993)
    http://edventure.com/release1/0693body.html

51. S Kirsner, "Community Theater" *CIO Magazine* (December 1997)
    http://www.cio.com/archive/webbusiness/120197_main.html

52. W A Galston, "(How) does the Internet affect Community? Some
    Speculations in search of Evidence" John F Kennedy School of
    Government Harvard University (1996)
    http://www.ksg.harvard.edu/visions/galston.htm

53. "Virtual World Communities Survey" *CIO.com* (1998)
    http://www.cio.com/forums/behavior/survey4.html

© Fergal Lawler 1999

7
Computers: Our Greatest Tool?

NEW TOOLS

It is not a bad definition of man to describe him as a tool-making animal. His earliest contrivances to support uncivilised life were tools of the simplest and rudest construction. His latest achievements in the substitution of machinery, not merely for the skill of the human hand, but for the relief of the human intellect, are founded on the use of tools of a still higher order.

So stated Charles Babbage (1791-1871),[1] the inventor of the analytical engine and widely acknowledged 'father of the computer'. From early times, a number of factors have differentiated humans from other animals. These included:

- the size of our brains;

- our capacity to communicate using complex language;

- our capacity to work in groups;

- our capacity to make and use tools.

Tools have always been central to our progress as a species. Our 'ages' – the Stone Age, the Bronze Age, the Iron Age, the agricultural age, the industrial age, the digital age – are in fact called after the ingredients that went into making our tools.

Marshall McLuhan, another 'father' – this time of the digital age – subtitled his seminal 1960s book, *Understanding Media*,[2] with the phrase, *The Extensions of Man*. Indeed, tools have always extended our ability to do things. The technology-based tools that we are making today are no exception. In fact, the word 'technology' may be defined as the organised study of techniques for making and doing things.

If someone uses a tool long enough, do they begin to take on the characteristics of the tool? If someone works in a factory long enough, do they begin to exhibit characteristics of the factory? To put it another way, though 'man' maketh the tool, does the tool, ultimately, re-maketh the man?

These are important questions, and while not within the scope of this book, are worth keeping in mind as we tread fearlessly forward. As Gene I Rochlin put it in *Trapped in the Net: The Unanticipated Consequences of Computerization:*[3]

> Humans seem always to regard what they have made as something that they can therefore control. That our history has been shaped by the form and use of our tools in ways totally unanticipated by their inventors is, as always, conveniently forgotten.

THE RISE OF COMPUTERS

"The line between human and computer at some point will become completely blurred," predicted Alvin Toffler in his 1981 book *Third Wave*.[4] Few tools have become as central to the functioning of society as the computer. The computer is everywhere.

As Kevin Kelly wrote in his "New Rules for the New Economy" article for *Wired*:[5]

> The notion that all doors in a building should contain a computer chip seemed ludicrous ten years ago, but now there is hardly a hotel door without a blinking, beeping chip. Soon, if National Semiconductor gets its way, every FedEx package will be stamped with a disposable silicon flake that smartly tracks the contents.

To put it all into some sort of context, let's have a brief look at how to computer has evolved over the last 50 years to its present all-encompassing position.

A (Very) Brief History of Computers

There is debate as to who exactly invented the first computer, though most would agree that it was the Second World War that first brought it to prominence. However, the computer didn't really have a major impact on business until the 1960s. Even then and into the 1970s, it was only large business that used its giant mainframes.

It was the 1980s, with the introduction of the personal computer (PC), that the computer began to have a wider influence on business and society. The PC was a revolution, in that it opened up to a broad range of people to the power and potential of computing. Before the PC, the computer was something almost mystical, something hidden away in some 'computer room'. With the introduction of the PC, things would never be the same again.

The PC had a modest beginning. As the *New York Times* put it:

> In June 1982, the IBM personal computer, only a few months on the market, offered a maximum of 256 kilobytes of memory, a choice of one or two floppy disk drives and an optional colour monitor. Fully configured it cost close to $7,000. A hard drive was not an option, but the entire operating system, which IBM had purchased from a 32-person company called Microsoft, fit easily on one 128k floppy disk with room to spare.

The article went on to explain that a 1998 PC would have 1,500 times the memory and that its hard disk would be 47,000 times the size as the original floppy drive.

With the 1990s, computing power kept increasing and its price kept dropping. As George Gilder stated in 1997:

> Computing power has risen 100 million-fold since the late-1950s – a 100,000-fold rise in power times a thousand-fold drop in cost.

As the decade comes to a close, PCs are in more than 40 per cent of American homes, and computer chips are everywhere.

A Select Chronology of Computers

1833 The 'first' computer, the analytical machine is invented by Charles Babbage.

1911 Computer Tabulating Recording Company is formed in the United States – it will later become known as IBM.

1937 The binary calculator is invented by George Stibitz at Bell Labs.

1939 Z2, what some regard as the first modern computer is invented by Konrad Zuse in Germany.

1945 The ENIAC, which, in most textbooks, is regarded as the first modern computer, becomes fully operational. It weighs 30 tons, is 100 feet long and 8 feet high. It contains almost 18,000 vacuum tubes.

1947 A dead moth has been found to cause a malfunction and the term 'computer bug' is invented.

1947 The transistor is invented.

1949 According to the magazine *Popular Mechanics*: "Computers in the future may weigh no more that 1.5 tons."

1954 The first mass-produced computer is introduced by IBM.

1960 There are some 2,000 computers in use in the United States.

1965 Gordon Moore establishes 'Moore's Law'. It basically predicts that computer chips will double in power every eighteen months and halve in price. Moore's Law has remained true over three decades.

1971 Intel introduces the first microprocessor.

1975 Bill Gates and Paul Allen found Microsoft (formally known as Traf-O-Data).

1976 Steve Jobs and Steve Wozniak form the Apple Computer Company.

1978 There are some 500,000 computers in the United States.

1980 Microsoft is given the contract to write an operating system for IBM. Bill Gates buys DOS for $50,000.

1981 Bill Gates predicts that, "640k should be enough for anybody".

1981 IBM releases the first personal computer (PC).

1982 The computer is named 'Man of the Year' by *Time* magazine.

1983 There are over 10 million computers in the United States.

1984 The Macintosh is introduced by Apple.

1986 There are over 30 million computers in the United States.

1989 There are over 100 million computers worldwide.

1993 Intel's Pentium is released.

1997 Sub-$1,000 computers become more common.
1998 Apple releases the iMac.

Key Impacts of Computers

Computers are having a number of specific impacts on business and society. These include the following.

- Automation.
- Commoditisation.
- Mass customisation.
- Individual empowerment.
- Rapid change.

Automation

One of the central objectives of computer design has been to automate processes historically carried out by humans. We see this in everything from the bar code tracking of products in supermarkets, to automated bank teller machines in streets, to the robot-assisted assembly of cars in factories. In time, we will have robots that will automate housework.

Commoditisation

Computer chips are turning more and more of our products into commodities. With computers inside practically everything these days, the actual difference between competing products is diminishing. Basic performance levels are evening out in an increasing number of product sectors. In this sort of environment, you gain competitive advantage by strong branding (with a focus on style) and by developing lasting relationships with your customers.

Mass Customisation

A computer-automated production environment greatly lends itself to mass customisation. We have always had customisation – from custom-built cars to custom-made clothes – but it was of necessity for people with significant income. However, the flexibility of computer-controlled production processes allows customisation to reach the masses in an economical manner. Perfect examples of mass customisation are the Dell and Gateway websites.

Individual Empowerment
With the advent of the PC, a key characteristic of computers became decentralisation and by extension empowerment of the individual. The large mainframes centralised everything but the PC brought power to the desktop and ultimately to the home. Without the PC and the ensuing individual empowerment, the Internet could not have grown at the pace it has. The PC empowers the individual more than it empowers the organisation.

Rapid Change
Computers are infiltrating all areas of society. The fact that computer processing power is increasing so rapidly and computer prices are dropping equally as fast and new models are coming out so often, means that society is in a flux of change.

The Emperor's New Computers?
Nobody doubts that computers are one of humanity's greatest inventions, or that they have had a huge impact on society and will continue to have an even greater one. However, I believe that many are now questioning the human costs of this impact, probing it to see what exactly computers have delivered, how in reality they have improved our quality of life. People are rightly asking the question: Are we undergoing progress just for progress' sake?

We have seen in the Chapter 5, *Truths and Myths of the Information Society*, that computers have not delivered that dreamed of leisure society, and that they have moved very many people from relatively high-paying manufacturing jobs to lower paying services jobs. There are many other areas in society where the computer has not lived up to expectations.

The Paperless Office
Remember the 'paperless office' that computers were supposed to introduce? A 1998 report funded by the Electronic Document Systems Foundation[6] found that people still want paper, predicting that in twenty years, "reading, printing and publishing will still be recognisably similar to what it is today". Xplor International, a document research organisation has stated that while 90 per cent of the information in the office was paper-based in 1994, that will drop to 50 per cent by 2004.[7]

That doesn't necessarily mean that we will have less paper to deal with. According to market research firm Norwell, the number of pages produced by American offices is rising by 6 per cent each year and is expected to hit 1.54 trillion by 2000. The *Financial Times*[8] has reported that the volume of paper used in offices around the globe grows at 20 per cent per year. One would think that with the introduction of e-mail, for example, the paper flow would slow. Not so, according to Hewlett-Packard[9], who stated that when e-mail is introduced in an office, printing skyrockets by 40 per cent.

Computers and the Productivity Puzzle

Thomas Landauer in his 1995 book *The Trouble with Computers*,[10] piles fact upon crushing fact illustrating that for all the massive spending on information technology, productivity gains have been minimal. In fact, perversely, studies have shown that in numerous sectors, heavy investment in information technology brought about productivity *loss*.

Landauer's book makes the points that:

a) computers have not contributed nearly as much to labour productivity as we had hoped – or by rights, they should;

b) for the jobs most people do in service enterprises, most computer applications make work only a little more efficient;

c) the efficiency effects of computer applications designed in traditional ways are improving very slowly, if at all;

d) efficiency effects of applications designed with the new, user-centred methods improve very rapidly.

In the United States, productivity growth for the period 1973-1993 was less than half that for the period 1950-1973. While the oil crisis of the 1970s certainly played its part in reducing productivity, it does not go to explain the whole picture. Certainly, one would have expected that with the very high spending on information technology that occurred in that period there would have been significant productivity gains as well as losses.

Spending on information technology has indeed been significant and accelerating for most organisations over the last 25 years, as Morgan Stanley's Stephen Roach, pointed out in his 1997 paper, "The Boom for Whom: Revisiting America's Technology Paradox".[11]

Over the 1990-96 interval, corporate America spent a total of
$1.1 trillion (current dollars) on IT hardware alone, a rate of
investment that is fully 80 per cent faster than the rate in the
first seven years of the 1980s.

Roach went on to point out that:

60 per cent of annual corporate IT budgets go toward
replacement of outdated equipment and increasingly frequent product replacement.

Even asides from the lack of significant productivity contribution
by computers during the 1980s and early-1990s, one would have
expected that the major trend of 'downsizing' would have contributed to an upswing in productivity. Downsizing in essence has
meant replacing people with computers, so as to cut costs.

However, a 1994 paper entitled "Downsizing and
Productivity Growth: Myth or Reality?"[12] by Martin Baily, Eric
Bartelsman and John Haltiwanger, found that downsizing does
not necessarily improve productivity.

"In contrast to the conventional wisdom," the paper stated, "we find that plants that increased employment as well
as productivity contribute almost as much to overall productivity growth in the 1980s as the plants that increased
productivity at the expense of employment."

As Louis Uchitelle put it in an article for the New York Times in
1996:[13]

At the end of the 19th century, railroads and electric
motors were expected to transform America, making a
young industrial economy far more productive than any
seen before. And they did. At the end of the 20th century,
computers were supposed to perform the same miracle.
They haven't.

THE REAL PROBLEM WITH COMPUTERS

We have a problem, Silicon Valley.

This problem, in my opinion, lies with a mechanistic, logical and industrial view of the world that was driven deeper into the thinking of our societies with every pump of an engine, grind of a tooling machine and calculation of a computer. For everything there is a theory, for everything there is a model, for everything there is a logical solution, is how this mechanistic thinking goes.

From its invention in the 1940s to the early-1990s, the computer has been seen by many as the Holy Grail of machines and logic. Many of those who established the theory and science of computers and programming took a view that in fact *people were the problem* and the computer was the machine that would sort out that problem.

Down through the years, a significant number of programmers and champions of information technology saw people as little more than illogical nuisances. While software and hardware may have been designed by humans, they were not designed *for* humans.

The essence of the 'trouble with computers' is well illustrated by a quotation Thomas Landauer attributes to a senior vice-president of a major supermarket chain.

> If the customer walks in with a magnetic-strip-reader card and identifies herself as customer X, we can track every single thing she buys and do all kinds of wonderful things with that information.

In this manager's mind, the pesky customer is an object that should behave in a defined, planned way.

A mitigating factor here is that in the early years of computer design, processing power and storage was very expensive and difficult to come by. Getting computer time was no easy process. Therefore, it became ingrained in the minds of many computer programmers and engineers that computers should only be used for the most important of tasks, such as making nuclear bombs, solving huge mathematical problems or landing on the moon. In that period, the very idea that such a valuable resource should be used to allow people to *communicate* with each other was seen as an outrage and affront.

A traditional computer programmer is a strange breed. Historically, they have often prided themselves in making things difficult. Their special joy is in 'figuring out' and they cannot understand why the rest of the world doesn't get a kick out of figuring out too. To this day, there is a definite resistance among many in the computer industry with regard to engaging with the great 'unwashed' public. Although we have marketing phrases such as 'plug 'n' play' (plug 'n' pray), making things genuinely easy goes against the grain for many computer programmers. The computer as a 'consumer product' is a certain kind of blasphemy.

Some programmers shrink at the idea that there will soon be a computer in every home, feeling that the 'specialness' and uniqueness of owning a computer is then diffused. These people design computers and software, not for people to use, but for other computer programmers to admire. The more lines of code, the more hip functions, the more kudos they get. Consequently, much software is cumbersome and difficult to use.

In *The Trouble with Computers*, Thomas Landauer estimates that, if software programmes were designed with the user in mind, then productivity within the service sector would rise by 4 to 9 per cent annually. He notes that the average user interface has more than 40 flaws. If the easiest twenty of these flaws were corrected then usability would improve by an *incredible* 50 per cent. Landauer notes that if users are factored in from the beginning, then extraordinary efficiency improvements of over *700 per cent* can be achieved.

Little has changed since the publication of Landauer's book. A 1998 survey by Standish Group International[14] found that 45 per cent of a software application's features are never used, 19 per cent rarely used, 16 per cent sometime used, 13 per cent often used and 7 per cent always used. Yet, in spite of this fact, software gets bigger and bigger. Microsoft Windows went from 3 million lines of code (Windows 3.1) to 14 million lines (Windows 95) to 18 million (Windows 98).[15]

Inventor of Pascal, Niklaus Wirth, has put forward two new laws for software: 'software expands to fill the available memory' and 'software is getting slower more rapidly than hardware gets faster'. As you watch Intel's processors get faster and Microsoft's software get fatter, you begin to feel that you are spending to stand still. As someone wryly commented to me, "I bought my first computer in 1994 and I've been upgrading ever since."

Designed with Contempt

No wonder computers have not contributed to productivity the way they should have. And to think of the promise held out by computers in the 1950s and 1960s. To think of the sheer infatuation many of the computer pioneers had for the new machine, which in many cases was only matched by the contempt they had for people.

In 1958, Herbert A Simon and Allen Newell predicted that computers would before long be able to do anything a human could do.[16] Marvin Minsky in 1968 believed that all you needed were some good "semantic models" if you wanted computers to "write really good music or draw highly meaningful pictures".[17] George Miller in 1972 made the statement that:

> Many psychologists have come to take for granted in recent years...that men and computers are merely different species of a more abstract genus called 'information processing machines'.[18]

Professor John McCarthy once stated that:

> The only reason we have not yet succeeded in formalising every aspect of the real world is that we have been lacking a sufficiently powerful logical calculus. I am presently working on that problem.[19]

The same professor also asked the question: "What do judges know that we cannot tell a computer?"

In 1960, Herbert Simon predicted that:

> Within the very near future – much less than 25 years – we shall have the technical capability of substituting machines for any and all human functions in organisations. Within the same period, we shall have acquired an extensive and empirically tested theory of human cognitive processes and their interaction with human emotions, attitudes and values.[20]

Simon's timing was somewhat off, but his thinking and approach to problem solving has imbued many an organisation over the last 30 years. In 1970, J W Forrester stated that:

It is my basic view that the human mind is not adapted to interpreting how social systems behave...Until recently there have been no ways to estimate the behaviour of social systems except by contemplation, discussion, argument and guesswork.[21]

In 1974, B F Skinner stated that:

The disastrous results of common sense in the management of human behaviour are evident in every walk of life, from international affairs to the care of a baby. We shall continue to be inept in all these fields until a scientific analysis clarifies the advantage of a more effective technology.[22]

What strikes me most about the above comments is the contempt with which they have for people – you and me. No wonder computers have not helped people in the way they could have. They were not meant to. No wonder people have, historically, had a fear of computers. In the eyes of so many pioneers, people were the problems that computers were going to solve.

The Great Addiction

The really worrying thing is that computers have become indispensable to society without in fact delivering significant value and productivity, as Joseph Weizenbaum pointed out in his book, *Computer Power and Human Reason: From Judgement to Calculation.*[23]

Our society's growing reliance on computer systems that were initially intended to help people make analyses and decisions, but have long since surpassed the understanding of their users and become indispensable to them.

As Gene Rochlin put it in his book, *Trapped in the Net: The Unanticipated Consequences of Computerization:*[24]

...the complacent acceptance of the desktop 'personal' computer in almost every aspect of modern life is masking the degree to which computerisation and computer networking are transforming not just the activities and instruments of human affairs, but also their structure and practice.

The adoption of computers to organise, manage, integrate, and co-ordinate a wide variety of human activities has greatly augmented human capabilities and increased the scope and connectivity of human activities...But at what cost to resiliency and adaptability? Office networking allows considerable interactive flexibility, as do market transfer systems, electronic banking, and the Internet, but the requirements for compliance and strict adherence to standards and protocols are stringent. Just-in-time industrial systems offer great flexibility in manufacturing, but, as was discovered in the recent Kobe earthquake, they are essentially inoperable if the electronic system that co-ordinates and schedules the required network of tightly coupled activities is damaged or destroyed.

BRINGING IT ALL BACK HOME

The Internet offers the opportunity of bringing it all back home. Because, the Internet makes the computer – and those who design them – focus primarily on the needs of people, not the desires of technicians. The Internet has changed the computer from being a tool, the major focus of which was on computation and processing, to one that also embraces communication.

This is a fundamental and necessary shift. The Internet humanises the computer. The Internet makes the computer a truly useful consumer tool. With the Internet, the computer embraces society. That is why the Internet is so revolutionary and important.

REFERENCES

1. Charles Babbage, http://www-groups.dcs.stand.ac.uk/~history /Mathematicians / Babbage.html

2. M McLuhan, *Understanding Media: The Extensions of Man* (MIT Press)

3. G I Rochlin, *Trapped in the Net: The Unanticipated Consequences of Computerization* (Princeton University Press: 1998)

4. A Toffler, *Third Wave* (Bantam Books: 1991)

5. K Kelly, "New Rules for the New Economy" *Wired* (September 1997) http://www.wired.com:80/wired/archive/5.09/newrules.html Now available in book form: K Kelly, *New Rules for the New Economy* (Viking Press: 1998)

6. Electronic Document Systems Foundation, http://www.xplor.org/

7. *Ibid.*

8. *Financial Times,* http://www.ft.com/

9. Hewlett Packard, http://www.hp.com/

10. T K Landauer, *The Trouble With Computers: Usefulness, Usability and Productivity* (MIT Press: 1996)

11. S S Roach, "The Boom for Whom: Revisiting America's Technology Paradox" (Morgan Stanley: 1997), http://www.ms.com/

12. M Baily, E Bartelsman and J Haltiwanger, "Downsizing and Productivity Growth: Myth or Reality?" CES 94-4 (May 1994) http://www.census.gov/ces/abstracts/abs94_4.html

13. L Uchitelle, "Measured in Productivity Gains, the Computer is a Disappointment" 191*New York Times* (8 December 1996) http://uainfo.arizona.edu/~weisband/411_511/product_nyt.html

14. The Standish Group, http://www.standishgroup.com/

15. Niklaus Wirth, http://www.cs.inf.ethz.ch/~wirth/

16. J Weizenbaum, *Computer Power and Human Reason: From Judgement to Calculation* (W H Freeman & Co: 1976)

17. *Ibid.*

18. *Ibid.*

19. *Ibid.*

20. *Ibid.*

21. *Ibid.*

22. *Ibid.*

23. *Ibid.*

24. G I Rochlin, *Trapped in the Net: The Unanticipated Consequences of Computerization* (Princeton University Press: 1998)

© Fergal Lawler 1999

8
Understanding the Internet

REQUIEM FOR THE ARPANET

Like distant islands sundered by the sea,
We had no sense of one community.
We lived and worked apart and rarely knew
That others searched with us for knowledge, too.

Vint Cerf ('Father of the Internet')[1]

KNOW YOUR ROOTS

To understand how best to do business on the Internet, it is important to truly *understand* the Internet.

Understanding the roots of the Internet is like understanding the grammar of a language. Understanding its history is like understanding the history of your country and world. If you don't know where the Internet came from, why it was invented and how it evolved, then it will be difficult for you to put into context what is happening on the Internet today and what might happen next month. More importantly, it will be difficult for you to get the best out of the Internet.

The best way to succeed on the Internet is to imitate the things that make it a success. If you don't understand it, at a roots level, then you can't hope to implement such a strategy.

As a first step in understanding the Internet, let's step though a selected timeline. One of the things that will strike someone about this timeline is that, although the basic network for the Internet has been around since the 1960s, it was not until the 1990s and the introduction of the World Wide Web, that the Internet became a true phenomenon.

SELECTED INTERNET TIMELINE

1957: The Soviet Union launches Sputnik and sends a major wake-up call to the United States.

1964: RAND proposal (brainchild of Paul Baran) outlining the principles of what would evolve into the Internet.

1965: The Pentagon's Advanced Research Projects Agency (ARPA) – which was a formal response to the Soviet launch of Sputnik – begins work on its network. Ted Nelson coins the phrase 'hypertext'.

1968: First test network using RAND principles established by the National Physical Laboratory in Great Britain.

1969: ARPA launches more ambitious project to be called ARPANET (which is the forerunner of the Internet). Four research institutes/universities form the original net-work.

1971: 23 host computers on ARPANET.

1972: 37 host computers on ARPANET. The first e-mail message is sent.

1973: First international connections to ARPANET.

1974: Telenet, the first commercial version of the ARPANET is launched. The term 'Internet' is used for the first time.

1975: 4 billion minutes of international telephone calls.

1979: Newsgroups are established.

1980: Over 10,000 people are connected to ARPANET.

1981: There are over 200 host computers connected to APRANET. IBM releases the first PC.

1984: National Science Foundation begins to support the growth of the Internet. There are over 1,000 host computers on the Internet.

1985: Whole Earth Lectronic Link (WELL), the first 'online community' is formed.

1986: E-mail mailing lists developed.

1987: There are over 10,000 host computers on the Internet.

1988: There are over 60,000 host computers on the Internet. First major virus attack occurs.

1989: ARPANET formally closed down. Tim Berners-Lee formulates the idea for the World Wide Web.

1990: There are over 300,000 host computers on the Internet.

1991: National Science Foundation lifts restrictions on commercial traffic.

1992: There are 1 million host computers on the Internet. The

World Wide Web becomes a reality. The Internet links some 17,000 networks in over 30 countries.

1993: Estimated that some 4 million people use the Internet, with 1.5 million host computers. In February, NCSA releases Mosaic, the World Wide Web browser that would truly ignite the revolution.

1994: Netscape is formed. The first Internet commerce is transacted and there are 3 million host computers. About 8 million Internet users.

1995: 7 million host computers. National Science Foundation discontinues its Internet funding; commercial organisations take up the slack. Netscape goes public and makes Wall Street history by doubling its share price within a day of its first public offering. There are approximately 20 million Internet users.

1996: There are almost 10 million host computers on the Internet connecting upwards of 150 countries. There are approximately 50 million Internet users.

1997: MCI predicts that the total volume of data traffic will supersede the total volume of voice traffic on global phone systems by 2000. 80 billion minutes in international telephone calls. A transatlantic call costs 1.5 per cent of what it cost 60 years previously. World Bank predicts that by 2010 it will have fallen by another two-thirds. There are approximately 100 million Internet users.

1998: Four out of five Internet users in the United States say the Internet has improved their lives. Three out of four American Internet users shopped online during the Christmas season. There are approximately 150 million Internet users. (And a lot of other things happen as well.)

WHY WAS THE INTERNET INVENTED?

When I searched the Internet to find out information about its history, I found conflicting reports with regard to why it was invented. Most said that it was because of the threat of nuclear war but some refuted that idea.

What is interesting here is the fact that the Internet – being the world's greatest library and information resource – offers many opinions and theories on a huge range of subjects. The information child and adult of the future will not take their 'facts' from one source, but must be able to interpret between differing opinions to find the 'truth' of the matter.

It seems to be agreed that the specific event that would result in the Internet being invented was the launch of Sputnik by the Soviet Union in 1957. Before Sputnik, America had felt that it was on top of the world; unassailable. The launch of Sputnik was a huge shock to the American system. How had communism managed to 'get ahead' of capitalism?

As a result of the Sputnik launch, a number of agencies and initiatives were established, one of which would result in the nascent Internet. Specifically, the Internet was invented because the US military needed a communications system robust enough to withstand a nuclear strike from Russia. More particularly, the military did not want to have one or even a small number of central points in its communications infrastructure, which would have meant that if the Russians targeted them they could cripple America's capacity to effectively communicate.

We should examine this need carefully because everything that the Internet is today and everything that it will be tomorrow was born out of it. The US military accepted that if their telecommunications capacity was destroyed then their capacity to fight a war was severely hampered. In this acceptance was the recognition that communications is at the heart of the military and that in the modern world secure communications is *decentralised* communications.

The US military recognised that, in a modern world, the enemy can more easily target centralised infrastructures. Historically, to target and destroy such infrastructures, enemy soldiers would have had to physically infiltrate and place bombs. However, with modern long-distance satellite spy and guidance systems and nuclear weapons, a building or centre could be targeted from thousands of miles away.

This new problem was as a result of new technology. Basically, new technology was having a domino effect, forcing old technology and old thinking to be upgraded. The US military was recognising that it was entering a new world arena and that it had to change with the changing times.

At the turn of this century, William Butler Yeats wrote that:

Things fall apart,
The centre cannot hold.[2]

The Internet was an acceptance that in a modern world the centre cannot hold. The Internet succeeded because everywhere on its network was a centre, because everywhere was the centre of somewhere. Everywhere had the capacity to be the centre, thus things were spread out.

HOW DOES THE INTERNET WORK?

What sort of a communications infrastructure do you put together that will withstand a nuclear strike? (Or perhaps more importantly: Why do you need a communications infrastructure if there's nobody left to communicate with?)

In his excellent article "Short History of the Internet",[3] Bruce Sterling wrote that:

> RAND mulled over this grim puzzle in deep military secrecy, and arrived at a daring solution. The RAND proposal (the brainchild of RAND staffer Paul Baran) was made public in 1964. In the first place, the network would have *no central authority*. Furthermore, it would be *designed from the beginning to operate while in tatters*.
>
> The principles were simple. The network itself would be assumed to be unreliable at all times. It would be designed from the get-go to transcend its own unreliability. All the nodes in the network would be equal in status to all other nodes, each node with its own authority to originate, pass and receive messages.

The messages that would travel over this network would be broken up into 'packets'. For illustration purposes, let's imagine that you have a message that is ten sentences long and that to travel over the network, your message is broken up into ten packets, each containing one individual sentence.

Now, all the packets are sent on their merry way. They know their destination but other than that they can take whatever route they like to get to that destination. Each of the ten packets can reach the final destination using totally different routes.

Only one packet has to get through to ensure success. Each packet knows that it is part of a larger message, and that until all the packets have arrived, the message is not complete. If the other packets don't come then the packet that arrived at the destination will keep sending back reminders to the place where the message originated saying, 'Hey, where's those other lazy packets. I'm all alone.'

This whole process is the ultimate in decentralisation and democratisation. In this technical solution lies what is perhaps an inherent irony upon which the Internet was built. Although it was built for military purposes, the philosophy behind its design and many of the people who worked on it, were not untouched by the liberal winds that were blowing through America in the mid to late-1960s.

A question that is often asked is: Why is it so cheap to communicate on the Internet? The reason it's usually no more than the price of a local call to communicate with a great deal of the world using the Internet, is because the Internet makes much better use of telephone wires and other telecom delivery systems.

When you are having a telephone conversation you rent the entire line for the period you are making the call. However, you really only use a small percentage of the line's capacity. On the Internet, packets share the telephone lines with other packets. At any one time there could be quite a number of packets whizzing down the line. Thus, there is much greater and more economical use made of the telephone line, resulting in substantially cheaper communication prices.

There is a drawback here. Because Internet traffic shares lines, it is very difficult to guarantee real-time communication. If not many people are using the Internet at a particular time, then you will be able to enjoy your Internet phone calls, your live video or sound. However, if the Internet gets very busy and lots of packets are trying to squash into already full lines, then delays will occur.

PRINCIPLES UPON WHICH THE INTERNET WAS BUILT

It is not the purpose of this chapter to give a strict history of the Internet, nor is it to be a technical journey into the bowels of this giant network. Rather, I researched this area from a business and social perspective. I was trying to find out if there was something in the way the Internet was thought up and designed that did indeed lay the seeds for its phenomenal blossoming in the 1990s.

Or was it some accidental process that through coincidence and good luck evolved to where it is today?

I believe that there is enough evidence to indicate that the pioneers who created the foundations for the Internet were indeed driven by ideas that were unique and far-reaching. The principles upon which the Internet was designed and upon which it has evolved over the last 30 years were not randomly assembled, nor half-baked. The Internet, from the beginning, was readied to grow into what it is today.

The key principles upon which the Internet was built are as follows.

1. The computer as a communicator.

2. Co-operation and community.

3. Open standards, open thinking.

4. Long-term vision (sustained government support).

The Computer as a Communicator

What made the Internet unique from day one is that its creators had a radically different vision as to what a computer should and could do. Instead of just calculating things, they felt that the computer could also be used to communicate.

Michael Hauben in his article "Behind the Net: The Untold History of the ARPANET and Computer Science,"[4] quotes The ARPANET Completion Report, published jointly in 1978 by BBN (the builders of the first Internet) and ARPA, which states that:

> The ARPA theme is that the promise offered by the computer as a communication medium between people, dwarfs into relative insignificance the historical beginnings of the computer as an arithmetic engine.

In the 1960s, promoting the computer as a communications device within the computer and scientific community was frowned on by many. At that time, computers were hugely expensive and processing power and computer memory very hard to come by. Computers were seen as almost sacred computational tool solving hugely complex problems. Communication was seen as a common thing; something not worthy of a computer's precious time.

It was a brilliant scientist, J C R Licklider, who had the vision to look ahead. From the 1950s, Licklider had had a vision of computers, not simply as giant calculators, but also as communications devices. It was this sort of vision that became the foundation stone for Internet research and development.

Co-operation and Community

Community and co-operation were a central part of Licklider's vision for the Internet. As Michael Hauben wrote in *Behind the Net*:

> Robert Taylor, Licklider's successor at the IPTO, reflects on how this foundation was based on Licklider's interest in interconnecting communities. 'Lick was among the first to perceive the spirit of community created among the users of the first time-sharing systems…In pointing out the community phenomena created, in part, by the sharing of resources in one timesharing system, Lick made it easy to think about interconnecting the communities, the interconnection of interactive, online communities of people…'
>
> The 'spirit of community' was related to Licklider's interest in having computers help people communicate with other people. Licklider's vision of an 'intergalactic network' connecting people represented an important conceptual shift in computer science. This vision guided the researchers who created the ARPANET. After the ARPANET was functioning, the computer scientists using it realised that assisting human communication was a major fundamental advance that the ARPANET made possible.

The Internet evolved in a period where contradictory forces were at play. Cold War paranoia mixed with 1960s idealism. The objective may have been to create a military technology. However, the core development happened during the late-1960s, a time of popular protest against war.

People were demanding more of a say in how their countries were run. The Internet was developed using a system that encouraged people to have their say and contribute ideas. This open, co-operative environment was consistent with the cry for more democracy which students and others were raising during that period.

Graduate students contributed significantly to the development of the Internet (ARPANET), working closely with ARPA, a military research institute. It was the work of students in other

areas that would expose the military campaign in Vietnam.
Ironies and contradictions abounded.

Robert Braden of the Internet Activities Board, reflected on
the value of collaboration and co-operation.

> "For me, participation in the development of the
> ARPANET and the Internet protocols has been very excit-
> ing," Braden wrote. "One important reason it worked, I
> believe, is that there were a lot of very bright people all
> working more or less in the same direction, led by some
> very wise people in the funding agency. The result was to
> create a community of network researchers who believed
> strongly that collaboration is more powerful than competi-
> tion among researchers. I don't think any other model
> would have gotten us where we are today."[5]

This whole co-operative model is what would go on to drive the
'free software' movement (dealt with in detail in the Chapter 10,
Things Digital). Operating systems, such as Linux, would not
have been possible were it not for the World Wide Web and the
co-operative atmosphere the Internet facilitated.

> "Linux was the first project to make a conscious and suc-
> cessful effort to use the entire world as its talent pool," Eric
> Raymond wrote in "The Cathedral and the Bazaar".214[6] "I
> don't think it's a coincidence that the gestation period of
> Linux coincided with the birth of the World Wide Web, and
> that Linux left its infancy during the same period in 1993-
> 1994 that saw the take off of the ISP industry and the explo-
> sion of mainstream interest in the Internet. Linus
> [Torvalds, creator of Linux] was the first person who
> learned how to play by the new rules that the pervasive
> Internet made possible."

The Internet has changed the way many people work. Don
Tapscott wrote about his popular book on children in the digital
age, *Growing Up Digital*,[7] that it was, "written on the Internet.
The research team collaborated with several hundred children
and adults located in six continents. The analysis, drafting and
editing was conducted by a core team in five locations using a
shared digital work space, electronic mail and computer confer-

encing. The main reference source was the Web. It would not have been possible to write this book without using these tools".

This sense of co-operation has made the Internet a wonderful problem solver. Starting off in the academic and scientific community it has emerged as a global tool for addressing complex issues through co-operation and interactivity.

Open Standards, Open Thinking

The Internet was developed in an atmosphere of openness. This is perhaps best exemplified by how open thinking was actively encouraged in the Network Working Group (NWG) that originated the Internet.

> "The content of a NWG note may be any thought, suggestion, etc., related to the HOST software or other aspect of the network," the NWG suggested. "Notes are encouraged to be timely rather than polished. Philosophical positions without examples or other specifics, specific suggestions or implementation techniques without introductory or background explication, and explicit questions without any attempted answers are all acceptable. The minimum length for a NWG note is one sentence."[8]

The above is an extraordinary model for development and would have run counter to the way much scientific research would have been carried out. It encourages free-form thinking and the mix of thoughts and ideas with other thoughts and ideas. It is a model that allows minds to interact and fuse. The Internet now allows a vast network of minds to interact and fuse and it was this sort of thinking that made it all possible.

As Michael Hauben put it in "Behind the Net":[9]

> This open process encouraged and led to the exchange of information. Technical development is only successful when information is allowed to flow freely and easily between the parties involved. Encouraging participation is the main principle that made the development of the Net possible.

The Internet was developed very much using a bottom-up model. Based on the principle of 'open standards', the code and technical data was made free and easily available. People were encouraged to examine things, to join committees and to make suggestions as to how the Internet could be improved.

Linked to all this is the concept of 'pure research'. The ARPANET and Internet were allowed grow without any particular initial commercial or military imperative. Brilliant thinkers were given scope to think.

It would be also true to say that the Internet was a result of co-operative research. From early on, academic institutes were encouraged to contribute possible solutions to various technical problems that were being encountered. Basically, the ARPA philosophy was to find the very best people in academic research and to give them room and let them explore.

Long-term Vision (Sustained Government Support)
It is ironic that some of the most ardent champions of the Internet have been most against government involvement in the Internet. If ever there was a case of biting the hand that feeds or extreme delusion, then such people have exhibited it in vast quantities.

The Internet would not exist were it not for sustained US government – and later worldwide government – support and funding beginning in the late-1950s and continuing up to the present day. If ever there was an example of the fruits of the investment in long-term research and development then the Internet is that example.

Human society can often be criticised for having very short-term focus and objectives. Pollution, global warming and massive waste are examples of taking the cheap and easy way out to the detriment of the planet and future generations of all life.

The Internet is a credit to the long-term view. It is probable that the Internet would never have been invented by private industry, because of the incessant pressure of profit making and meeting short-term objectives.

WHY DID THE INTERNET EXPLODE IN THE 1990S?

The Internet grew very slowly for some twenty years and then exploded in the 1990s. Why? Well, there are a number of reasons. Firstly, the World Wide Web was invented. Secondly, the PC was popular and becoming cheaper. As the 1990s come to an end, we are seeing PCs in the United States for US$300. The PC is becoming a mass consumer item.

Kevin Kelly in *New Rules for the New Economy*,[10] explained that what brought the Internet forward at such thunderous pace in the late-1980s and early-1990s was the, "dual big bangs of jelly bean chips [cheap computer chips] and collapsing telco prices. It became feasible – that is, dirt cheap – to exchange data almost anywhere, anytime. The Net, the grand net, began to nucleate. Network power followed".

This brings me to my third point. Everytime there are significant shifts in how we communicate, there are significant shifts in how we live and do business. From language, to printing, to the telephone, to television, to the Internet, new communication tools have made the world go round.

In 1866, the cost of transmitting eight words per minute by telegraph from England to the United States was US$100 in gold. Even then, *The New York Tribune* was writing how "the miracle of annihilation of space is at length performed". If the cost of communication was still the same today, do you think we'd be talking about globalisation and the Internet?

In the last twenty years, the price of communication has plummeted.

> "In 1994, the ten largest telecoms giants made bigger profits than the 25 largest commercial banks," *The Economist*[11] reported. "Demand is soaring: over 38 million new subscribers were connected to the fixed network in 1994, more than twice as many newcomers as in 1986. Another 19 million joined the mobile network in 1994 alone. Yet costs have tended to fall faster than prices, which is why the industry has been so profitable."

In 1998, Dr Pekka Tarjanne, Secretary-General of the International Telecommunication Union stated that:

> The telecommunication sector is one of the major components of the world's economy. The value of telecommunication sales (equipment and services combined) is expected to exceed US$1 trillion in 1998. Furthermore, telecommunication networks are a major facilitator of trade in other goods and other services. For instance, the value of financial services transferred over the SWIFT international telecommunication network exceeds $US1 trillion each day.[12]

KEY FEATURES OF THE INTERNET

For most people, there are really only two main sections of the Internet: e-mail and the World Wide Web. Before examining these in more detail, there is another area worth covering: newsgroups. Although not used as much today, newsgroups played a very important role in the early Internet.

When you enter your local supermarket, you will probably pass a noticeboard advertising guitar lessons, yoga classes and an 'as new second-hand bed for sale'. Internet newsgroups are a bit like noticeboards, only they are on a global scale and cover practically every subject imaginable.

It is presently estimated that there are some 20,000 newsgroups. This incredible number of gathering places for people to trade information, services, abuse and flagrant self-promotion, has come under a lot of stress in the last couple of years.

Basically, many of the newsgroups have been abused by mass advertisers and by others who basically enjoy causing arguments and controversy. Because of these reasons, a significant number of people have either stopped using newsgroups or never bothered with them in the first place. However, the principle of the newsgroup is valid and properly used can be a useful means of communication and community building in an online context.

E-mail

If you don't understand e-mail and how to use it effectively, you are at a severe disadvantage in the digital age.

The World Wide Web may be the most talked about and reported aspect of the Internet, but on a day to day basis, e-mail is its most practical and used element. We must remember that the Internet was designed in a fundamental way as a communications system, and that communications has and will be at the heart of what it is and does.

The influence of e-mail may be relatively undetected but it is nonetheless profound. Consider the following findings from various surveys and reports in 1998.

- 36 per cent of executives said they used e-mail more frequently than any other communication tool, making it the most preferred tool for communication amongst this group. (26 per cent preferred the telephone.)[13]

- Business people were sending and receiving up to 190 e-mails, resulting in a major change in day to day working practices.[14]

- 52 per cent of US lawmakers received a daily e-mail tally of how many of their constituents are in favour of or oppose a specific issue.[15]

- E-mail advertising received a higher approval rating among online users compared with other forms of Internet-based advertising.[16]

- The widespread adoption of intranet technology was attributed to e-mail, which was the most important application for half of companies with intranets.[17]

- Very few companies had policies on the use of e-mail. (Something that became very obvious in the Microsoft trial, where e-mail was used extensively to defend and attack arguments.)[18]

From the very early days, what enthused the people who used ARPANET, the forerunner of the Internet, was not so much the ability to share data and access remote computers, but rather to send and receive messages from friends and colleagues.

E-mail is a form of communication. However, it is different to communicating face to face, or by phone, fax or letter. Sometimes these differences are subtle, but they are always important. An organisation that doesn't understand how to use e-mail is like an organisation whose staff shouts into the phone.

'Netiquette' is a term used with regard to using e-mail and the Internet properly. Like etiquette, netiquette needs to be learned and practised. Many of us have learned netiquette in a 'trial and error' way. However, while such an approach was perhaps inevitable in the early days of the Internet, there is less room today to behave in a way that shows you are inexperienced using the medium. This is particularly so when you are dealing with a customer. Therefore, organisations need to implement training and policies with regard to the proper and effective use of e-mail. Otherwise, the organisation will look unprofessional.

If a January 1999 survey published by e-mail specialist company Brightware[19] is any indication, then organisations have not at all integrated e-mail into their overall communications mix. Brightware surveyed the *Fortune 100* companies, asking them a simple question: "What is your mailing address?"

One third of the companies didn't respond at all. Only 4 per cent responded within fifteen minutes, while for a further 26 per cent, it was not possible to find an e-mail address to which this simple question could be sent. While organisations may be still be very poorly prepared to manage e-mail, consumers are embracing it. A January 1999 published study of Internet users by the Pew Research Center[20] found that e-mail, "continues to be the top Internet draw".

Maybe consumers like e-mail because as a form of communi-cation, it gets straight to the point. E-mail can be like an ongoing conversation. E-mail is fast. It can be too fast. Always pause before you send off an e-mail in anger.

E-mail is the original 'push' technology. It comes to you, whereas you have to make a conscious decision to go to a web-site. It should, therefore, be a *primary objective* of anyone who has a website to get the people who visit their website to join an e-mail newsletter or discussion list. If you achieve this you have in some way 'hooked' them, and you can then start developing a potential profitable relationship with them. However, you will only get people to join such lists if you have valuable informa-tion to send them.

As I wrote earlier, information overload is a huge issue for people. E-mail 'spam' – unsolicited e-mail that is mass-mailed to thousands of people – is becoming an increasing problem. People have less and less time and if there is too much noise and rubbish in the e-mail people receive, then it will inevitably inter-fere with their capacity to get the best out of e-mail.

Spam or otherwise, many executives are getting and sending upwards of 180 e-mails a day. There is very little space in their head for anything that is rambling or 'off-subject'. The worst thing that can happen to your or your organisation is that you are seen as someone whose e-mails should be ignored. If that happens you are in serious trouble.

There is, unfortunately, a dark side to e-mail, in that it is one of the prime contributors to information overload. Before 7 January 1999, the American Senate, with its 100 senators, was receiving an average of 70,000 e-mails per day; that's an average of 700 e-mails per day per senator.[21] With the commencement of the impeachment trial of President Clinton, the overall number rose to 500,000 per day. (The American House of Representatives was receiving over 1 million message per day in late-1998.)

Knight Ridder News Service reported that this flood of e-mail was, "overloading the computer system responsible for delivering them to electronic mailboxes. E-mails are arriving hours, even days and weeks, after constituents send them – when they arrive at all".

> "It's been rendered almost useless," Tara Andringa, spokeswoman for Senator Carl Levin, told Knight Ridder. "We've been told not to rely on the e-mail system and not to use it to respond to constituents."

When the Stephen King website launched in late-1998, it was expected that there might be a couple of hundred e-mails per day. When the figure reached flood levels at over 1,600 per day, it was time for damage control. The website announced that:

> Due to the overwhelming flood of e-mail, which Stephen's assistants are wading through, we are temporarily suspending e-mail sent to his office. Please check back when they've had a chance to get caught up.

The website manager was quoted as saying that in future only discussion boards would be available, and that e-mail communication would no longer be accepted.

To do your part in easing information overload, understanding the basic principles of e-mail communication are important. David Skyrme, of David Skyrme Associates[22] has developed a number of basic rules for communicating using e-mail. These include:

- all e-mails should have an appropriate subject line or title that accurately describes what the content of the e-mail is about;

- e-mails should generally have a 'call for action'. What do you want the receiver to do as a result of getting your e-mail?;

- where possible, stick to one topic per e-mail;

- e-mails should be informal. They are like conversations.

E-mail Discussion Lists
I have learned more through participating in e-mail discussion lists than through any other medium or tool of learning.

Earlier in this book I wrote about the concept of the 'massively parallel society'. Without e-mail, or more particularly, without e-mail discussion list structures, this concept could not evolve. E-mail discussion lists allow a number of people to participate in the ongoing discussion and exploration of a particular subject or problem.

When you send an e-mail message to the list, it is distributed to everyone. You have joined a communications network, where your communication reaches every other person on the network and vice versa. This process can last for a week or for several years, depending on what you want to discuss.

On these lists, ideas, opinions and 'facts' are put forward. However, if these ideas, opinons and 'facts' do not have substance, you can be sure that someone on the list will point out their lack of logic or inaccuracy. Used properly, e-mail discussion lists are a very effective way of exploring opportunities and solving complex problems.

Patricia Wagner and Leif Smith of Pattern Research have written about the importance of 'listening' while being part of e-mail discussion lists.

> "On Internet newsgroups and e-mail discussion lists, listening is called 'lurking'," they write. "Newcomers are always advised to lurk for a while, get the lie of the land, get a sense of what is being said and how it is being said. Only after a period of lurking should people contribute, because otherwise their contributions might seem awkward and ill-informed. Of course, some Internet settings, such as chat forums, are much more spontaneous, but in newsgroups and discussion lists the above procedure is the norm."[23]

A key factor in the success of an e-mail discussion list is a moderator. A moderator is like an editor, manager, commentator and motivator combined. Without a moderator, an e-mail discussion group has a much-reduced ability to be productive. (For a more comprehensive discussion on moderation, see the 'Leadership/ Moderation' section of *Characteristics of Online Communities* in Chapter 5.)

An interesting thing I have observed about the Internet through being part of e-mail discussion lists for years, is that definable behavioural patterns and life cycles can be observed. In 1994, e-mail discussion list contributor, Kat Nagel, posted an excellent piece entitled *The Natural Life Cycle of Mailing Lists*. The following stages were isolated.

1. **Initial enthusiasm**: people think this is the best list in the world.

2. **Evangelism**: people make great plans for the list.

3. **Growth**: loads of people join, attracted by the energy.

4. **Community**: lots of activity, some of it good, some bad. Everyone is friendly and wants to help out.

5. **Discomfort with diversity**: some cracks begin to show, as old hands get tired of things, such as newbies asking the same questions and other people repeating their pet theories.

Finally

Smug complacency and stagnation: this list becoming sterile as new people are scared away and people with energy and a genuine desire to learn move on.

or

Maturity: the list develops a strong culture, which allows it to address the various mini-crises while still focusing on discussing in an energetic way the type of topics it was set up to discuss.

E-mail Newsletters

E-mail newsletters are one of the most effective ways of communicating and building brands on the Internet. They are also a very hard thing to do right. Because of the nature of the Internet, it is very difficult to deliver an e-mail newsletter in anything other than standard ASCI format. What this basically means is that it's down to the very bare, unadorned text; no bold, no italics, no formatting of any sort, and certainly no graphics.

In this sort of minimal communications environment, you really need to have a message. You really need to have something to say that's useful to the reader. It needs to be factual and accurate: because if it isn't then one of your readers will get back and point out your mistake. And if someone doesn't, then that's probably because you have precious few readers.

An e-mail newsletter has got to deliver. If it does deliver then it's one of the best ways possible to build a brand, since it attaches to that brand substance, integrity and knowledge.

More than any other factor, Nua, the company I founded, was built on e-mail newsletters. Since 1996, week by week, we have delivered a number of free newsletters, "Nua Internet Surveys" [24] and "New Thinking"[25] being the most widely known. Nua Internet Surveys charts Internet trends and by 1999 had a weekly readership of some 150,000 people. New Thinking's objective is to "contribute to a philosophy for the digital age". Its readership is at roughly 15,000.

Both newsletters have increased their subscription levels every single week since they were launched. They have helped Nua win numerous awards, worldwide press coverage and major contracts. Both newsletters are 'only as good as their last issue'. They value their readers time and pursue a policy of constant excellence in the information they deliver.

Nua newsletters have been primarily responsible for building for Nua an international profile and brand. The majority of Nua's key clients (Lucent Technologies, Thomas Publishing, Gateway, Procter & Gamble) started off as subscribers to our newsletters. After a period of receiving our publications, we had established with them a reputation for quality information and thinking. They began to trust and respect us as an organisation that truly understood the Internet. Our newsletters were that essential 'foot in the door'.

E-mail newsletter publisher Al Bredenberg,[26] in a succinct post to the excellent I-Sales discussion list, while agreeing that e-mail newsletters could be very effective warned that:

> ...it's getting harder and harder for an e-mail newsletter to get noticed because of the constant stream of new entrants. In addition, busy Net users and business people are hesitant to sign up for e-zines, because so many of them are of poor quality – mostly made up of badly written free articles and thinly-disguised sales pitches.

Bredenberg recommended a number of things to keep in mind when planning an e-mail newsletter. These are as follows.

1. Think of an e-zine [e-mail newsletter] as a way to serve your audience on the Internet and build a trusting relationship with them, not as a forum for pitching your products or services.

2. Choose a clearly defined and specific niche.

3. Let your first priority be to offer real value to the reader through good-quality content.

4. Make a clear distinction between editorial content and advertising in the format of your e-zine.

5. Build your e-zine list on an opt-in basis only. Don't sign people up without their permission.

6. Be selective in accepting articles from outside writers. Prefer to pay money for a good article rather than to take a bad article for free.

7. Develop a thorough editorial process. Copy-edit every article to eliminate typos, poor grammar and vague and confusing passages. Also, do a good job of content editing, to make sure that you are publishing coherent, well-structured articles.

8. Commit yourself to a regular publishing schedule.

9. Exercise patience, recognising that positive results may be long in coming.

10. Be prepared to spend time and money to promote your e-zine and build readership.

The World Wide Web

For many of us involved in the Internet, it is hard to imagine a time when the World Wide Web, or the 'Web' as it's popularly known, did not exist. Yet it was only February 1993 when Mosaic, the Web browser that would truly ignite the revolution, was released by NCSA.

The first time I used Mosaic, was an incredible moment for me. I was sitting in front of a computer in Dublin, Ireland, and as if by some form of magic, text and images were appearing on my screen from all over the world (but mainly America). To this day, I still marvel at the World Wide Web.

Tim Berners-Lee invented the Web when working for European research agency, CERN. In presenting a MacArthur Fellowship to Berners-Lee, it was stated that he was receiving it for pioneering "a revolutionary communications system requiring minimal technical understanding to locate and distribute information throughout the world at very low cost".

In 1996, Berners-Lee himself wrote that:

The World Wide Web was designed originally as an interactive world of shared information through which people could communicate with each other and with machines. Since its inception in 1989, it has grown initially as a medium for the broadcast of read-only material from heavily loaded corporate servers to the mass of Internet connected consumers.[27]

The Web is like a giant worldwide library or network of libraries. People can access information and add information to this library. (Some have described the Web as a giant library, with all the books on the floor…and the lights turned out.) The Web is a worldwide marketplace. People can find out about and purchase products and services. They can offer information, as well as the ability to purchase, products and services.

In theory, the Web can accommodate anything digital. Text, images, video, animation can be made available and accessed through it. However, bandwidth shortages have meant that in most situations it is only practical to provide/access text and images that have a small file size.

It's not essential to understand what bandwidth and file size mean. Just imagine that when trying to deliver a video over the Internet, it can be like pushing an elephant through a telephone wire. Text, on the other hand, swims through the wires like a tiny tadpole. Bandwidth will improve and the Web will change, but for a number of years, low bandwidth will be a critical issue for many users, particularly – though by no means exclusively – those in poorer countries.

From Clay Tablets to the Web

Information tools have been with us for thousands of years, and the Web is at heart such a tool. It is also a tool that more accurately imitates the way the mind works as an information storage and processing tool, than that other great information tool – the book. For this reason and more, the Web is likely to play a central role in the future evolution of society.

Since writing was invented, it has always been a challenge to find the perfect medium for the storage and communication of that writing. The earliest writers used everything from wood to slate to clay tablets. Ink and parchment followed, with paper and printing being available in China from 200AD. From China, printing spread to the Islamic world where many fine libraries were established. It was not until 1450 and the invention of the printing press by Johannes Gutenberg that printing began to develop in Europe.

In the 20th century, we have seen an explosion of information tools, such as typewriters, film, radio, television, computers, wordprocessors and the Internet. We have seen hard disks and databases for information storage. Today, the world has never had so many information tools in its possession.

The Web is perhaps one of the most important information tools ever invented, combining the elements of cheap computer storage, search and information processing capacities, with the worldwide connectivity that modern telecommunications offers.

Hypertext, an information tool with profound implications, has risen to prominence with the Web. Hypertext allows individual information to be navigated through and combined with other information in a wide variety of ways.

Until the emergence of hypertext, it was really only possible to organise information in a linear fashion, one page or one chapter after the other. In some ways it could be said that hypertext better reflects how we think and how the mind is constructed and is thus a more natural way for humans to store and explore information.

I wonder whether over time we have become our tools. I'm particularly thinking about books (one of which you're reading!). The book is a wonderful invention, and without it much of the progress of the last couple of hundred years could not have occurred.

Our books, and our libraries, are a store of knowledge that is used in everyday life and will be passed on to future generations. The book is an incredible tool as a record of knowledge, though it is less useful as a tool of learning. Otherwise, why would we have schools and universities? We need teachers to bring books alive, to add the 'multimedia' of experience and expression to them.

You see, the book is a linear tool. It has a beginning, middle and end. It goes from page 1 to page 200, with each page number logically following from the previous one. It is interesting to examine the evolution of books and more particularly the evolution of the styles used in creating books over the centuries.

My own knowledge of this is in an Irish context and the first book that comes to mind is the *Book of Kells*, which, it is believed, was created in Ireland in the 8th-9th century. This is not really a 'book' as we know it today. Rather, it is a multimedia experience: a work of visual as well as written expression.

In the *Book of Kells*, in those early days of 'writing', it was like the words were seen as slightly impotent by the scribes in their capacity to express and communicate. Therefore, the letters of these words had to be exploded with colour, shape and size. The *Book of Kells* is not to be read. It is rather to be looked at, gazed at and experienced. The words themselves are by no means the primary object of the exercise. Rather, the colour and images predominate.

Published in the early 19th century, William Carleton was one of the first 'ordinary' Irish writers, coming from a small farm in County Tyrone. His stories jumped and moved all over the place, like they were being wrestled down by the page and always trying to escape to the heart of the story. Carleton would start off writing about something, but before long he would mention some character, event or place. Beside the mention of this character he would put an asterisk and at the bottom of the page he would go into great detail about this character. This was hypertext before the word existed. This was the way people told stories, because nothing really has one beginning, one middle or one end.

The mind is not linear. The mind is rather a network, where millions of brain cells set about to establish complex tasks through co-operation and non-linear processes. In our minds there are always a series of things happening, and most of us find it very hard to focus on one particular subject for a sustained period of time.

The Internet is a network in a variety of ways. Firstly, in the way people and computers are connected on a worldwide basis. Secondly, by the use of hypermedia, the way information is stored and presented.

Hypermedia is an environment where text, images, sound, video and animation can be linked together to create a variety of paths or routes. (Hypertext refers only to the linking of text.) Hypermedia is a major breakthrough and diminishes the linear dominance in the storage and presentation of information. Hypermedia is much more reflective of how the brain operates.

Hypermedia is indeed a network, in that it links one content 'node' to another. Without hypermedia, the Web would be a very flat and limited place. In our mind, we jump from place to place, from idea to idea, from association to association. Hypermedia is a tool that facilitates this process.

Hypermedia, hypertext, multimedia, are all essentially saying the same thing: that the world is a connected place and that the media that reflects the world should be connected too. That sound, images, text and programming should interact to tell the whole story and show the whole picture.

For now, the Internet is largely limited to text and simple images, so it is text that must weave and thread its way. But as bandwidth increases, the Internet will open up to sounds and moving images, creating an unbelievable web of information.

Website Development Principles

As the Web spreads its net around the world, few organisations will be able to resist its pull. As a general point, remember that a website is a medium through which you communicate with people. It becomes like a window through which the world can look in at you. When developing a website you should keep the following principles in mind.

- Simple and succinct.
- Fast to market.
- Information rich.
- Facilitate relationships.
- Open and linked.
- Resource properly.
- Plan for the long haul.
- Have a long-term vision.
- Ask the question: Why?

Simple and Succinct

If you save people time today, you increase your chances of making money. One of the best ways of saving time in this hurried, overloaded world, is to be simple and succinct. If people want to be amazed, they'll go to the circus or the cinema. When they come to your website, they just want the facts.

On the Internet, simplicity is next to godliness. Always ask the question: Is this as simple for my user as it can possibly be? Keep the information succinct. In other words, don't write 1,000 words when 500 words will do. Simplicity has the added – and vital – bonus of ensuring that your website will download quickly.

Fast to Market

You need to develop for the Internet quickly. A website is not a masterpiece. Rather, it is an evolving, interactive environment. Get something of quality up quickly, see how your target market reacts to it, then evolve it.

Information Rich

The Internet is an information-driven environment, which means that an organisation represents itself by the information it delivers. The organisation that delivers poor information will be seen as a poor organisation. Remember that the three properties of information are: content, structure and publication. Keeping this in mind, it is also important to remember that your information should be:

- kept up to date: an out of date website is an embarrassment;

- written with hypertext in mind. Porting information from brochures or books rarely works.

Facilitate Relationships

At a most basic level, a website should allow the user to contact the appropriate section of the company in the easiest manner possible. A good website must be engaging and reach out to the user; it must facilitate relationships. From a marketing perspective, a website must contain a number of 'calls to action'.

When someone visits your website, you should try your best to get them into a database by, for example, asking them to join a product e-mail newsletter. Of course, we need to remember that we are dealing with information consumers on the Internet and that they need to be always treated with respect. At every opportunity we should empower them to investigate the product or solution most appropriate to them.

Open and Linked

The Internet is an evolving environment and your website must evolve with it. Therefore, your website needs to have an open design that will allow for such rapid evolution. One of the most remarkable things about the Internet is that it is 'platform' independent. In other words, is doesn't matter what computer or software you're using, you can communicate and access information using the Web.

As inventor of the Web, Tim Berners-Lee has stated:

Anyone who slaps a 'this page is best viewed with Browser
X' label on a Web page appears to be yearning for the bad
old days, before the Web, when you had very little chance
of reading a document written on another computer,
another wordprocessor or another network.

Your website is part of the Internet network. The more links that
there are from other websites to your website, the better. If you
look at the best and most popular websites on the Internet – such
as Yahoo, for example – you will find that they are linked to from
a great number of other websites. If you are getting a lot of links
to your website then you are definitely doing something right.

Resource Properly

To do a website right is expensive. It requires quality information and quality relationship building on a day to day basis. For
one, that requires quality people who have experience of the
medium. This sort of people are difficult to find and when you
do find them, they are – to make an understatement – not
cheap.

Plan for the Long Haul

This may well be the age of instant gratification but precious few
websites deliver like you've just won the Lotto. Be prepared for
a slow build. Launching your website is only the first stage in the
process. If you win business one customer at a time in the offline
world, be prepared to win them one customer at a time on your
website. The Web is all about working hard and diligently on a
day to day basis – just like real business.

Have a Long-term Vision

If you are planning for the long haul, then you need a long-term
vision. While you need to have flexible plans and be able to react
quickly, it is vital that you have a strong vision of where you
want your website to go.

Ask the Question: Why?

I've left the best wine until last. You really have to ask yourself:
Why are we doing this? It's got to make sense for your business.

Is our target market online? Can we afford the time and money required to create a quality website? One of the ways of judging if it makes sense or not is to look at the ways a quality website can deliver a return on investment to your organisation.

Website Return on Investment
A reasonable question that needs to be asked when developing a website is: "Where is the return on investment?" The ways a quality website can deliver a return on investment can be broken down into two main sections: direct returns and indirect returns

Direct Returns

- Pre-sales support.
- Sales/E-commerce.
- After-sales support.
- Distribution and packaging.
- Print and publishing.
- Personnel and employment.
- Organisational empowerment.

Indirect Returns

- Opportunity costs.
- Product/Service development.
- New market opportunities.
- Investor and media relations.

Direct Return on Investment: In the initial phases of an Internet development, most websites are more likely to save an organisation money, or aid in the sales process, rather than create substantial income through direct sales. (There are exceptions, of course.)

The Internet is an ideal medium for the consumer to gain product information that will support them in their purchase decision. Dell Computers and Gateway have found that customers who ring them after having visited their respective websites are significantly more likely to purchase and will require less phone calls in that purchase process, than customers who ring without having visited the website.

For certain product categories – computer software and hardware, books, travel and tourism, news and information, financial information, business to business sales – the website is becoming an increasingly important sales channel.

A quality after-sales website service is available 24 hours a day to a customer. After-sales support can include the provision of manuals, frequently asked questions, discussion forums, etc. More advanced structures, such as case-based reasoning support systems, bring the customer through a particular problem, and then offer solutions.

For those products that are digital in nature – software, information, images, etc. – the Internet can radically reduce distribution and practically eliminate packaging costs. At trade shows in America, the trend is not to hand out a brochure but to hand out a business card with a website address on it. A quality website will in time have a significant impact on print and publishing costs.

A website becomes a permanent advertisement for employees, thus saving employment costs. A well-structured personnel section can streamline potential employee data, thus saving administrative costs. Increasingly, potential employees are visiting websites to judge whether the organisation in question is worth working for.

A dynamic and well-designed website will increase operational efficiency by providing a rich information resource for staff, thus reducing the time a member of staff spends looking for any particular piece of information. This is an important step in helping establish a learning organisation, in that it enhances the flow of information throughout the organisation.

Indirect Returns on Investment: The indirect benefits of developing a quality Internet presence can be summarised by using the phrase, 'If you're not in, you can't win'. As Bill Gates, CEO of Microsoft has stated:

Not every company that bets on the Internet will win, but those who bet against it are certain to lose.

The Web has, and will continue to have, such a huge impact on world commerce and society, that it should not be so much a question of what are the short-term costs of developing a quality Internet presence, as what are the long-term costs of not developing one?

The Internet allows you to get closer to your customer; to interact with them. It also allows your customer to get closer to you. Your customer can tell you what sort of product/service they would like from you in the future. You can test out new product ideas, achieving a constant stream of feedback. The end results are products and services that better match customer needs.

A quality website can be a driver to open up markets that historically were too expensive to service or exploit. It can help create brand new marketplaces and product opportunities that simply did not exist before the advent of the Internet. Again, if you're not in, you can't win.

In the digital age, an organisation must be prepared daily to tell its story on its website to both media and investors. If it is doing things it must record that it is doing such things in a professional and involving manner. A website is an ideal medium from which to deliver this flow of information.

INTERNET MYTHS

In the early days of any revolution, tall tales are told. Soundbites become facts because they sound good and because there is such a void of factual information and experience. The Internet has had its share of myths, a number of which have become accepted truths. It is time to put the following myths to bed.

- The Internet was born in chaos and must therefore remain in chaos.

- Nobody knows you're a dog.

- Information wants to be free.

- The Internet is cheap to develop for.

- Everyone is a publisher.

The Internet was born in Chaos and must therefore remain in Chaos

It became almost a mantra of early Internet enthusiasts that the Internet was born in chaos and must by some inevitable logic remain in chaos. These early Internet pioneers – almost exclusively white, male and rich – fervently championed ideas such as freedom of speech and independence from rules and government control. They talked about the World Wide Web as if it represented the world. Of course, it didn't. It was a small club and its 'chaos' was within that small club atmosphere.

It is important to understand that long-term the Internet will have the same demographic profile as the rest of society, with the major exception in that it will be many years before it is used in any substantial way by lower income people. It will, therefore, require the same type or order that present society requires to function properly.

The Internet exists in a rapidly evolving environment. It is a mistake to take every present characteristic of the Internet and to attempt to turn them into long-term rules and standards. For example, some people say that you cannot control the Internet, that it is by its very nature chaotic. Some say that you cannot tax the Internet.

When it is time to control the Internet, the Internet will be controlled. When it is time to tax the Internet, the Internet will be taxed. The control may be different, the taxation may be different, but control and taxation there will be.

Do not assume that what pertains on the Internet today will be what will pertain tomorrow. Assume rather that in time the Internet will reflect and be reflected by the attitudes, behaviours and structures of the wider society.

Nobody knows you're a Dog

Many of us have seen the wonderful cartoon of the two dogs and the computer. One dog is sitting on a chair, its paws on the keyboard. The dog at the keyboard looks into the wondering eyes of the other dog, saying, "On the Internet, nobody knows you're a dog."

On the contrary, on the Internet there is a capacity to know an incredible amount about you. There is software that can track you every movement online, building up a profile of your every purchase and every website you visit. E-mail leaves a trail and what you might consider as casual conversation can build up in an archive, to be perhaps used at some future point against you. (Ask Bill Gates.)

It is, therefore, no surprise that in the last couple of years, the rights of privacy have been foremost in the minds of Internet users. On the Internet, nobody may yet be able to see you but that doesn't mean they can't see into your life and lifestyle.

Information wants to be Free

Another wonderful phrase which grew like wildfire in the
Internet grapevine was, 'information wants to be free'. For anyone
that experienced the early days of the Internet when all information basically was free, this seemed to have an irrefutable logic.

Not so. While much free information is required to grease the
great wheels of the Internet, there is no law or requirement to
make all information free. Free information can only remain free
as long as it creates some form of value. Creating value costs and
must get a return or else that value will not continue to be created. For publishers, the value free information may create is in
bringing people to their website, where at some point they will
agree to subscribe to paid-for information services.

The Internet is cheap to develop for

Another early myth was that it was cheap to develop for the
Internet. In the early days there was perhaps a certain truth in
that. Because there were so few websites in 1993/1994, any website that launched was a type of event. Even if you weren't interested in buying a car, you still went to the new car website just
to see what it was like. It was also true that that most of the early
websites were developed by the pioneers themselves. The costs
of long nights and pioneering expertise were usually not
accounted for, thus making the development seem good value.

The Internet of today is a different animal entirely. With 8 million websites and growing, launching a new website can seem like
burping in an elevator. As search engines become bogged down
by hundreds of millions of pages, getting your website known is
becoming and increasingly difficult and expensive process. There
may well indeed be 200 million people with access to the Internet
through the world, but that doesn't guarantee that even one of
them will visit your wonderful new website.

Expertise is scarce on the ground too. The pioneers are all running their own companies now, so finding quality staff to run
your development is another difficult and expensive exercise.
All in all, developing a quality Internet presence that reaches its
target market and achieves its objectives, is an increasingly difficult task.

Everyone is a Publisher

To publish is to make public. Publication is the final property of
information. A website is no longer by definition a publication.

With Yahoo registering only 8 per cent of the Internet and the search engines charting no more than 30 per cent, it is likely that many websites are receiving little or no traffic on a weekly basis. If your website is not reaching a public, then you are not a publisher.

There is another related Internet myth here which implies that publishing is somehow easier on the Internet than elsewhere. Publishing requires craft and effort. Just because you can slap a few hundred quickly put-together words into HTML and onto a website doesn't mean anything.

Okay, maybe you can slap up a website and maybe you can even get people to come and visit it (once). All that you will have achieved is that these people will think that you're a bad publisher.

Yes, if you do it right, the Internet can be a publishing medium for you, and in the digital age, most organisations must become publishers in some form or another. But remember, publishing is a skilled trade. Digital age organisations need to learn that trade. It's not easy, or cheap.

WHERE NEXT FOR THE INTERNET?

Ever since the Internet exploded onto the world scene in the early-1980s, there have been those who have been predicting its demise. It was predicted that the Internet infrastructure would not be able to cope with the massive increase in traffic and use. It was said that the Internet would not be able to cope with the introduction of electronic commerce. It was said that the Internet was boring, that text and simple images would never keep people's attention. It was said that the phenomenal growth of the Internet had to slow down.

But the Internet has survived the incredible growth. In 1988, K G Coffman and A M Odlyzko writing in *First Monday*, stated that:

...the Internet appears to be growing at 100 per cent per year, compared to 15-20 per cent for private line networks and under 10 per cent for the voice network. Thus if current trends continue, and there seems to be no reason they should not, data traffic will overtake voice traffic around the year 2002, and will be going primarily over the public Internet.[28]

As Robert Metcalfe, vice president of Technology at International Data Group put it:

> One of the beauties of the Internet is that it can change in several places simultaneously. There are five or ten next generation internets coming.

Most agree that the Internet is really only at its beginning.

> "I think where we are with the Internet where we were 100 years ago with electricity," Paul R Gudonis, president of GTE internetworking has stated. "We're still in the early stages of this."[20]

So, where next? Well, every year we hear about the coming bandwidth bonanza. We read about how full multimedia, video-on-demand and interactive television are ready to hurtle down the wires. By and large we are left waiting. And while we wait for the Godot of high bandwidth, underneath our noses real learning, real interactivity and real business can be achieved with the text, numbers and small images that travel over the present Internet.

> *There is so much than can and is being achieved with the Internet as it is!*

For the average organisation and user, it is unwise to plan for the Internet based on the coming bandwidth bonanza. From a bandwidth point of view we may in fact see multiple 'internets'. For example, the Web for emerging economies will be very slow for years to come, while the Web in Silicon Valley will be very fast.

Sooner or later, the Internet will stabilise – its network will speed up and growth will indeed slow down. The Internet infrastructure may be totally overhauled. They may even change the name of the Internet. It won't really matter.

What is important when looking to the future is not to worry about what will happen to the Internet. You see, it doesn't really matter what happens to the Internet, the network and the principles of the network will survive. No matter what changes occur, we will be living and working in a networked world for the foreseeable future. If we understand the network, then the future can be managed.

In the digital age, we live in the *network economy*. We must all live network, think network.

Vint Cerf, regarded by many as the 'father of the Internet', introduced this chapter with a stanza from his poem, "Requiem for the ARPANET. In 1998, Cerf expounded to *ZDTV* on the future of the Internet, talking about how he saw an interplanetary network which would link the earth, moon and even Mars. Crazy talk. But then anyone who would have said that the ARPANET of 1969 would turn into the Internet of 1999 would have been deemed crazy too.[30]

REFERENCES

1. V Cerf, "Requiem for the ARPANET"
   http://www.netmom.com/cares/cerf_requiem.htm

2. W B Yeats, "The Second Coming" *The Collected Poems of W B Yeats* (Macmillan: 1982)

3. B Sterling, "Short History of the Internet" *The Magazine of Fantasy and Science Fiction* (February 1993)
   http://www.art.acad.emich.edu/faculty/chew/Internet/short-history-of-Internet.html

4. M Hauben, "Behind the Net: The Untold Story of the ARPANET and Computer Science" *First Monday* (August 1998)
   http://www.firstmonday.dk/issues/issue3_8/chapter7/index.html

5. *Ibid.*

6. E S Raymond, "The Cathedral and the Bazaar"
   http://www.tuxedo.org/~esr/writings/cathedral-bazaar/

7. D Tapscott, *Growing Up Digital: The Rise of the Net Generation* (McGraw-Hill: 1997)

8. M Hauben, "Behind the Net: The Untold Story of the ARPANET and Computer Science" *First Monday* (August 1998)
   http://www.firstmonday.dk/issues/issue3_8/chapter7/index.html

9. *Ibid.*

10. K Kelly, "New Rules for the New Economy" *Wired* (September 1997)
    http://www.wired.com:80/wired/archive/5.09/newrules.html
    Now available in book form: K Kelly, *New Rules for the New Economy* (Viking Press: 1998)

11. F Cairncross, "The Death of Distance" *The Economist* (30 September 1995) http://www.economist.com/

12. P Tarjanne, "Secretary-General's Report to the Second World Telecommunication Policy Forum" (March 1998) http://www.itu.int/wtpf/sg_rep/1_draft/sg_rep-e.htm

13. R Morgan, "Hold all Calls, Please, I've E-Mail to Read" *Media Central* http://www.mediacentral.com/Magazines/MediaCentral/Columns/Morgan/19980415.htm

14. Pitney Bowes, "E-mail is Changing the Working Day" Nua Internet Surveys, http://www.nua.ie/surveys/?f=VS&art_id=897306427&rel=true

15. G Barrett, "Constituents trading paper for e-mail" *USA Today* (26 January1999) http://www.usatoday.com/life/cyber/tech/ctd117.htm

16. Nikkei Multimedia, "Internet Users Positive on E-mail Ads" AsiaBizTech http://www.nikkeibp.asiabiztech.com/Database/98_Jul/16/Mor.01.gwif.html

17. "E-mail is No. 1 Application Tool" *Computer Intelligence* http://www.ci.zd.com/

18. "Poor E-mail Policy on British Web Sites" Buchanan E-mail, http://www.buchanan.co.uk/

19. Brightware, http://www.brightware.com/

20. Pew Research Center, http://www.people-press.org/

21. J L Fix, "Senate's E-mail System hits Gridlock" *Knight Ridder News Service* (15 January 1999), http://spyglass1.sjmercury.com/breaking/docs/063702.htm

22. David Skyrme Associates, http://www.skyrme.com/

23. P Wagner and L Smith, "The Networking Game" Pattern Research, http://www.pattern.com/

24. Nua Internet Surveys, http://www.nua.ie/surveys/ To subscribe to Nua Internet Surveys, send an email to "surveys-request@nua.ie" with the word **subscribe** in the body of the message.

25. "New Thinking" http://www.nua.ie/newthinking/current.html To subscribe to New Thinking, send an email to newthinking-request@nua.ie with the word **subscribe** in the body of the message.

26. A Bredenberg, http://www.copywriter.com/newsltr.htm

27. T Berners-Lee, "The World Wide Web: Past, Present and Future" W3 (1996)
    http://www.w3.org/People/Berners-Lee-Bio.html/1996/ppf.html

28. K G Coffman and A M Odlyzko, "The Size and Growth Rate of the
    Internet" *First Monday* (October 1998)
    http://www.firstmonday.dk/issues/issue3_10/coffman/index.html

29. B Burke, "The Internet 1998: The End of the Beginning" *BusinessToday*
    (1998), http://www.businesstoday.com/techpages/wsj2100598.htm

30. I Bloxsom, "Vint Cerf on the Internet's Future" *ZDTV* (20 August 1998)
    http://www.zdnet.com/zdtv/newscobrand/features/story/0,3730,21303
    18,00.html

© Fergal Lawler 1999

9
Think Network:
People are the Network

WHY THINK NETWORK?

In recent years, a common enough phrase within the computer industry has been, "the network is the computer". This phrase was meant to signify the move away from the dominance of stand-alone computers and the rise in the importance of the network.

With the advent of the Internet – the great network of networks – we could extend that original phrase and say that:

The network is the economy. The network is the society.

Looking at it in another way, we could say that the network has always been a central part of our economy and society. We could quite easily look at civilisation and see a whole engine of networks; from road networks to human networks.

Most of us are probably aware of the old saying, "when in Rome, do as the Romans do". Well, to paraphrase that pearl of wisdom, "when on a network, do as the network does".

This Internet network is different. It is digital, it is global, and it grows and changes faster than practically anything changed in the industrial age.

If you, as an individual or business, want to play an active part in the digital age network economy, you need to understand it in a very deep way. Much of that understanding may involve discarding knowledge and wisdom that has served you well in the industrial age economy. Discard that knowledge you must, for bringing old thinking into a new age will be like trying to mix oil and water.

If you and your organisation don't think like the network, don't behave like the network, don't embrace and run with the network, don't become like the network, then you will be left behind by the network economy.

Networked people, and networked organisations, are what thrive in a networked world. This chapter is about trying to get to the core of what networks mean, how they function, how you create value within them, and what their main characteristics are. Before we get into the detail, let's stand back and remember one thing:

People are the network.

Yes, there are wires. Yes, there are computers, modems and routers, websites and the like. There are all these things that all work – or should work – to help people interact and share information with each other. That's what it's all about when it comes down to it.

The network economy is just another name for the caring economy because the network is all about people: people are the network.

THE MEANING OF NETWORKS

The Internet is the single greatest network that humanity has ever invented. It allows millions upon millions of people to communicate with each other and to access and provide information.

The network is *not* about the tool although much of the technology-driven media would make you believe that it is. It is not about the wires. It is not about the computer. When the Internet reaches its maturity, the tools will become invisible. People are the network. Everything you do in a network you should do with people in mind, whether they are your staff, customers, public, media, investors or whoever.

It is important to explore the various meanings of the word 'network', as many of us have come to associate the word in a narrow sense with something technical. Networks are an inherent part of life and have been around long before any computer or telephone wire was invented.

The word 'network' is both a noun and a verb; it is both a thing and an activity. In the English language, 'network' originates from the word 'net'. The *Chambers Dictionary* defines a 'net' as "an open fabric, knotted into meshes: a piece or bag, or a screen or structure, of such fabric used for catching fish, butterflies, etc.".

Chambers defines the noun 'network' as "any structure in the form of a net: a system of lines, as, e.g. railway lines, resembling a net: a system of units, as, e.g. buildings, agencies, groups of persons, constituting a widely spread organisation and having a common purpose".

The 'inter-net' has become synonymous with the World Wide Web. Among the definitions *Webster's Dictionary* uses for 'web' include: "textile fabric, especially as in the piece or as being woven in a loom: The network of delicate threads spun by a spider to entrap its prey; a cobweb: Any complex network: a web of highways; anything artfully contrived or elaborated into a trap or snare: a web of espionage".

An interesting thing to note here is the idea of a 'web' being something that can trap or ensnare. (Imagine thinking of the Web as the World Wide Snare?) Indeed, a network can be closed in the sense that it keeps things in or out.

Physical networks have been a central building block of civilisation. Without its road and water networks, to name but two, the Roman Empire would never have achieved the status it did. We already live in a network society, as Ilan Salomon of the Hebrew University, explained in an article entitled, "Telecommunications and the 'Death of Distance': Some Implications for Transport and Urban Areas".[1]

> We are a network society because we rely on water and sewerage networks, and transportation networks which include roads, rail and air networks, and telecommunication networks, of course. These, combined, have brought about the concept of the network society. Location decisions are very much affected by those networks; we cannot locate where we do not have water or where we do not have sewerage, so this is one constraint on our location.

In modern times, we have come to associate networks very much with computers and telecommunications. According to the Institute for Telecommunication Sciences, a 'network' is an "interconnection of three or more communicating entities" with an 'interconnection' being defined as, "the linking together of interoperable systems". Whatis.com defines a 'network' as "a series of points or nodes interconnected by communication paths. Networks can interconnect with other networks and contain subnetwork".

The Cyberspace Lexicon[2] defines 'network' as "a system that links computers and other information/telecommunications technologies together, either by cable or by 'wireless' (radio or optical means), so that they can exchange information".

These may be technical definitions but we can draw from them a universal law that is applicable to all networks. It is that a network has two essential components.

1. **Information centres**: which in a basic sense may include a computer, website or a person who has access to the network.

2. **Communication channels**: which is the system of wires or radio waves that connect up the information centres.

In exploring the meaning of networks, it is interesting to investigate what would be considered to be the opposite of a network. As white is the opposite of black, there probably is no exact opposite to a network. However, by examining the above definitions we can isolate what might be close to its opposite.

As in nets and webs, a single thread is not a network. As in societies, a hermit is not a network. Broadly, we can say that the more 'threaded' you are and the more you interact, the more you are part of the network. The opposite to being networked is being alone. The opposite to thinking network is thinking 'me'.

VALUE IN A NETWORK

Unless a network delivers value, it has no real function and will wither away. Who does it create value for? For people. How does it create that value? Now, that's a more complex question. It is impossible to measure in an exact manner the particular value that a network creates. However, we can go some way in establishing the factors that make up that value equation and in establishing some form of indicative value.

We have already explored how a network has two essential components – information centres and communication channels. Therefore, the value of a particular network is based on some combined result of the synergy created by information centres and communication channels synching up.

The overall value of a particular network is made of the following basic elements.

1. *The number of information centres on the network.* On the Internet this includes both websites and people with access to the network.

2. *The quality of these information centres.* From a website's point of view this would relate to how well it delivers accurate, up to date information. From a people point of view this would relate to how knowledgeable they are and, equally importantly, how willing they are to share information and collaborate over the Internet.

3. *The quality of the communication channel.* This is dependent on such things as the quality of the bandwidth available, the quality of your Internet service provider, etc.

There is no real formula that can be applied here that I am aware of. We can say though that points 2 and 3 are very linked. Solving the bandwidth problem won't be very beneficial if all that happens is that you get faster access to poor quality information. It would be like driving down a wider highway to a library and arriving to find that the books are still scattered on the floor... and the lights are still turned out.

Establishing Network Value

To establish the value in using a particular network, we need to establish its 'network cost'. This cost then needs to be measured against the cost of using other networks, to see if it is good value or not. Network cost has three main elements.

1.   The time spent using the network.

2.   The financial cost of using the network.

3.   The quality of information received.

Time Spent

The time spent is calculated from the following.

1. **The set-up time**: the time it takes me turn on the computer and get online.

2. **The search time**: which involves the time it takes me to find what I'm looking for, which ranges from using a search engine, to waiting for a particular website to download, to browsing through that particular website.

3. **The action time**: which is the time it takes me to act on the information I've received.

Time is the scarcest resource of the digital age. The Internet came to prominence for many as an amazing way of finding information that would otherwise have taken considerably longer to find. However, as Internet information overload intensifies and bandwidth remains a problem, the Internet is losing some of that advantage.

Allowing people to act on information is very important. Increasingly, the Internet is becoming an e-commerce medium, which allows people to purchase things as a result of information they have received.

Network Financial Cost
This would include:

a) equipment costs (computers, modems, etc.);

b) Internet service provider costs;

c) telephone costs.

In countries, such as the United States, the above costs have continued to drop, making the Internet a viable option for more and more people. However, in other parts of the world, the costs of getting and staying connected are still very substantial.

Quality of Information
This would include the:

a) actual quality of the information;

b) trust you can put in the information;

c) completeness of the information.

If the information is poor quality then value is reduced. If you can't trust the information, then that again reduces value. It is difficult to establish trust in a virtual space such as the Internet, where you cannot actually meet people or visit their premises.

If the information is not complete – there are ten information sources and only five of them are available to you – value is reduced. Although the Internet has a very wide range of information, in certain disciplines it may not be as complete as a specialised library.

Information Centre Value
As already explained, an 'information centre' is a person (user) with access to the network or a website. So, how do we measure the value of a particular information centre? Let us look at the two types of information centres separately.

Network User Value
Let's first look at how you measure value for a person who uses the Internet network. But before that maybe we should step back and ask the question: Why should I deliver value to the network? What's in it for me?

If I am an information worker, then I make my living from the knowledge I deliver. I live in a rapidly changing environment and I must constantly be on the lookout for future opportunity. By spreading some of my knowledge liberally throughout the network, I leave trails and links back to me for people and organisations that might want to pay for or quote my knowledge in the future. Thus, if I intend to make my living within the network, the more visible I am within that network the better. I can say personally that I have followed this strategy of maximising my visibility on the Internet for many years and that it has been a tremendous success for me.

The opposite approach would be for me to hoard all my knowledge and to expect the network to come to me without me making any effort to reach out to it. (To think 'me' instead of 'network'.) This approach has some merit if I am some form of internationally acclaimed guru. However, remember what I said in an earlier chapter about information in the industrial age being like gold and information in the digital age being like milk?

If I hoard my information then I may find it is increasingly going out of date before it achieves any value for me. If I want to achieve value (income) from it, I must thus carry out an active campaign of informing the network that I have this information. The best way of doing this is by providing some of it for free, thus providing a taster of what can be got if someone is willing to pay. (I could, of course, advertise it, but then providing some of it for free is a type of advertising.)

There is another factor at play here. A lot of the information, which workers need today relates to the nature of the Internet itself. In other words, there is a huge need to understand the medium itself, to see what works and what doesn't within it. In a way we are all apprentices in the digital age these days, learning our trade on the shop floor of the network economy.

Apprentices work hard to learn their craft and don't get paid much. We information workers and organisations need to learn our craft on the Internet every day. The more we interact with the Internet the more we learn. And we cannot really have any useful interaction with the medium unless we ultimately have information to bring to the table. Giving away some of our information for free gives us greater presence within the network and is a very valuable way for us to learn. Thus, we gain knowledge by creating value.

Having explored why an individual needs to create value, let's explore the range of value that can be created. At a very basic level, if I have access to the network then I have the opportunity to bring value to the network if I contribute to a newsgroup or online chat forum. However, the only connection I leave is my name, unless I have moved to the next important level and acquired an e-mail address. With an e-mail address I allow the opportunity for others to get directly in touch with me.

As with every other environment, there are advantages and disadvantages of any action taken in a network. While spreading my e-mail address throughout the network means that I am more contactable by the people I want to contact me, it also means that I am more contactable by spammers and people sending me useless mail.

This is an interesting situation. In establishing my value within the network, I have been very liberal with spreading my e-mail address about. However, once I have achieved the value I want, the fact that I have value encourages others seeking value to get in touch with me more. The more value I achieve (the more famous or respected I become), the more people will want to get in touch. Getting the balance right – of being well-connected within the network and yet not overloaded by the communications I receive – is a major challenge for the information worker.

The ongoing value I create as a user within the network is dependent on the following.

1. The quantity of contributions I make to the network.

2. The quality of these contributions.

3. The connections and links I leave behind.

There must be a certain quantity, yes, but if the contributions are not of a certain quality then the network will begin to ignore me and even filter me out, as other network users avoid my contributions. Making sure my e-mail or website address is available, is a daily task that must be undertaken.

There is no better builder of an individual's network value than through word of mouth. We all know that there is no better compliment to receive than for someone who is not directly connected to you to compliment you. If people start quoting you in the network regularly, then you are beginning to accrue serious network user value. Equally, if people start criticising your contributions, pointing out inaccuracies that you are unable to defend, then you are accruing a negative network value.

Network Website Value (Reverse Distribution)

In the physical economy, distribution is a fundamental element in economic activity. In a digital economy, and particularly where the value of a website is concerned, traditional distribution is not so much a factor. From a website point of view, it is not about getting the website 'distributed' to you target market, but rather a matter of getting your target market to come to your website. This we might term as 'reverse distribution'.

There are no 'roads' to your website when it is launched. Thus, a primary objective is to create a comprehensive 'road network' that facilitates your target market coming to your website in the easiest possible manner.

There are a number of ways of creating this network for your website, which include getting:

• your target market to make your website their 'homepage';

• your target market to bookmark your website, so that whenever they look at their bookmarks they will see a 'route' to your website;

• other relevant websites to 'link' to your website.

Geting your target market to have your website as their homepage is the ultimate goal of any website. What this means is that when the user opens up their browser the first page it opens at is yours.

Netscape is the prime example of this. When you install a browser the homepage it generally defaults to is that of the maker of the browser. (Research has shown that the majority of Internet users do not know how to change their homepage.) It was the Netscape browser that exploded the use of the Web. At one stage some 85 per cent of Web users used the Netscape browser. The Netscape website was the most popular on the Internet.

However, Netscape did not see this diamond underneath its nose, and did not fully exploit its potential. The fact that the Netscape website was not as useful as it could have been – not to mention the entry of the Microsoft browser into the market – meant that over time the number of visits to the Netscape website dropped significantly in comparison to other websites, such as Yahoo. During 1998, Netscape finally recognised the potential and turned its website into much more of a portal entity.

Research has shown that the average Internet user has no more than twenty favourite bookmark websites that they will go back to on a regular basis. Getting your website into the top twenty bookmarks of your target market is therefore a prime objective. Of course, this is not a simple task and is basically down to how useful the Internet user finds your website.

In the virtual environment that the Internet is, word of mouth is a powerful ally. In getting a link from another website, you could say that you have achieved imbedded word of mouth. Someone at that website has decided that your website is of a quality that they will create a link to it encouraging people who visit their website to consider visiting yours.

If you look at some of the most successful websites on the Internet, you will generally find that they have managed to get a substantial number of other websites to link to them. I've used a tool from alexa.com which compiles the number of links there are to a particular website to illustrate this. Alexa is not totally scientific, but it does give a reasonable indication of how many other websites have linked to a particular website. I have drawn up a brief table as follows.

**Selected Website Linking Information
(December 1999)**

Website Name	Links to that Website
Amazon.com	1,023,629
Yahoo	477,580
Microsoft	463,259
Netscape	149,346
ZDNet	95,568

Source: *alexa.com*

Creating positive network website value in 1999 is a difficult, costly and time-consuming task. Companies, such as Yahoo and Amazon, had first mover advantage. Yahoo, for example, did practically no advertising before it went public. Word of mouth drove it forward.

On the Internet of 1999, there is little or no first mover advantage left. Getting links to your website, having people bookmark it or make it their homepage, requires a substantial investment. You must fight for attention among millions of websites and hundreds of millions of pages.

It is a task, however, that every organisation, which has a website, must undertake with vigour. Because if a website does not have network value then it is a weak entity within the network. As the Internet network becomes more and more important within the economy, being a weak entity within it becomes a severe disadvantage.

In the near future network website value (as well as the network user value of the information workers within an organisation), will become a significant component in how the overall value of an organisation is calculated.

Negative Network Value
If people and websites can say good things about you and link to you in a positive manner, they can equally say bad things about you and link to you in a negative manner. And as the saying goes, 'good news travels fast, bad news travels faster'.

If your website is poor, if the information on it is inaccurate, if you are not skilled in contributing to a chat forum and thus say something foolish, then you risk creating negative network value. As bad as having no network value, negative network value can damage your reputation and hurt your bottom-line.

Countering people who were damaging your reputation in the offline world often meant saying nothing or sending them a solicitor's letter. It's not so simple on the Internet. While the basic laws are the same, the fact that cyberspace crosses a multitude of international borders means that it is often difficult to ascertain where the defamatory statement originated. For various reasons, the Internet also lends itself to anonymity (although this is changing), and it may be hard to track exactly who sent what message without considerable cost and effort. If you are based in Ireland, taking legal action against someone in Sweden who has created a defamatory website against you, with the website itself being hosted in the United States, is no easy task.

The Internet is the world's greatest grapevine.

If you ignore the grapevine, particularly if there are people saying things about you or your organisation, you do so at your peril. You need to engage with it, you need to see every time you or your organisation is mentioned – even in a negative manner – as a potential opportunity to increase your network value.

If the information being provided is inaccurate, then correct it in a balanced way. If someone is criticising you then respectfully engage with them. Try to turn their opinion around, but at least show the Internet that you are interacting, that you are informing. There is the other option and that is not to interact, not to provide information. To do nothing and ignore the Internet. The Internet can charge a high price for doing nothing.

Intel and the Price of doing nothing

When I searched AltaVista from 1 January 1994 to 31 December 1994, with the word 'Pentium' (Intel's popular chip), the first ten responses I got *all* had to do with a bug in the original Intel Pentium chip. (When I searched using 'Intel', three out of the first ten responses referred to the Pentium bug.) Information on the Pentium bug arose first on the Internet towards the end of 1994. A hefty debate developed and before long the offline press picked it up. The rest, as they say, is history.

The Pentium bug was rare, and in the larger scale of things, relatively minor. However, the huge press coverage and debate which arose from it was as much a reaction to Intel's poor record of public relations and customer interactivity than the design fault itself.

On 12 December 1994, Andy Grove, President and Chief Executive Officer of Intel, was quoted as saying with regard to the likelihood of a user encountering the error in the Pentium chip that:

> You can always contrive situations that force this error. In other words, if you know where a meteor will land, you can go there and get hit.[3]

Consumers who had bought Pentiums were not impressed and the Intel defensive stance became the real bug in the ointment. Within weeks, Andy Grove released a statement offering a 'Pentium replacement policy'. His tone had changed considerably, and in offering to replace Pentiums with the error, he stated that:

> We at Intel wish to sincerely apologise for our handling of the recently publicised Pentium processor flaw. What Intel continues to believe is technically an extremely minor problem has taken on a life of its own. Although Intel firmly stands behind the quality of the current version of Pentium processor, we recognise that many users have concerns.[4]

The Pentium bug had indeed taken on a life of its own. On the growing grapevine of the Internet, where everyone has the potential to voice their opinion, wild fires of speculation were raging along the communication channels.

There were a flurry of Pentium joke websites and even a 'Pentium joke generator'. One Internet user hysterically claimed that "the fallout from the Pentium disaster is likely to be worse than Chernobyl". Another anonymous user claimed that the November 1994 Republican election victory might have been due to the Pentium bug.

In the end, the Pentium bug was not that serious and the replacement policy took much of the sting out of the criticism. In fact, very few Pentiums were actually sent back for replacement. A 1996 notice on the University of Pittsburgh website typified the reaction. It stated that:

> While it has been more than a year since the defect in Intel's Pentium chip was announced, many owners of University Pentium machines *have not yet contacted* CIS to arrange for the free replacement of the flawed chip.[5]

What happened to Intel, one of the largest and most powerful companies in the world, as a result of the Pentium bug, was not purely down to the Internet and its grapevine. However, it was reflective of the new age and the information consumers who populate it. Information consumers don't like getting talked down to. They don't like their concerns being ignored. If you annoy them they simply won't accept it. They'll send some e-mails, comment on newsgroups, maybe even build a website for the cause. In this sense, the Internet puts publishing at the fingertips of millions.

The Internet doesn't forget either. In its network archive, so much of day to day history is recorded and thus becomes visible and accessible to people willing to search back for it. In the past, only researchers with lots of time and access to expensive databases could have accessed the type of information the Internet now offers essentially for free.

I, for example, spent a few hours searching the Web to compile this story on Intel. Without access to the Web, it would have been almost impossible for me to collect the information I needed. On the Internet, so much can be measured and accounted for. Everywhere we go, we leave trails that others may follow up in the future, piecing together a story that might be negative or positive.

If as people and organisations we do not fully inform and interact with the Internet, we face a number of possible results.

1. The Internet will ignore us and will treat us as if we do not exist. As the Internet grows in social and economic importance, not existing in its eyes will mean not existing in the eyes of millions upon millions of people.

2. The Internet grapevine will chew us up and spit us out. The Pentium bug is just a famous example of this process. I have seen many more over the years, and expect to see many, many more. (I will cover more of them in Chapter 12, *Building Brands Online*.) Remember, on the Internet, you are measurable, transparent and ultimately accountable.

IN A NETWORK, NETWORK

The verb 'to network', in some ways, is as old or older than human civilisation. Families, groups, clubs, gangs and communities network. The ability to network is one of humanity's greatest strengths.

Why do we network? We network because there is benefit in networking. If I participate in a network, I have the opportunity to gain information and contacts which are valuable to me either in a social, economic or spiritual manner. If I didn't network I wouldn't have these contacts.

Networking is generally a natural part of what we all do on a day to day basis. Because we take it so much for granted it is interesting to read a quotation from the American National Institute on Disability and Rehabilitation Research,[6] as it advises people with disabilities with regard to how they should go about seeking work.

"When we use the terms 'networks' or 'personal connections', we are referring to the range of people you see and interact with in the variety of activities you do (and have done) at work, in school, and in your community," the Institute states. "They may include family or close friends, former bosses or co-workers, professionals, and people working in stores that you frequent. We all know people, and we all have networks."

Profnet,[7] a business networking organisation, makes the following statement about networking.

> In it's simplest form, networking simply means making connections to make exchanges easier. This can be social, personal, professional, or even technical. In the professional setting, networking is getting to know people and businesses, and developing trust and communication to make the process of business easier and more profitable. This usually involves the exchange of 'leads', or referrals to potential customers, between businesses.

Patricia Wagner and Leif Smith of Pattern Research[8] explain that networking "is the art of discovering patterns in the world and making useful connections for ourselves and for others".

Political philosopher and foreign policy expert, Dr Francis Fukuyama, speaking to the Merrill Lynch Forum[9] talked about, "networks of trust", and about how you need to understand how the social networks operate within a particular country before you start doing business in it.

Jessica Lipnack, president of the Networking Institute[10] in Boston, told *The Washington Post* that there is a greater need than ever for people to network today so that they can build their own 'social capital'. Lipnack said this kind of capital has three components: trust, reciprocity and dense social networks. Trust is integral to any relationship where people must rely on one another, she stated, and reciprocity makes possible a true give and take of information and resources, rather than just a take. A dense social network increases the potential for exchange, Lipnack concluded.

The Rules of Networking

There are precious few successful business people who have not spent at least some of their professional lives networking. The reason, for example, many of us carry business cards is so that we can network, as the business card is a primary networking tool.

While the Internet can never replace human contact – and it would be a very foolish person who might think that it would – there is no doubt that it can be a tremendous aid in the networking process. I know, for one, that some of my most valuable business contacts have originated, and have been kept in touch with, as a result of e-mail.

The rules of networking are reasonably well-established, and I would say that anyone who wants to truly make use of the Internet should understand and use them on a day to day basis. Patricia Wagner and Leif Smith of Pattern Research have developed a number of such networking rules. In summary, these are:

- be useful;
- taking can be as important as giving;
- don't be boring;
- don't abuse your contact;
- listen;
- ask quality questions;
- don't make assumptions.

Nancy Roebke, executive director of Profnet Inc.,[11] a professional business leads generation corporation, has developed what she terms, 'the Ten Commandments of networking'. In summary, these are:

a) be prepared – always carry your business cards;

b) be a good listener;

c) give first to get later;

d) follow-up;

e) be specific;

f) choose effective networking events;

g) choose contacts effectively (your competitors can be contacts too);

h) share your resources;

i) keep good records;

j) never stop – networking is a never-ending game.

The rules were not written specifically with the Internet in mind, but each one of them has relevance. Your e-mail signature file is your business card. Providing free information follows the 'give first to get later' rule. Interestingly, John Hagel III and Arthur G

Armstrong opened their influential book *Net Gain*[12] with the following quotation:

> One man gives freely and yet gains even more. Another withholds unduly, but comes to poverty.
>
>   Proverbs 11:24

The Internet is a network. On a network, network.

THE NETWORKED ORGANISATION

The Internet connects people. Connections facilitate networking and networking is a form of co-operation and collaboration. A company is a group of people who have established structures, including networks, which allow it to achieve certain goals.

With the advent of modern transport and telecommunications networks, and now the Internet, what we have found is that as a company's ability to extend its networks has expanded, the company itself has extended itself. We have seen in Chapter 3, *Cyberspace: The New Space*, how teleworking has become a viable option for millions of people.

The term 'virtual corporation' has been coined to describe a company that is established with the express intention of fully exploiting virtual structures, such as the Internet. Such an organisation might not have a physical 'head office', or any real office at all for that matter. Instead, it is structured around a telecommunication and Internet network, sharing the physical office space of its members where appropriate.

A virtual organisation is often some combination of other organisations and individuals. It can be assembled quickly in response to a sudden shift in the marketplace. It can be set-up to pursue a specific goal and then disbanded as quickly when that goal has been achieved. Such an organisation can save costs in a number of areas and if properly planned and executed can be very successful.

However, we all know the saying, 'easy come, easy go'. Virtual organisations are by their very nature fluid and unstable. Having some of your workforce telecommuting is one thing, but trying to create a cohesive entity where the majority of the workforce is not in the one place throws up major challenges.

David Skyrme, of David Skyrme Associates,[13] in a paper entitled "Principles for Networked Organisation", outlines a number of key factors necessary in building a successful work environment on a network. He writes about how people need to be willing to trust and support each other, of how a positive attitude must reign. It is also interesting that Skyrme reiterates a principle that I keep coming across when reading about networks and networking – give before thinking of getting.

Skyrme also stresses the central importance of building effective teams.

> Teams are the organisation units that create focus and allow work to proceed. The most productive teams for knowledge work are small multi-disciplinary groups. For example, 5-8 people with a variety of backgrounds and personality traits.[14]

Skyrme notes that information workers need to belong to more than one team so that they can gain a broader perspective and hone different skills. This is very true in the sense that as such information workers are physically isolated, they need to develop a broader range of skills so as to be able to prosper independently.

"Miscommunication is probably the worst obstacle to effectiveness in any organisation," Skyrme writes. This is so true. While the Internet can indeed facilitate co-operation and collaboration, it can often be a hotbed for miscommunication and distrust. Communicating by e-mail can become a very cold and mechanical process. The very speed of e-mail can light wildfires. E-mail can be something to hide behind. Instead of taking the time and effort of meeting up with someone to tell them something important, an e-mail can become a convenient cop-out. It is therefore vital that all virtual organisations plan regular physical get-togethers so that people can build genuine trust and understanding.

Operating within a virtual environment is all well and good, but we need to always remember that humans are flesh and blood, not virtual. Touch, feelings and emotions are essential parts of living, working and doing business. Until we become like hardware and software, they will continue to play a central role in human existence.

GROWTH IN A NETWORK

The growth of a network follows exponential rather than linear growth. For example, if there are only two people on the network, then all that can happen is that one connects and/or communicates with the other. If the number doubles to four then we see more than a doubling in the amount of connections and communications that can occur. One can communicate with three others individually, with the three together, with two out of the three. Thus, as the network grows, the number of possible connections, combinations and communications explode.

Networks need to reach a certain 'connectivity threshold' before they become truly useful, but when they reach that threshold their growth tends to gather pace considerably. Fax machines and the Internet are examples here. The Internet grew very slowly for most of the 1970s and 1980s. (The fax machine was an overnight success in the 1980s after being around for twenty years.)

There were many other 'competing' networks to the Internet. A number of the larger organisations ignored or tried to create their own 'Internets'. However, by 1995, the Internet had gone beyond the critical connectivity threshold point. It had gained a momentum that drew everything else along with it.

In reality, the Internet is not one network but a 'network of networks', a network of different individuals, organisations and needs. This multifarious environment can have different connectivity thresholds, depending on who is using it and what for.

For example, during the 1970s and 1980s the Internet had a relatively small number of users who were nearly all scientists and academics. For them, it had already reached its connectivity threshold, and had become an extremely useful medium through which they communicated with their peers and shared information.

As the Internet exploded with new users in the early-1990s, many academics and scientists began to complain about 'their' network being 'saturated'. At the same time, business was complaining that the Internet had not yet reached the connectivity threshold for profitable commerce to occur. In this situation, one organisation's connectivity threshold was another's saturation point. Then the spammers came, sending useless messages that wasted bandwidth and filled up everyone's e-mail boxes.

The general point here is that exponential growth rapidly

expands the network environment, which at certain points creates positive value for different constituencies. However, exponential growth can suddenly blossom out of control, guzzling bandwidth and creating that dreaded beast – information overload.

SECURITY AND RELIABILITY OF NETWORKS

The issue of Internet security is essential to the future of Internet commerce. It is not even so much about how actually secure the network is but how comfortable consumers feel about security. In trying any new medium, particularly in giving your credit card number, consumers are naturally cautious. A 'trust environment' will need to be created and this will require high security levels so as to create that necessary comfort factor.

It is certainly true that security is an increasing concern on the Internet. Consider the following.

- In 1998, the American National Computer Security Association (NCSA) claimed that 98 per cent of all organisations experience virus problems each year.[15]

- In 1998, the NCSA also claimed that an organisation was ten times more likely to be infected by a virus than twelve months previously.[16]

- 1998 findings from The Computer Security Institute showed that 64 per cent of the 520 companies surveyed had experienced computer security breaches within the previous twelve months, a rise of 16 per cent rise on the 1997 figures.[17]

- Hackers testifying before an American Senate Committee in 1998 claimed that they could render the Internet unusable in the United States in fewer than 30 minutes, stating that Internet and computer security was "almost non-existent".[18]

A 1997 report by IT analyst group Ovum[19] pointed out that the real problem with Internet security was the organisation's reluctance to manage risk.

Users are in a very difficult position. Internet security is complex, many-layered, and changing rapidly. Aggressive marketing of security products adds to the confusion, as does the ease with which rumours about security spread. The Internet is one of the best sources of misinformation about Internet security.

The report identified two essential concepts organisations need to take into account when planning an Internet security strategy. These are that insecurity:

a) is an intrinsic part of the Internet;

b) cannot be eliminated, rather it can be managed.

To understand how we might best deal with security online, it is instructive it explore how we have dealt with security offline. Most of the early cities that humans built were walled so as to keep out undesirables. As civilisation evolved, cities grew and commerce flourished, with security forces, such as police and army, replacing the walls. Walls became historical artefacts as it was recognised that the best way to deal with infringements and unlawful acts was not with static walls, but rather with a flexible security presence.

The Internet network is evolving in the same way. The nature of its success has been about openness and if it wants to continue that success it will require flexible, vigilant security policies. The firewall that protects an organisation's internal network may never fully be replaced – as ancient city walls have been – but what we will see is an increase in 'network security policing'. As with all core activities on the Internet, it is people who need to be central to the process and not technology.

Reliability

We're not simply talking about security issues when it comes to the Internet network. The basic reliability of the network must also come in for scrutiny. Many are amazed at how a system designed originally for thousands of users has been robust enough to facilitate many millions of users. However, the hackers who testified before the American Senate made the very relevant point that "the Internet was not designed to be bullet-proof by today's standards", pointing out that it was based on network protocols more than twenty years old.

If your business depends on online transactions then it needs to be up 24 hours a day, 365 days a year. This is a costly process. If you have 'rush-hours' in your online business (you get a lot of orders in a compressed period of time) then your website might well fall over as a result of too much traffic. In 1998, the Internet itself almost fell over as major news stories broke and people rushed online in their millions to get information. (Perhaps the best example in 1998 was the Louise Woodward child murder trial in the United States. The judge's verdict was released first on the Internet causing large sections of it to overload as a result of the huge traffic.)

Much of the software and hardware for websites is like the Web itself, only a few years old. There can be bugs and glitches. Consider that the Internet's most important brands, such as Amazon, America Online, Egghead Software, all faced reliability issues in 1998, and you will realise that this is a most serious issue requiring urgent attention.

The Internet is too important for reliability issues not to be properly addressed. However, there may be some rocky roads ahead as the network is restructured to meet the growing demands of its role as one of the world's primary social and commercial environments.

Measurability and Privacy in Networks

An electronic network is a 'measurable' environment. The Internet, being an electronic network and as open as it is, can be like a window into much of what you do on the network. Everything that happens on it leaves a trail. All of its activity can be measured, calculated and analysed in various ways.

With the introduction of Intel's Pentium III chip, such measurement capacity moved a significant step forward. Each chip has a unique identification number, meaning that the owner of the computer can be readily tracked once they go online.

As always, there are positive and negative sides to measurement and tracking. Organisations can establish structures that can help measure the satisfaction of their customers and the happiness of their workforce through the use of ongoing surveys and other measurement tools. Used this way, the Internet can deliver vital feedback to the organisation, indicating which strategies are having a positive impact and which are having a negative one.

Where measurement techniques begin to impinge on privacy rights can be a grey area. Certainly, if a consumer or worker is not aware they are being measured and tracked, their privacy is definitely being violated. However, sometimes consumers and workers can sign away rights assuming that there is much less measurement than is actually happening.

A few years ago, a software technology called 'cookies' was developed for the Internet. This software can track you as you

move from website to website, building up a log of your movements. In many cases, cookies were placed on people's browsers
without their knowledge.

As of 1998, the position of the American government towards
privacy was very much one of laissez-faire, reflecting its general
thinking towards the Internet. (The European Union has been
more proactive with regard to protecting privacy rights.) As far
as privacy was concerned, self-regulation was the best regulation
in America's opinion. However, in my opinion, asking private
industry to set the standards for consumers' privacy is a bit like
asking a reformed alcoholic to manage a pub. The temptation is
great.

In 1988, a report by the Center for Public Integrity[20] claimed
to provide an in-depth study of how the American Congress had
continually put the interests of Corporate America ahead of privacy concerns of its citizens. In the same year, Electronic Privacy
Information Center (EPIC)[21] made a statement claiming that
online privacy policies were being developed but not imple-
mented. They found that, for example, only three out of 40 surveyed websites had posted promised privacy policies. "Pathetic"
was how the EPIC summed up the attempt at self-regulation.

Businesses need to understand that people are genuinely concerned about their privacy. In 1998, the respected ongoing online
user survey by Georgia Tech found that privacy was the number
one concern of Internet users.[22] While the 1998 Privacy Concerns
& Consumer Choice survey,[23] by Louis Harris & Associates survey found that:

- Almost 9 out of 10 Americans (88 per cent) say they are concerned today about general threats to their privacy.

- More than 8 in 10 (82 per cent) feel that consumers have lost
all control over how companies collect and use their personal
information.

- Almost 8 in 10 (78 per cent) believe that businesses tend to ask
for too much personal information.

- 4 out of 10 respondents (41 per cent), representing 78 million
adults, say that they have personally been the victim of an
invasion of their privacy as a consumer.

- Only 51 per cent say they believe that American businesses in
general use the personal information they collect "in a proper
manner".

- Women are even more privacy-oriented than men in consumer-privacy matters and it is the prime consumer audience of better educated and higher income groups that register the strongest privacy concerns.

"Concerns over threats to personal privacy remain at very high levels and, in some cases, are increasing," the executive summary to the survey stated. "Most people feel that businesses ask for too much personal information, and that consumers have lost all control over how this information is used. Moreover, few people express strong confidence that businesses are using consumers' personal information properly."[24]

A 1998 survey by the American Federal Trade Commission,[25] found that only 14 per cent of commercial sites informed surfers of their policies on collecting and selling online data. Heeding the obvious lack of privacy policies by websites, and the growing worries of consumers, in April 1999, IBM informed its online advertisers that they must have published privacy policies on the websites if they wanted IBM to continue advertising with them.[26]

IBM suggested to these websites that they follow guidelines set up by an industry watchdog called The Online Privacy Alliance. These guidelines include the following.

1. Telling website visitors that personal information is being collected.
2. Indicating what will be done with that information.
3. Giving visitors the opportunity to limit what the website operator can do with that information, other than for the purpose for which it was collected.
4. Notifying visitors if cookies are being used.

"We think what IBM has done shows some important leadership in an area that's absolutely essential for the industry," Rich LeFurgy, Chairman of the Internet Advertising Bureau, a coalition of advertisers, told the *San Francisco Chronicle*.

No matter how well-intentioned, privacy is not an issue that can be left up to private business alone. Governments have a vital role to play in guaranteeing privacy and general rights. There are enormous legal, social and commercial issues that require the very best minds and a broad consensus between the private and public sectors if they are to be properly addressed. If governments do not engage in a positive manner with the Internet, they will in time be seen as negligent; a negligence that they will surely pay for.

COMPLEXITY AND THE NEED FOR TRAINING

If people are the network, then the more people on a network the more complex it becomes. (As of 1998, there were 150 million Internet users worldwide.) That's because people are complex. They have complex feelings, needs and wants. To create a cyber-space where people feel comfortable enough to establish communities, do business, spend their leisure time, etc., requires considerable technical complexity, but more importantly, a deeply complex social environment.

The more complex a system is the more difficult it is to predict and control. Consider for a moment the engines of the Internet – computers. Already it could be said that humans have effectively handed over much of the development process of future generation computers to previous generation ones. Before you start calling me a science fiction head, just remember that the new computers we make today could not be designed or tested without the software and processing power of already existing computers. There are precious few people in the world today who have a deep understanding of the inner-workings of a humble PC. PC support has, in very many cases, become about replacing parts, not fixing them.

The more useful a network becomes, the more complex it becomes and the more dependent on that network you can become. Your network can become a comfortable trap within which you begin to carry out increasing levels of your information sourcing, communication, interaction and commerce, ignoring or withdrawing from other networks and forms of information sourcing and interaction.

If I were to have an Internet nightmare, then it would see me several years from now, having become very dependent on the Internet in a number of areas of my life, staring at a frozen screen. If such a complex system as the Internet went down, all I could do, along with millions of others, would be to wait until it came back up again. (Perhaps prayer will come back into fashion as the digital age progresses?)

To even begin an understanding of such a complex environment as the Internet requires a life-long learning approach. For
many, we are moving into an information age, an intellectual environment. We are moving into cyberspace; a place created by and
for the mind and imagination. Thus, the blocks and obstacles within this environment for all of us will be our own minds, our own
attitudes, our own lack of understanding of the environment.
Ongoing training and education is essential for all individuals and
organisations that want to play an active part in cyberspace.

If the Internet is indeed the 'information superhighway', as
American Vice-President Al Gore once named it, then most of us
drive on it without a licence. Searching for, and organising, information are complex tasks, and yet people are asked to search for
information and build websites without hardly any formal training. Learning how to use e-mail effectively requires skill, and yet
most people are expected to pick up this skill as they go.

In some ways, it's all rather simple. If you want to succeed on
the Internet, the key skills you need to learn are social, not technical. As pointed out already, the Internet survival kit is filled
with networking, collaborative and co-operative tools.

VERSATILITY AND CHAOS IN THE NETWORK

The original Internet was designed so that it didn't have a centre
that could be targeted by a nuclear strike. The great achievement
of this design was that everywhere had the capacity to become a
centre. If everywhere on the Internet has the capacity to be a centre then everywhere has potential power.

The Internet network is this versatile, malleable, flexible, ever-
changing kind of environment. When Intel had the bug in its
Pentium, joke sites sprouted up from nowhere within days.
When the Heaven's Gate cult committed suicide their website
became the centre of attention. Outposts can suddenly become
centres if the right event occurs.

A 1998 IBM report entitled "Banking in the Network
Economy"[27] wrote about the potential of the Internet to create a
"particle economy. In this particle economy, components would
be assembled from multiple suppliers to create product offerings
that are mass individualised to the needs of the customer. The
strategic focus of the network economy moves banks from a
product orientation in the 1980s to mass-segmentation in the
1990s and to individualised offerings or value propositions by

the next millennium. Whatever the outcome, the impact promises to be extraordinary".

The network of the coming years is a heady place, where speed and the ability to change reign. It is full of exciting potential, and full of danger. Whatever, we cannot hide from the network; we must embrace the Internet.

INTERNET NETWORK CHARACTERISTICS

From what we have explored in this chapter and from other sections of the book, it is possible to establish a set of key characteristics of the Internet as a network. These characteristics are:

- digital;
- global;
- fluxed;
- connected;
- interactive;
- co-operative and collaborative;
- exponential;
- versatile;
- measurable;
- complex;
- insecure;
- open.

Digital
This is the digital age and the Internet is its digital foundation. Things digital are married to things computer and we have already explored the huge impact computers are having on society. The network is digital, the economy is digital, and that is a key difference between the industrial age physical networks and economies.

Global
We are not talking about a local network here, but a truly global one. In one way or another, the Internet is reaching into practically every country in the world. This is a global network like we

have never seen before. As we shall see later, the impact of globalisation should not be overstated – the local will be central to most of our lives for a long time to come. However, it is a characteristic of the Internet that must be taken into account.

Fluxed

"The world is in a state of chassis," a character in a Sean O'Casey play stated around the turn of the 20th century. What would he have said about today, I wonder? The world that we live in is constantly in a state of flux, and this great Internet network is the most fluxed of all. Doubling in size every year since 1988, filling with millions of websites, millions upon millions of pages of information and heaving with so many million e-mails.

This network has a long way to go before it settles into anything approaching maturity. Therefore, it would be a foolish person that would claim to understand exactly how it will behave when it does settle. It would be a foolish organisation that would set down rigid plans and strategies for the Internet. In such a fluxed world, there's no point in waiting for the perfect moment to truly engage with the Internet. Truly engage today and learn as you go.

Connected

The essence of a network is the connections it creates. The Internet is no different and those that thrive within its environment are those that make the right connections – and lots of them!

Interactive

People are the network and to get the best out of the Internet you need to interact with other people and/or information other people have created. If you can't, or are unwilling to interact, then you shouldn't be doing business on the Internet.

Co-operative and Collaborative

The Internet can become an environment where virtual teams can assemble from different geographic places to co-operate and collaborate. However, never forget the vital function of face to face interaction if such processes wish to be genuinely cohesive and productive.

Exponential

As we have seen, networks grow at exponential rates. Remember, in 1994 the Internet hardly had any user base and there was little or no commerce done on it. By 1998 it had 150 millions users and was becoming a central hub for future world commerce.

Versatile
Electronic networks are versatile environments. The very design of the Internet was to ensure versatility, adaptability and flexibility. Everywhere on the network has the potential to be a centre; everywhere has thus the potential to influence and be powerful. In a versatile environment you need to be versatile if you are to truly exploit it.

Measurable
When you move within an electronic network you leave a trail and that be tracked. You can also leave a record of your satisfaction and dissatisfaction. Privacy issues are central to measurement issues.

Complex
The more people you have within an environment, the more complex it becomes. When you bring together millions of people from very many nationalities and backgrounds, you create an environment teeming with complexity.

Insecure
If you want to live a safe and secure life, do nothing. The Internet is an open environment and is thus potentially open to attack. However, as cities of old found that walls hinder growth more than they protect, the Internet is faced with managing insecurity rather than finding a once-off solution for it.

Open
One of the defining differences between networks in the industrial age and digital age is that industrial age networks were generally closed and exclusive and that digital age networks, such as the Internet, are more open and inclusive.

The Internet, as we have already seen, is the result of open thinking, design and behaviour. As a result of open standards, the Internet has managed to reach out to the world, to seed its network wherever there are computers and telephone lines. No company or set of companies – with their proprietary approaches to developing technologies – could have ever created as open and growing a place as the Internet.

REFERENCES

1. I Salomon, "Telecommunications and the 'Death of Distance': Some Implications for Transport and Urban Areas" Urban Design, Telecommunication and Travel Forecasting Conference (1996) http://www.bts.gov/tmip/papers/tmip/udes/salomon.htm

2. B Cotton R Oliver, *The Cyberspace Lexicon: An Illustrated Dictionary of Terms from Multimedia to Virtual Reality* (Phaidon Press Inc.: 1994)

3. E Corcoran, "IBM Halts Sales of Computres using Flawed Pentium Processor" *The Washington Post* (12 December 1994) http://www-tech.mit.edu/V114/N63/pentium.63w.html

4. "Intel Adopts Upon-request Replacement Policy on Pentium™ Processors With Floating Point Flaw; will take Q4 Charge against Earnings" http://www-europe.mathworks.com/pentium/Intel_replace.txt

5. "CIS Still Replacing Defective Pentium Chips" University of Pittsburgh (1994), http://www.pitt.edu/~document/connections/back/mar96/feature5.html

6. National Institute on Disability and Rehabilitation Research http://www.ed.gov/offices/OSERS/NIDRR/

7. Profnet, http://www.profnet.org

8. Pattern Research, http://www.pattern.com

9. "Economic Globalization and Culture: A Discussion with Dr Francis Fukuyama" *The Merrill Lynch Forum* (1998) http://www.ml.com/woml/forum/global.htm

10. The Networking Institute, http://www.netage.com/index_tni.html

11. Profnet, http://www.profnet.org

12. J Hagel, A G Armstrong, *Net Gain: Expanding Markets Through Virtual Communities* (Harvard Business School Press: 1997)

13. David Skyrme Associates, http://www.skyrme.com

14. D J Skyrme, "The Networked Organisation" David Skyrme Associates (1996) http://www.skyrme.com/insights/1netorg.htm

15. National Computer Security Association is now ICSA
    http://www.icsa.net/

16. *Ibid.*

17. "Cyber Crimes Increase" Nua Internet Surveys
    http://www.nua.ie/surveys/?f=VS&art_id=889459927&rel=true

18. M Mosquera, "Hackers Debunk Myth Of Net Security" *TechWeb*
    (24 May 1998), http://www.techweb.com/wire/story/TWB19980524S0001

19. Ovum, http://www.ovum.com/

20. "Nothing Sacred: The Politics of Privacy" The Center for Public Integrity
    (1998), http://www.publicintegrity.org/nothing_sacred.html

21. Electronic Privacy Information Center, http://epic.org/

22. GVU's WWW User Surveys
    http://www.cc.gatech.edu/gvu/user_surveys/

23. "1998 Privacy Concerns & Consumer Choice Survey" Louis Harris &
    Associates and Alan F. Westin, http://www.privacyexchange.org/

24. *Ibid.*

25. American Federal Trade Commission, http://www.ftc.gov/

26. E Auchard, "IBM Presses Websites to take Online Privacy Stand"
    Reuters, (2 April 1999), http://nt.excite.com/news/r/990402/01/net-
    advertising-ibm

27. IBM White Paper, Banking in the Network Economy
    http://www.ibm.com/ibm/publicaffairs/banking/intro.html

© Fergal Lawler 1999

10
Things Digital:
Learning from Software

THINGS DIGITAL ARE FLUID THINGS

Once upon a time all societies were very much tied to physical things. The early tribes bartered fish and animals and whatever was of physical value. Then, along came money, a type of symbolic, virtual entity. With money we bought land, houses, cars and televisions. The money was virtual in that it represented value but the things it bought were very much physical.

Communication was very much person to person until writing arrived. Then came the book, the telex and the telephone. Communication whizzed over thousands of miles of space, as if that space did not exist. Along came the radio, film and television. Voices and images came as if from nowhere. Things were still physical but a lot communication was becoming virtual.

Along comes the computer, and with it software. Today, the computer and software are all around us, and in ten years it will be everywhere, in everything from our light bulbs to our clothes.

Microsoft didn't become powerful by making physical things. It made software, the digital stuff that makes computers useful. You cannot touch or hold software. Most software you license, rather than own. Software is a very different entity to physical products. It obeys different rules.

Software is digital and all things digital are made up of 1s and 0s, rather than atoms, which make up all things physical. Every word, every sentence, every number, is made up of sequences of these 1s and 0s. Software because of its inherent flexibility is endlessly reproducible at minimal cost. It is so easy to copy these sequences of 1s and 0s.

Things physical are made up of atoms and these are much more hardy and inflexible. They have a finite resource and must obey the laws of scarcity. Yes, you may be able to grab an image of a tree, but copying – getting another one to grow – takes years.

Digital things are fluid, flexible and changing and we are, therefore, entering a very fluid world. A world that flows and changes and shifts. You build a house of concrete and wood and glass. It is a solid structure. You create a software programme. If you don't save and back it up, then in one second all your work can disappear. Like as if it had never been. Software is like that. Things digital are like that.

This can be an advantage. Look at how fast the software industry has grown. Look at how quickly software products have advanced. There is a capacity to move, to find out and explore new possibilities and opportunities in a very rapid way. However, there is a volatility within the digital world that can be very unnerving. The pace can be frantic, the change radical.

You can fall into the trap of changing things because you can, not because you should. Driven by the pressure to change, you can introduce new products before they are fully developed and tested. Before long, you are building future versions on weak foundations. You may look like you're making progress simply because you are changing.

Software and the Internet

Software fits the Internet like a glove fits a hand. Software products are in a position to benefit more from the Internet than any other industry or sector. In 1998, IDC predicted that by the year 2008 close to 100 per cent of software licences will be acquired online.[1] The reasons are simple and clear.

- People who access the Internet are the perfect target market for software since most of them have computers, and therefore, use software.

- Software can be delivered over the Internet, thus greatly reducing packaging and distribution costs. There are implications here from pricing to the whole nature of what a software product can now be.

- The Internet can be an ideal environment for software development. Before the Internet, software developers were relatively isolated. They either worked on their own or else belonged to companies. On their own, they might physically meet with other developers and share knowledge and perhaps code, but they were generally limited to meeting people nearby. (Even finding out who to meet was difficult.)

For these reasons, software achieves a pioneering position in the evolution of the Internet as a marketplace and environment. New models for marketing and distribution, research and development, production, customer support and consumer and media interaction are evolving in the software domain.

Not all the lessons learned by the software industry will be applicable to other sectors and products. However, many will, if only perhaps in part. It is the objective of this chapter to examine carefully the new models emerging for software, and where appropriate, to show how these models illustrate general rules for doing business in the digital age.

THE PHENOMENON OF OPEN SOURCE SOFTWARE

"Open source software poses a direct, short-term revenue and platform threat to Microsoft."

Halloween Document' [2] Microsoft's investigation into
open source software, leaked at Halloween, October 1998).

*"Microsoft is 'seriously considering' opening the source code of
the Windows NT kernel to allow outside programmers to
improve on the technology, according to Microsoft Vice
President Brian Valentine."*

The Wall Street Journal, "Microsoft Alters Course on Windows Strategy"
(8 April 1999).[3]

Why should the world's most powerful software company be
worried about a 'bunch of volunteers' writing software in their
spare time? And, if Microsoft is worried – and certainly intrigued
– by open source software, shouldn't your organisation be as
well? Or, should you be excited, sensing a radical new opportunity? And just what the hell is open source software and how do
you create it? Is there something in the process of open source
software that can be used effectively in other business sectors?

In this section, I'll attempt to answer the above questions and
some more. First, however, I admit that I'm not a programmer.
But I am tremendously excited about open source software. And,
yes, I do admire the sense of idealism that many of the open
source software activists exhibit. But, equally, I subscribe to the
basic business case and economic principles and philosophy of
open source software.

In its analysis of open source software, Microsoft was perhaps
discovering that the open source model reflected a new model of
economic and business activity. The leaked Halloween
Document (and follow-up documents) was a comprehensive
analysis of open source software, with often interesting conclusions, which included the following.

• Open source software can achieve, if not surpass, the quality
  of commercial software.

• Open source software is more a process than a product; the
  'competitor' is not so much a company but a way of thinking
  and working.

• Open source software is being used in an increasing number
  of 'mission critical' environments.

• The best example of what open source software can achieve is
  the Internet itself, whose foundations are those of open source
  software.

• That the more the Internet grows, the more open source software will grow.

Some Background on Open Source Software

Open source software is based on the fundamental idea that not simply the software products, but also the code – the 'secrets' of how the software is made – should be made freely available for anyone who wants to use it, adapt it and pass it on.

Richard Stallman is seen by many as the 'father' of open source software. A former researcher at MIT's Artificial Intelligence Laboratory, in 1983 he established the GNU Project, with the objective of building an entire free operating system based on the operating system UNIX. Stallman went on to found the Free Software Foundation (FSF).[4] The FSF website, in answering the question, 'what is free software?' states:

> 'Free software' is a matter of liberty, not price. To understand the concept, you should think of 'free speech' not 'free beer'. 'Free software' refers to the users' freedom to run, copy, distribute, study, change and improve the software. More precisely, it refers to three levels of freedom.
>
> • The freedom to study how the program works and adapt it to your needs.
>
> • The freedom to redistribute copies so you can share with your neighbour.
>
> • The freedom to improve the program, and release your improvements to the public, so that the whole community benefits.

For most of the 1980s, the open source software movement was very dispersed and isolated. Small groups operated, often within universities and large companies, sharing code and advice, but the general environment was very restricted.

In late-1990, things began to pick up speed, with initial releases of the programming language Perl and operating system Linux. By the early-1990s open source software began to gather momentum as the result of the new distribution methods, such as CD-ROMs.

However, without question it was the Internet, and particularly the introduction of the World Wide Web, that gave a tremendous boost to the open source software movement. In an interesting and vital synergy, the development of the Internet was aided by open source software. In 1995, for example, open source Web server, Apache was released. By 1996, Apache was the most popular Web server with 29 per cent of the market. By 1998, it had more than 50 per cent, trouncing much larger rivals, such as Microsoft and Netscape.

An important ingredient in the evolution of open source software was universities and other educational establishments. Not only did programming students have time on their hands, but also open source software was the ideal educational tool, in that it allowed students to dissect and play with the software.

Out of one such educational hothouse – The University of Helsinki – was the Linux operating system born. Developed by Linus Torvalds, while still a student, Linux has become a powerful force in the last couple of years. By some estimates, by 1999 it had as many as 6 million users, and according to IDC was growing by more than 20 per cent annually.

Linux is the operating system of choice for many Internet service providers. It was used for special effects for the *Titanic* blockbuster. Oracle, Sun, IBM, Apple and Dell, all have shown a commitment to Linux.

> "Linux is subversive," Eric S Raymond writes in his highly influential paper, "The Cathedral and the Bazaar".[5] "Who would have thought even five years ago that a world-class operating system could coalesce as if by magic out of part-time hacking by several thousand developers scattered all over the planet, connected only by the tenuous strands of the Internet?"

(It would seem that Linux is a very practical example of the massively parallel society theory propounded earlier on in this book.)

In "The Cathedral and the Bazaar", Raymond explained about how the traditional way of designing software could be compared to how a cathedral is built. Very careful planning was required, with the software code being "carefully crafted by individual wizards or small bands of mages working in splendid isolation, with no beta to be released before its time".

However, as Raymond pointed out, the success of Linux threw this thinking largely on its head. The Linux development approach could be summarised as follows:

Release early. Release often. Delegate like mad. Be totally open to

*input and suggestions. Encourage, motivate and respect people
and their contributions.*[6]

To Eric Raymond, the Linux style of development "seemed to
resemble a great babbling bazaar of differing agendas and
approaches (aptly symbolised by the Linux archive sites, which
would take submissions from *anyone*) out of which a coherent
and stable system could seemingly emerge only by a succession
of miracles".

It should be noted here that the Linux design philosophy is
very similar to that espoused by JCR Licklider and the Network
Working Group, who helped develop the ARPANET (the precur-
sor of the Internet) in the 1960s. The Network Working Group
encouraged "any thought, suggestion, etc.". Contributions were
to be "timely rather than polished. Philosophical positions without examples or other specifics, specific suggestions or implementation techniques without introductory or background expli-
cation, and explicit questions without any attempted answers are
all acceptable".[7]

In this sense, Linux, open source software and the Internet,
draw from the same philosophical well.

NETSCAPE GOES FREE

On behalf of everyone at Netscape, I want to thank you for
helping us get to this point in the first place. Your thinking
and writings were fundamental inspirations to our decision.[8]

These were the words of Eric Hahn, Executive Vice President and
Chief Technology Officer at Netscape in early-1998. They were
written to Eric Raymond with regard to his paper, "The
Cathedral and the Bazaar", which examined open source software development strategies and sought to draw some principles from them.

"The time is right for us to take the bold action of making
our client free, and we are going even further by commit-
ting to post the source code for free for Communicator 5.0,"
said Jim Barksdale, Netscape's Chief Executive Officer. "By
giving away the source code for future versions, we can
ignite the creative energies of the entire Net community

and fuel unprecedented levels of innovation in the browser market."[9]

Netscape is a morality tale for the Internet – its time came and its
time went. Its initial phenomenal success, its subsequent loss of
market share to Microsoft, and finally its acquisition by America
Online, is a stern lesson in taking anything for granted in this war
of change we are living through.

Once upon a time, the Internet *was* Netscape. For a great
many, their first introduction to the Internet was through the
Netscape Navigator browser. Released in late-1994, it was a piv-
otal moment in Internet history.

Pricing for Navigator was a little unusual. Basically, you were
free to download it to test it or for educational reasons. Most people just downloaded it and didn't even consider paying. Because
Navigator was essentially free, and also because it was a great
product, it grew like wildfire. At one stage it had something like
90 per cent of the browser market. (Netscape was following a de
facto 'freeware' strategy (which I'll explore later), not an open
source software one.)

Netscape, of course, was delighted with such market share,
and didn't seem to mind too much that a lot of Navigator users
were not paying. The corporate user and Internet service
provider (ISP) was different, however. No 'wink 'n' nod' pricing
models were applicable here; the asking price had to be paid for
fear of litigation.

In 1995, Microsoft arrived on the scene with Internet Explorer.
Nobody paid much attention at first as Microsoft had been writ-
ten off as a company that had missed the Internet wave.
However, asides from being the software Goliath that it is,
Microsoft had also done something very clever.

Internet Explorer was and would always be freeware, it stated. (In fact, the real Microsoft objective was to integrate the
browser with its operating systems.) Microsoft was out to take
away the browser platform from Netscape, by particularly focusing on the ISP and corporate marketplaces.

Microsoft attacked the browser market with maximum
aggression. Its Internet Explorer quickly gained market share. By
early-1998, studies were putting it ahead of Netscape Navigator
in market share. Netscape was reeling. A company that had
achieved a market valuation high of some $5 billion a short while
earlier was now under pressure. The big game had been lost.

PRINCIPLES AND STRENGTHS OF THE
OPEN SOURCE SOFTWARE MODEL

There now follows a set of basic principles which underlie open software development.

- The co-operative principle.

- The rapid evolution principle.

- Copyright and copyleft.

- Rewards are essential.

- The user is a developer principle.

- Egalitarian leaders are essential.

- The 'obey the unwritten rules' principle.

- There must be a base point to start from.

The Co-operative Principle

The foundation stone upon which open source software development is based is co-operation. It is not surprising, therefore, that open source software development has blossomed on the Internet.

Linus Torvalds expanded on this fundamental principle in a 1998 interview with *First Monday*[10] magazine.

> "Imagine ten people putting in one hour each every day on the project," Torvalds explained. "They put in one hour of work, but because they share the end results they get nine hours of 'other people's work' for free. It sounds unfair: get nine hours of work for doing one hour. But it obviously is not."[11]

This open source software co-operative approach has already been used in other business sectors. Alex Balfour in a piece entitled, *The Only Model of Web Publishing that Really Works*, writes about how the 'Linux Model', as he calls it, works very well in the publishing arena.

> "Successful Web publishing is all about leveraging the power of the Internet," Balfour writes. "That means building communities. Encouraging user participation. Exploiting global reach. Don't tell me, you've heard this all before. Now

hear this. Successful website management and development is no different. It's all about building communities, encouraging user participation and exploiting global reach."

The Rapid Evolution Principle

As has been already noted, 'release early, release often' is a fundamental motto for open source software development. This creates what I would describe as a 'rapid evolution' environment.

For some time now, I have felt that the Internet behaves like a living entity that is the combination of the efforts and interactivity of millions of people. Of course, I am not the first to put forward this kind of view. Kevin Kelly in *New Rules for the New Economy*,[12] states that:

> If the Web feels like a frontier, it's because for the first time in history we are witnessing biological growth in technological systems.

The rapid evolution principle of open source is of course ideally suited to a digital age which, in itself, is in a period of rapid evolution. In some senses, open source is following the aphorism, 'when in Rome, do as the Romans do', 'when on the Internet, do as the Internet does'.

> "The real strength of the freeware community is in the rapid turnaround and the rapid pace of interaction between the developers," developer of Perl, Larry Wall, explained to *Techweb* in 1998. "And that's why it's so important to have source code that is open, at least to the developers, and preferably to everybody."[13]

In many ways, the open source environment is like an evolutionary hothouse where things are always coming to life, fighting for survival, to either die off or grow stronger and further evolve. As Eric Raymond puts it:

> In the open source world, innovators get to try anything, and the only test is whether users will volunteer to experiment with the innovation and like it once they have. The Internet facilitates this process, and the co-operative conventions of the open source community are specifically designed to promote it.[14]

In this software evolutionary hothouse, only the strong code survives, as it is tested and tested by programmers from all sorts of disciplines, with all sorts of ideas, from practically every country in the world. This inspection and debugging process is generally much superior to that which happens for commercial software. Cleaner, more robust and tested code, is a key strength of the open source software model.

Copyright and Copyleft

In many ways, software is much closer to an intellectual product, such as a film or a book, than it is to a physical product, such as a car or a box of washing powder. Richard Stallman of the Free Software Foundation, in his promotion of the open source software model, has made some interesting points with regard to copyright and intellectual property.

> People have been told that natural rights for authors is the accepted and unquestioned tradition of our society. As a matter of history, the opposite is true. The idea of natural rights of authors was proposed and decisively rejected when the US Constitution was drawn up. That's why the Constitution only permits a system of copyright and does not require one; that's why it says that copyright must be temporary. It also states that the purpose of copyright is to promote progress – not to reward authors. Copyright does reward authors somewhat, and publishers more, but that is intended as a means of modifying their behaviour. The real established tradition of our society is that copyright cuts into the natural rights of the public – and that this can only be justified for the public's sake.[15]

Open source/free software advocates realised that they needed a different approach to dealing with the rights surrounding software. They came up with a number of solutions which generally fell under the title of 'copyleft'. The copyleft licensing principle was as it implied, almost the opposite of copyright. Copyleft licensing allowed you to work with and adapt open source software in any way you like, with an important rider: under copyleft, it is 'illegal' to hide the source code that results from your work and adaptations. In other words, you must make your new source code available to the wider community.

In adopting the copyleft formula, open source advocates, such as Stallman, were making the point strongly that copyleft was more natural that copyright. In that, they were contributing to a very old argument. Intellectual property, whether it is literature, music or other arts, has always walked a thin line between the rights of creators and the rights of the wider society.

A phrase that has always rung true for me is "geniuses steal, beggars borrow". As an author myself I want to get paid. I realise, however, that much of what I have done in putting this book together – and in putting all my other writings together – has involved borrowing and 'stealing'. To create a piece of writing I take 'code' (ideas) from loads and loads of people and assemble them together with some of my own ideas and structure, and hopefully create a credible, intellectual offering.

However, there are numerous ways of getting paid. I don't charge money for my New Thinking[16] publication every week, but I do get a return. It has given me a worldwide audience, has enhanced my reputation as a thinker, has resulted in invitations for me to speak at important conferences and it has opened doors to contracts for my company. All in all, I am more than happy with the return.

Of course, I am in good company. Shakespeare may be one of the greatest writers of all time, but like most open source software developers, he fashioned many of his greatest plays using plots that were already in existence. Woody Guthrie, one of America most important folk singers, hardly ever wrote an original tune. James Joyce borrowed liberally both structures, plots and techniques when writing his books.

Linus Torvalds was a bit of a rogue himself. He didn't write Linux from scratch, as Eric Raymond points out.

> Instead, he started by reusing code and ideas from Minix, a tiny Unix-like OS for 386 machines. Eventually all the Minix code went away or was completely rewritten – but while it was there, it provided scaffolding for the infant that would eventually become Linux.[17]

Focusing exclusively on the individual and the simplistic Hollywood 'one man saves the world' myth makes it easier for us to understand and package life. However, if we are to look closely, we will find that human creativity is not exclusively the story of individual acts of brilliance. All geniuses stand on the shoulders of those who have gone before them. All geniuses lean heavily on the society at large. Because we are so focused on naming things and on individual triumph, the individual genius keeps stealing all the limelight and getting all the credit.

But that's not really how it happens on the ground. Progress has always been the result of the effort of a great many people. Open source software development is merely embracing rules and customs and ways of doing things that have existed for millennia. Co-operation has always made sense, has always been at the core of human civilisation.

There are fundamental principles at play here that are broadly applicable. The digital age organisation is a co-operative one. It is one that, instead of focusing on protecting its information, spreads that information around, seeking to create new value. It seeks advantage, not in what it has, but in the momentum it has achieved and what it is going to do.

Rewards are Essential

Open source software development may not be based on monetary rewards for those who contribute to the development, but that doesn't mean that the developers do not expect and receive rewards. The rewards in many ways are 'ego-based'. Developers, who work hard on a piece of quality software and then release it to the wider community, get *respect*. The better the software they write and they more of it they release, the more respect and kudos they get.

In open source software development, the reward system encompasses a number of areas:

- people need to be made aware on a regular basis that their effort is valued;

- people need to see that their work is making a genuine difference by being incorporated in the next release;

- people need to see that there is an overall sense of momentum; that progress is being made, or that new and exciting challenges lie ahead.

  "If volunteers believe that their work is helping to build something which they will find useful," Alex Balfour writes. "If they can see that their work and ideas making an immediate difference, and if they are properly credited for their effort so their stock rises among their volunteer peers, they will work hard."

The User is a Developer Principle

A key characteristic of the open source software community is that it is a peer-based community. In one way or another, everyone is a developer. Everyone is interested in the product and wants to make it better.

> "I think the open development model tends to work best for areas where the developers are themselves users," Linus Torvalds told *First Monday.* "I don't think that is really anything fundamental, but being a user and a developer adds motivation that would otherwise have been replaced by the normal money-concerns of commercial software."[18]

This peer developer/user environment tends to occur mostly with software products that deal with core infrastructure problems, such as the operating systems for computers. For mass market software applications, the vast majority of users (myself included), couldn't care less about how a wordprocessor works or what might have caused the problem, we just want to get that report or letter finished. Those who work with operating systems, on the other hand, are, by definition, a much more select group who are often as interested in *how* the system does things as much as what the system does.

Herein lies perhaps the core strength and potential weakness of open source software development. The more involved in the product the users are, the stronger the system becomes, as everyone is pulling their weight. The developers may be giving away their software free, but what they are getting in return is detailed feedback on how to improve the next version of the software. If that feedback is not forthcoming, then the value proposition begins to break down.

> "Especially in the early days of Linux, the users were also acting as guinea-pigs for new features and so on," Linus Torvalds told *First Monday.* "They (sometimes unwittingly) put in a lot of effort in determining whether something worked or whether it really should have worked another way. And for that work they put in they got the reward of seeing better and better systems.

"I have written on the value of readers," Torvalds continued. "Usually one assumes that readers (users) should
pay writers (developers) but it often works the other way
round. With Linux, as with many things, it worked both
ways in balance, so nobody gets paid! So it's a fair
exchange, perhaps? Collaborative development between a
user base and developer base, with the dividing line
between them pretty blurred?"[19]

Egalitarian Leaders are Essential

For an environment that claims to be very democratic and often
anti-commercial, it is surprising how many 'cult' figures open
source software produces – Linus Torvalds being perhaps the
best example.

In open source software development, we often hear the
phrase 'benevolent dictator'. However, leadership and other levels of status are achieved differently in the open source software
community than in a traditional business environment.

Because the success of any particular open source software project is based on attracting as many quality developers as possible to
work on it, leadership tends to be given, not taken. Leaders emerge
because they have written a brilliant piece of software, and, perhaps as importantly, have had the ability to motivate other developers to work to improve that software. You don't call yourself a
hacker in the open source software community. You earn that title
after your peers have decided to call you one.

As open source software proponent, Tim O'Reilly, wrote in
Web Review in 1998:

In this rough and tumble community, you gain status by
what you give away. A good idea has to be backed up by a
good implementation, one that can be tested and improved
by your peers.[20]

Open source leaders may well be charismatic, but they also know
how to lay down the law.

"I try to maintain artistic control over the development of
the language itself," Perl inventor, Larry Wall states.
"Therefore I've reserved kind of an absolute dictatorial
power over Perl. Within that, people can basically do what
they want, you know, as long as I'm agreeable to it."[21]

Eric Raymond believes that the qualities of a leader in an open source software community requires someone who not simply has good ideas and good programming skills, but who is also able to recognise the good ideas of other people.

> "The next best thing to having good ideas is recognising good ideas from your users," Raymond writes. "Sometimes the latter is better...Often, the most striking and innovative solutions come from realising that your concept of the problem was wrong...I think it is not critical that the co-ordinator be able to originate designs of exceptional brilliance, but it is absolutely critical that the co-ordinator be able to recognise good design ideas from others."[22]

The 'Obey the Unwritten Rules' Principle

There is nothing chaotic about the open source software community. In fact, it has an elaborate set of largely unwritten rules, which the vast majority of its members abide by. Herein lie some strange contradictions. While the source code of open source software is open to anyone to adapt, there are, generally, strict rules with regard to who is allowed implement software patches into the 'official' version. This has managed to reduce the danger of 'forking', where a project can begin to diverge off down various different paths.

> "According to the standard open source licenses, all parties are equals in the evolutionary game," Eric Raymond writes in "Homesteading the Noosphere" for *First Monday*. "But in practice there is a very well-recognised distinction between 'official' patches, approved and integrated into the evolving software by the publicly recognised maintainers, and 'rogue' patches by third parties. Rogue patches are unusual, and generally not trusted."[23]

The point to understand here is that communities, which evolve around a particular open source software or other product, develop elaborate customs and rule-sets to ensure their stability and growth. Anyone wanting to work with these communities must understand and abide by these rule-sets.

There must be a Base Point to start off from

All indications are that the open source software development environment works well only when someone brings to it a software product that already has foundational work done on it. In other words, this environment is not seen as suitable for developing products from scratch.

> "It's fairly clear that one cannot code from the ground up in bazaar style," Eric Raymond writes in "The Cathedral and the Bazaar". "One can test, debug and improve in bazaar style, but it would be very hard to originate a project in bazaar mode. Linus didn't try it. I didn't either. Your nascent developer community needs to have something runnable and testable to play with."[24]

It is also true to say that the software project brought to the open source development community must be of a particular type. The Microsoft Halloween Document[25] succinctly summarised what it takes to create a successful 'bazaar' or open source development environment. It isolated three key criteria.

1. **Large future noosphere**. The project must be cool enough that the intellectual reward adequately compensates for the time invested by developers.

2. **Scratch a big itch**. The project must be important/deployable by a large audience of developers.

3. **Solve the right amount of the problem first**. Solving too much of the problem relegates the open source software development community to the role of testers. Solving too little before going open source reduces 'plausible promise' and doesn't provide a strong enough component framework to efficiently co-ordinate work.

Weaknesses of the Open Source Software Model

The Internet of 1994-1998 was not unlike rock 'n' roll. Most of its critics and evangelists hungered for big events and major earth shattering statements. *Wired* magazine was perhaps best known for this approach. Things were either 'wired' or 'tired' as far as *Wired* was concerned. Something was always dead and over with. Something else was always going to change the world.

The open source software model will not change the world. It is not going to sweep before it the commercial software model. It will have an impact, certainly, but it has limitations that need to be recognised.

It is no surprise that Linux was originally developed by Linus Torvalds when he was a student at the University of Helsinki. Nor is it surprising that the Free Software Foundation founder Richard Stallman benefited from a significant fellowship. Or that the Internet itself was nurtured firstly within the military and then within the academic world. Open source software has evolved because of abundance created by the commercial world. Its programmers can afford to give of their time free because they have a day job that pays the rent, or because some government or private institution is funding them.

The problem of software support reflects a paradoxical strength and weakness of the open source software community model. A community is a wonderful environment for members of that community. However, communities by their very nature tend to repel outsiders. Many in the open source community are programmers or those with a high interest and knowledge of the software they are using. This peer community offers tremendous support to its members.

However, if you are not a programmer, and couldn't care less how the software works, but just want to install the bloody thing, support tends to be less forthcoming. There is, for example, no official Linux website. Interestingly, one of the popular ones, www.linux.org, was mysteriously out of service for a full week towards the end of 1998.

A *News.com* piece discussing the shutdown also went on to state how the site owner had been criticised by "those who objected to his recent decision to run banner ads on the Linux site" saying it violated the not-for-profit ethic that pervades the Linux community. But MacLagan said the banner ads generate critical revenue that pays the $2,500 to $3,000 in monthly expenses required to keep the site running. "Somebody has to pay the T-1 bills," he said.[26]

Somebody always has to pay the bills. In some ways, open source software reminds me of the Irish Gaelic Athletic Association (GAA). This is a truly amateur association whose unpaid, part-time players exhibit an extraordinary professionalism. The GAA can afford to pay its bills, not to mention a IR£100 million stadium, because of voluntary effort and match fees. However, there is a type of spiritual debate about whether players should be paid or receive sponsorship. One side says that their effort deserves it, the other worries about whether this would destroy the spirit and sense of community that amateurism has nurtured.

Open source software faces a similar challenge. It has grown up within a closely-knit community, which is passionate about the co-operative ideal, and is striving to establish a different way of doing things. Ignored by the commercial world, this community has in certain areas, created clearly superior product.

However, those involved in community organisations will well know that when nobody is making money out of the effort, everything is fine. It's when money begins to be made that the whole environment can change radically. There are those in the open source software environment who are worried that the embrace of their products by the commercial world will kill the inspiration that created them.

It is still open for debate whether open source software can successfully move from a peer based development/user world to a producer/consumer one. If it cannot then its impact will be very limited. Because not everyone wants to hack code – most of us just want to consume. And we – the consumers – are where most of the bucks are for software.

If open source software is to achieve this shift, it must address the following issues.

1. Comprehensive support structures need to be established which effectively solve problems for inexperienced users.

2. Comprehensive testing among ordinary end-users.

3. A much stronger focus on the average consumer's requirements needs to be established.

4. Open source software needs to tap into mass market marketing and distribution channels.

5. Open source software needs to create a cohesive overall operating environment where each software application fits logically with the next, creating a seamless, easy to use environment for the consumer.

These are significant challenges, and while open source software is an intriguing development that should be studied carefully, it needs to be remembered that it is no magic bullet, no sudden nirvana. It will not replace systems of commerce that already exist. Rather it is another approach to doing commerce. In certain sectors it will have a major impact, in others its impact will be negligible. However, it is well worth exploring in a comprehensive manner because in how it evolved and operates are many solid lessons for those of us who wish to achieve the full potential that the Internet offers.

> "Open source software works," publisher Tim O'Reilly states. "BIND has absolutely dominant market share as the single most mission-critical piece of software on the Internet. Apache is the dominant Web server. SendMail runs probably 80 per cent of the mail servers and probably touches every single piece of e-mail on the Internet."[27]

Not bad going for software created by volunteers.

OTHER SOFTWARE MODELS

Open source software is not by any means the only new or alternative model for software development that the Internet has had a significant influence on. Other models include:

- shareware and freeware;
- beta testing;
- software and new support models;
- 'penny software' – rethinking the product.

Shareware and Freeware

There is probably no particular time when the shareware software model was developed. However, although there are indications that there was such software available before the IBM PC, it really was the introduction of the PC that encouraged the trend in a major way. If there were two 'fathers' of the modern shareware model, then they would be Andrew Fluegelman and Jim Button, who in 1981 simultaneously launched PC-Talk and PC-File.

Fluegelman originally called his software 'freeware', a term which he had in fact copyrighted. (From a naming point of view, the whole software arena can be very confusing, with different names being used by different people to mean the same thing.) Freeware would later be used as a term to refer to software that you were allowed to use for free. However, the name 'shareware' was chosen as the best term for this sort of software after a competition in a *PC Magazine*.

Historically, shareware software consisted of small programs that were useful, but that programmers felt they couldn't really market or sell using traditional channels. In the early days, support was rarely offered. However, as a general principle, shareware can be seen as a marketing method for software, rather than a particular type of software.

The economic principle of shareware is that you can try the software for free and that if you like it, and find it useful, you should then pay for it. In essence, it is a 'try before you buy' marketing approach.

In the early-1980s, there were some very successful shareware products, include PC-Write and PC-File, which itself became a multimillion-dollar business. As the 1980s progressed, a great number of shareware distributors emerged. These businesses created catalogues and compilation disks of shareware and sold them to the public. While the market was generally booming, there were chaotic elements to it. Many distributors were advertising "open source software" once people bought their disks. Much shareware was hard to use or simply didn't work at all.

Shareware programmers had problems getting paid, not because people didn't necessarily want to pay but because it was so difficult. Most shareware operations were small, and, therefore, found it difficult to get merchant card accounts. Paying by cheque for people was cumbersome particularly if they intended to buy on behalf of an organisation (where a small cheque amount for something you already had didn't make a lot of sense to the finance/admin department).

Much of the shareware produced in the early-1980s was substantial in nature (databasing, wordprocessing). However, as time progressed, commercial software became cheaper and more sophisticated, with integrated packages, such as Microsoft Office, hard to beat from a price, performance and integration point of view. By the early-1990s, shareware was almost exclusively focused on games and utilities (add-ons to software programs or operating systems).

The game model for shareware is interesting and very effective. Most computer games involved levels of difficulty. With shareware, you were given, for example, a game whose first three levels were fully functional. Then, if you liked the game, you paid your money and received access to the remaining levels.

Getting paid for shareware was a subject close to the heart of many developers. Various approaches were used, from disabling elements of the programme, to time limits, to straightforward requests for payments, to repeated messages or 'nag screens' requesting the user to pay-up.

Disabling vital elements of the programme tended to annoy and frustrate users, who were not, therefore, able to try out the programmes full functionality. Time demos worked better. Surprisingly, straightforward requests for payments have worked quite well. Nag screens, again, tended to annoy and aggravate unless they were cleverly done.

The Internet has had a significant impact on shareware distribution. A user can now go to a site such as shareware.com and choose from a huge range of shareware, which they can then download and use. Low bandwidth, which makes it very time-consuming to download very large programs, as well as a distrust among certain consumers to give their credit cards online have been drawbacks, though.

iD Software has turned the shareware model into a multimillion-dollar business. In *Doom* and *Quake*, iD has produced some of the most popular (and violent) computer games ever released. iD sells its product as shareware as well as making its source code available to it public/users. In doing this, iD achieves many things.

• It creates a loyal, often fanatical, following.

• It creates a worldwide community and network for its games, as its users develop more and more levels for *Doom* and *Quake* fans to play.

• It creates an industry around its games, as companies test and adapt the source code, then license it so as to create new games.

• It creates a specialist skill resource, as enthusiasts around the world hone their programming and design skills base on iD standards, the best of whom would often end up working for iD.

• It sells an awful lot of games.

The difference between shareware and freeware is one of marketing. Freeware, such as Microsoft's Internet Explorer, is free to use, requiring no payment at any time. A company might employ the freeware marketing model when, like Microsoft, it has a platform or family of products. The freeware product acts as a sort of 'loss leader', attracting the target audience with the intention of getting them to then pay for the other products within the family. As we have already discussed, Microsoft used the freeware approach very effectively against Netscape's Navigator.

Beta Testing

"It's a rare (and foolish) software outfit these days that does not introduce its wares into the free economy as a beta version in some fashion," Kevin Kelly writes for *Wired* in "New Rules for the New Economy".

"Fifty years ago, the notion of releasing a product unfinished – with the intention that the public would help complete it – would have been considered either cowardly, cheap, or inept. But in the new regime, this pre-commercial stage is brave, prudent, and vital."[28]

The 'beta' Kelly was talking about is a pre-release or pre-commercial version of software. Beta testing involves sending the software outside the company to the general public for testing.

The beta testing approach is particularly useful for software that needs to be tested under the widest possible number of conditions and/or which is intended to be jointly used by a large number of people. Creating the same variety of conditions in a lab environment or getting a large number of people together to test software, is prohibitively expensive for most companies. Thus, the beta testing approach is often used.

Software beta testing has a very short history because beta testing is directed at the general public and before the 1990s, very few people had computers at home. In 1994, Corel was one of the first companies to use beta testing.

Tim Cassedy-Blum, in an article "Building Better Software", states that:

...the biggest milestone for beta testing was the test of Windows 95. Over 400,000 'preview' testers, myself among them, and 30,000 'official' testers received copies of Windows 95 in its early beta stages. Although the 90 per cent who were not 'official' testers were not required to submit bug reports, Microsoft included a bug reporting program anyway, and received thousands of bug reports from the preview testers.[29]

Why do people choose to beta test software? Beta software is
almost always offered for free, and there is a sense of excitement
in getting the software before its general release. Advanced betas
are usually quite reliable. The user thus gets their software for
free – or at a discount – with the only obligation to report what
bugs they find. It can also be the case that, if someone partici-
pates in a beta programme, they get the commercial copy of the
software for free – or at a discount – when it is released.

There is also the fact that for some enthusiasts, beta testing is
seen as interesting and fun. Companies that use beta testing are
usually careful to engender a sense of participation and community among their beta testers. Prizes and awards are sometimes
offered to those who find major bugs. Netscape for a period
offered a financial incentive or 'bugs bounty' for those who came
back with major bugs.

The beta testing approach can also work well with research
and development. iMagic Online, which runs a beta testing programme, states that:

> …we also want to know what you think about the game and
> ways you believe we can make it better. Many of the changes
> that we make start out as suggestions from our users.[30]

Establishing a beta programme can be very straightforward;
merely making the software available on a website for download
can be enough. But generally, there are forms to fill out before
downloading is allowed, so that the company can track how
many, and who, is downloading its software. After the download, there really needs to be a co-ordinated plan so that the company will get in touch with its beta testers on a regular basis, so
as to monitor how testing is progressing.

With ever decreasing product life cycles in this war of change,
the principle of beta testing is becoming more important.
(Internet browsers, for example, have a new version released on
average every six months.) The product gets out into the market
quickly to be tested and used. Done well, beta testing ensures not
only that you have a solid product for commercial release, but
also that your product (and its future releases) matches more
exactly the needs of your users.

New Support Models for Software
A well-planned Internet development can contribute significantly to the after-sales support process. A website is, by definition,

open 24 hours a day, thus offering at least some level of support whenever the customer requires it.

From a support point of view, a popular element of most software related websites (as well as other sites) is what is termed as Frequently Asked Questions (FAQs). Basically, the website assembles questions about its products that have been asked on a regular basis. This can reduce calls to support centres.

By putting product manuals and other information on a website, this can also help the customer. Many of us tend to lose or misplace the manual of the product we buy, and having that manual available online for browsing, search or download is a definite help. Software tends to go a step ahead here, by integrating the manual into the product in the form of a comprehensive 'Help' section.

Advanced online support systems involve the use of case-based reasoning and natural language search approaches. Case-based reasoning is a system that uses the solutions to previous problems to help solve new problems. The basic process that case based reasoning follows is described by Ian Watson and Farhi Marir in their book *Case-based Reasoning: A Review*.

> A new problem is matched against cases in the case base and one or more similar cases are retrieved. A solution suggested by the matching cases is then reused and tested for success. Unless the retrieved case is a close match the solution will probably have to be revised producing a new case that can be retained.[31]

Natural language search is a process that allows you to type out in sentence form the problem you are having with the product. For example: 'The software keeps crashing every time I try to print.' Natural language search then picks out keywords in the sentence, such as 'crashing' and 'print' and attempts to lead you towards the appropriate information to solve this problem.

Software creator Broderbund[32] has used advanced online support systems for a number of years. The Broderbund support section asks you to choose the product with which you are having a problem. Then you write a sentence describing the problem. From there, Broderbund asks you a number of questions, such as: 'What operating systems are you using?' 'What type of error message are you getting?' The intention is to zero in on your specific problem and then offer the appropriate course of action to solve that problem.

Online support systems will never fully replace the need for human support, nor should they aim to. Many of today's software is very complex and often developed under intense time pressures. Thus, we can get a substantial number of complex problems. Trying to solve all these problems through automated online support systems simply won't work. The customer will get confused and frustrated.

It should also be remembered that support is a great place to evolve a relationship with a customer. Support is where loyalty can be built and where sell-on can occur, where post-purchase satisfaction can be reinforced. As has been a theme of this book, too many people look at computerisation and the Internet as a way of shaving more costs out of the system, rather than facilitating growth and closer relationships with customers.

'Penny Software' – Rethinking the Product

The digital age forces us to rethink the very nature of what a product is, whether we own it or rent it, and how we pay for it. In the industrial age environment, many products were significantly defined and shaped by the type of packaging they required. Digital products delivered over the Internet require very little packaging. The fact that we had to package something often meant that we could not sell it in small quantities, as the packaging cost would have become greater than the product cost.

Some of us remember penny sweets and how we got them out of a big jar. Well, with the introduction of reliable electronic cash systems, we may well find ourselves buying 'penny software' and information over the Internet.

It may be hard to imagine the idea of penny software now but then that may be because we have a particular conception of what software or a product is. Perhaps software and digital products of the future might operate like pieces of a jigsaw? We might rent that indexing function for a wordprocessor for that one time that we actually need it. We might buy a selection of headline news for a penny per headline, with the choice to buy the full story if we want to. There are many possibilities, but the important point again is that the digital age forces us to think outside any package or box.

The Internet also throws up the question: Do we really need to own our products anymore?

"A striking vestige of manufacturing age thinking is the

still-dominant practice of charging for information age goods like software *by the copy*," Brad Cox wrote in an article entitled "What if there is a Silver Bullet and the Competition gets it First?" for the *Journal of Object-oriented Programming* in 1992.[33]

Cox pointed out that it doesn't make sense to sell things by the copy that can be so easily *copied*.

"Software objects differ from tangible objects in being fundamentally unable to monitor their copying but trivially able to monitor their use," Cox wrote. "For example, it is easy to make software count how many times it has been invoked, but hard to make it count how many times it has been copied. So why not build an information age market economy around this difference between manufacturing age and information age goods?"[34]

Why not indeed? This would change the whole way we think about products and commerce. We would encourage people to download and copy our products in the knowledge that they would begin paying for them as they started using them. Perhaps we could adapt an element of the shareware model and implement a timer, so that they got twenty uses free, and then paid from there on?

"Would you rather pay $39.95 at first for a game you might not play more than once?" Craig Thueson, Vice President of Sales for Wave Systems asks. "Or would you rather pay a dollar per use up to ownership at $39.95?"

This basic approach to paying from a usage point of view is not exactly new. Intellectual property is protected by copyright laws, which garner revenue as a result of performance of a particular piece of work. As I have stated earlier, software and other digital-based goods have a lot in common with intellectual property.

An indirect, though very important, benefit of pay-per-use is that it creates a direct link between the creator of the product and the user – there is an ongoing transaction and thus the potential for an ongoing conversation and sell-on.

This ongoing transaction is ideal for software and other information goods. Software is always changing – there are always new versions coming out. If there is an ongoing transaction, then there is the opportunity to deliver to the user what is always the latest version of the product. This is a valuable way of locking the customer into your product offering. Many software companies, such as anti-virus maker McAfee,[35] successfully implement strategies similar to the above.

Another benefit of the pay-per-use model – and other Internet-based software delivery models – is that it moves much of the labour element of the transactional cost to the consumer (filling out forms, etc.), thus reducing the overhead of the producer. When you consider that billing expenses can eat up almost half of the price of a phone call, you begin to realise just how much can be saved here. (For example, in America, it costs a dollar to process a cheque and 25 cents to handle a credit card transaction.)

Of course, these new ways of paying for things are dependant on an electronic cash environment; one where there is no charge for transactions, which thus allows micro-transactions, such as penny software, to occur. There are those who predicted that such a system would be in place by now, but certainly we should see electronic cash systems introduced within the next five years.

THE VALUE OF FREE

'Free' is a strange word. In society, most of the things that claim to be free are in fact not free at all. Many countries claim to have free education, free health care, free water. Governments tell us that they are working to create environments where you are free to walk the streets at night without worrying about crime. During the day we can visit free parks and free museums. We have freedom of information legislation that allows us to freely access essential information.

Of course, none of the above is actually free. Very, very little is free – there is always a price or a cost attached. We pay for our 'free' services through taxation. What, in fact, has happened is that the cost has been shifted to some other part of the value chain.

In open source software, freeware and shareware, the cost is also shifted. We are expected to pay in our time, to pay by buy-ing other products from that company, or to pay later once we have found the product useful. However, it is always the expec-tation that we will pay.

Why do we have taxation? Why don't we pay for everything

as we go? Because it's easier. Because it doesn't make sense to charge a child for the very act of walking into a sweet shop. Because it doesn't make sense to charge a loyal customer for the cup of coffee you hand them. There are lots of things that it makes no sense to charge for directly. We get our returns by charging indirectly for them or by charging over a longer period of time.

These things are often structural or utility elements within a society, business or technical environment. Open source software has helped build the foundations of the Internet. Its 'owners' charge has not been monetary but rather one of receiving the time, effort and admiration of the people, who used these foundations. Open source software is not so much a new model but rather an old model that goes back to the time when we were building societies and laying foundations that would allow communities to thrive. Everyone lent a hand because many hands made light work.

It may be that open source software will prove to be best suited to developing infrastructural or operating system-type software, rather than mass consumer software. Therefore, the lessons it offers may be best suited to organisations that are addressing such challenges. One other thing it has achieved, though, is to create, within a virtual environment, strong and committed communities, which have in their 'amateur' commitment achieved higher degrees of excellence than many of their professional compatriots.

The freeware, shareware and pay-as-you-use models all have interesting approaches that have been proven to work well on the Internet. As with open source software, they can make business sense by looking towards the longer term, rather than the short-term, return.

REFERENCE

1. IDC Research, "Online Software Sales to Rocket" Nua Internet Surveys
    (16 September 1998), http://www.nua.ie/surveys /?f=VS&art_id=
    905354364&rel=true

2. The Halloween Documents, http://www.opensource.org/halloween.html

3. *Ibid.*

4. Free Software Foundation, http://www.gnu.org/

5. E S Raymond, "The Cathedral and the Bazaar"
    http://www.tuxedo.org/~esr/writings/cathedral-bazaar/

6. *Ibid.*

7. M Hauben, "Behind the Net: The Untold Story of the ARPANET and
    Computer Science" *First Monday* (August 1998)
    http://www.firstmonday.dk/issues/issue3_8/chapter7/index.html

8. E S Raymond, "The Cathedral and the Bazaar"
    http://www.tuxedo.org/~esr/writings/cathedral-bazaar/

9. M Kane, "Netscape offers up Browser Source Code" *ZDNN* (23 January
    1998), http://www.zdnet.com/zdnn/stories/zdnn_display/
    0,3440,277371,00.html

10. *First Monday,* http://www.firstmonday.dk/

11. *First Monday* Interview with Linus Torvalds, "What Motivates Free
    Software Developers?" *First Monday* (2 March 1998)
    http://www.firstmonday.dk/issues/issue3_3/

12. K Kelly, "New Rules for the New Economy" *Wired* (September 1997)
    http://www.wired.com:80/wired/archive/5.09/newrules.html
    Now available in book form: K Kelly, *New Rules for the New Economy*
    (Viking Press: 1998)

13. D Sims, "Q&A with Larry Wall, Creator of Perl" *TechWeb* (8 April 1998)
    http://www.techweb.com/wire/story/TWB19980408S0020

14. E S Raymond, "The Cathedral and the Bazaar"
    http://www.tuxedo.org/~esr/writings/cathedral-bazaar/

15. R Stallman, "Why Software should not have Owners" Free Software
    Foundation (1994), http://www.gnu.org/philosophy/why-free.html

16. New Thinking, http://www.nua.ie/newthinking/current.html To sub-
    scribe to New Thinking, send an email to newthinking-request@nua.ie
    with the word **subscribe** in the body of the message.

17. E S Raymond, "The Cathedral and the Bazaar"
    http://www.tuxedo.org/~esr/writings/cathedral-bazaar/

18. *First Monday* Interview with Linus Torvalds, "What Motivates Free
    Software Developers?" *First Monday* (2 March 1998)
    http://www.firstmonday.dk/issues/issue3_3/

19. *Ibid.*

20. T O'Reilly, "Freeware: The Heart and Soul of the Internet" O'Reilly (1998)
    http://www.oreilly.com/news/freeware_0398.html

21. D Sims, "Q&A With Larry wall, Creator of Perl" *TechWeb* (8 April 1998)
    http://www.techweb.com/wire/story/TWB19980408S0020

22. E S Raymond, "The Cathedral and the Bazaar"
    http://www.tuxedo.org/~esr/writings/cathedral-bazaar/

23. E S Raymond, "Homesteading the Noosphere" *First Monday* (5 October 1998)
    http://www.firstmonday.dk/issues/issue3_10/raymond/index.html

24. E S Raymond, "The Cathedral and the Bazaar"
    http://www.tuxedo.org/~esr/writings/cathedral-bazaar/

25. The Halloween Documents, http://www.opensource.org/halloween.html

26. S Shankland, "Linux Online Outage Persists" *CNET News.com*
    (30 October 1998), http://www.news.com/News/Item/0,4,28166,00.html

27. Halloween I - 1.12, "Open Source Software: A (New?) Development
    Methodology" (November 1998)
    http://www.opensource.org/halloween1.html

28. K Kelly, "New Rules for the New Economy" *Wired* (September 1997)
    http://www.wired.com:80/wired/archive/5.09/newrules.html
    Now available in book form: K Kelly, *New Rules for the New Economy*,
    (Viking Press: 1998)

29. BetaBeta, http://www.betabeta.com/

30. iMagic Online, http://www.imagicgames.com/

31. I Watson, "Case-Based Reasoning Development Tools: A Review"
    University of Salford, UK
    http://online.loyno.edu/cisa494/papers/Watson.html

32. Broderbund, http://www.broderbund.com/

33. B Cox, "What if there is a Silver Bullet and the Competition gets it
    First?" *Journal of Object-oriented Programming* (1992) http://www.virtu-

alschool.edu/cox/CoxWhatIfSilverBullet.html

34. *Ibid.*

35. McAfee Software, http://www.mcafee.com/

© Fergal Lawler 1999

11
The Limits of Big

THE BIG ARE GETTING BIGGER

As I browsed through *The Economist* on Friday 27 November 1998, I read about America Online buying Netscape, the proposed Exxon and Mobil deal, "Britain's biggest merger of manufacturers," International Paper buying Union Camp, "America's two biggest disability insurers" merging, not to mention Deutsche Bank buying Bankers Trust, "to create the world's biggest financial-services firm".

Just one week in the year the big got bigger.

1998 ended up being the world's biggest ever year for mergers and acquisitions. More than US$2.4 trillion in deals were done, which was a full 50 per cent above 1997, which in itself had been a record year.

Federal Reserve Chairman Alan Greenspan went on record to warn against "overreaction" to mergers.

> "The United States is currently experiencing its fifth major corporate consolidation of this century," Greenspan said. "When trying to understand and deciding how to react to this development, I would hope that we appropriately account for the complexity and dynamism of modern free markets." (The other major merger waves in US history were: 1890s, 1920s, 1960s, 1980s and now.)[1]

"Size does matter," according to Janet L Fix, writing for the *Washington Free Press*. She quoted David Sowerby, economist for

Loomis Sayles, who stated that:

> Since 1994, stocks of the 50 biggest companies in the
> Standard & Poor's 500 have contributed nearly 40 per cent
> of the value gains in the index.[2]

It's the global village, or rather the global metropolis.

> "Globalisation – the accelerated integration of economic
> activity across national or regional boundaries – has
> become the catchword dominating economic and social
> policy discussion at the end of the 20th century," John
> Evans stated in a speech entitled "Economic Globalisation:
> The Need for a Social Dimension".[3]

The *Merriam Webster Dictionary* defines 'globalise' as "to make
global; especially: to make worldwide in scope or application".
Interestingly, it dates the origin of the word to 1944. Harold
Trabold, in a paper entitled, "Globalisation: Source of Woe or
Source of Wealth?"[4] wrote that globalisation stands for:

> "...greater global economic integration via trade, capital
> and technology flows, but also for growing competition
> from low-wage countries and for labour outsourcing via
> foreign direct investment.
> "The intensification of global economic integration is
> evidenced most clearly by capital flows," Trabold contin-
> ues.

John Evans backed up this analysis.

> International trade grew twice as fast as GNP during the
> 1980s, but foreign direct investment (FDI) grew twice as
> fast as trade. The growth of FDI slowed in the early 1990s
> but picked up in 1994 and has risen to record levels in
> 1995.[5]

He goes on to quote the OECD as stating that "never before have
so many firms from so many industries invested in so many
countries".

According to Dr Pekka Tarjanne, Secretary General of the
International Telecommunication Union:

The benefits of freer trade and more open markets are
clear: lower prices and more choice for consumers, new
market opportunities for suppliers and investors, and
higher rates of economic growth.[6]

The Economist, in a lead article on globalisation in 1998, stated
that:

That ugly, 13-letter word [globalisation] has become a
mantra of business, of politics, even of culture. This decade
has seen a remarkable increase in the openness to trade
and investment flows of country after country: partly
because of the demise of Soviet communism and of old
ideas of socialist self-sufficiency; partly because of liberali-
sations agreed upon during the Uruguay round of what
was then the GATT and is now the World Trade
Organisation; and partly because of the rapid, world-
shrinking spread of new information technology. Like it or
not, foreign businesses, foreign investors and foreign
(especially American) cultures have penetrated deeply into
most countries' domestic lives.[7]

How 'Global' is Globalisation?
In many ways, globalisation is just another word for 'bigness'.
Certainly, the big are global, but how 'global' are the big?

"Globalisation has always primarily been a process of
Westernisation," Gerald Segal, of the International
Institute for Strategic Studies, states.[8]

Is Westernisation not just another word for Americanisation?

"America's biggest export is no longer the fruit of its fields
or the output of its factories, but the mass produced products of its popular culture – movies and music, television
programs, books and computer software," the *International
Herald Tribune* wrote in a 1998 article entitled – without
irony – "The World Welcomes America's Cultural
Invasion".[9]
    "Entertainment around the globe is dominated by
American-made products," the *Tribune* continued.
"International sales of software and entertainment prod-

ucts totalled US$60.2 billion in 1996, more than any other
US industry, according to Commerce Department data
and industry figures...Films produced in English account
for between 60 and 65 per cent of the global box office,
according to the Motion Picture Association of America;
most of these ticket sales are generated by American-
made films."

The above would give the impression that the world has become
an American playground. Political philosopher, Dr Francis
Fukuyama, in a 1997 discussion with Merrill Lynch, would not
necessarily agree. While he admitted that globalisation was having a direct impact on nations and states politically, he felt that
"on a cultural level, it's not clear that homogenisation is pro-
ceeding nearly as rapidly. To a certain extent, there is a real resistance to cultural homogenisation".[10]

Backing up this view, John Naisbitt, author of *Global Paradox:
The Bigger the World Economy, the More Powerful its Smallest
Players*, writes that:

In the 1992 Olympics in Barcelona, 172 countries compet-
ed. More than 200 teams are expected in 1996. And in the
magical year 2000 there'll probably be more than 300 countries represented. As the world becomes more universal, it
also becomes more tribal. As people yield economic sover-
eignty and become economically interdependent, holding
on to what distinguishes you from others becomes very
important.[11]

The Economist would seem to agree. In a lead article in 1998 entitled "Here is the News", it stated that:

"On a typical day in 1898, *The Times* of London led with its
usual front page of advertisements; it then carried a page
reviewing some recent novels; and then acres of coverage
of the Balkan War. Altogether, the newspaper had nineteen
columns of foreign news, eight columns of domestic news
and three about salmon fishing. Exactly 50 years later, the
front page still carried advertisements and the leaders
commented on Italy, Canada, China and the crisis in
Western civilisation (no change, then). By 1998, the advertisements on the front page had been replaced by articles.

There were six of them and only one was foreign; it was about Leonardo DiCaprio's new girlfriend.

"Here then is a modern paradox," *The Economist* continued, "that in this age of globalisation, news is much more parochial than in the days when communications from abroad ticked slowly across the world by telegraph."[12]

America may be at the forefront of globalisation, but the American economy itself remains distinctly local. In a 1997 *Harvard Business Review* article entitled "How Fast can the US Economy Grow?", it was pointed out that while many American companies were facing increasing international competition, this should not be overstated.

> "Such global competition mainly occurs in the goods-producing sector – very few services are traded on international markets – and even within manufacturing there are many industries that remain largely isolated from foreign competitors (seen any Chinese refrigerators lately?)," the article explained. "Since we are mainly a service economy, this means that no more than 25 and probably less than 15 per cent of employment and value-added are actually subjected to the kind of global market discipline that the new paradigm emphasises."[13]

This, of course, is not unique. In his paper on globalisation, Harold Trabold examined two measures of globalisation: trade flows and capital flows. Examining trade flows, he found that globalisation was happening quite slowly and that "the degree of openness of the German economy, for example, has grown only slowly and relatively constantly".[14]

Dr Fukuyama would seem to agree with such an analysis.

> "I think that in many respects, globalisation is still superficial," he stated. "Although there is a great deal of talk about it currently, the underlying truth is that the global economy is still limited. It seems to me that the real layer of globalisation is restricted to the capital markets. In most other areas, institutions remain intensely local.
>
> "Trade, for example, is still predominantly regional," he continued. "Relatively little trade flows beyond local regions: Asians trade mostly with Asians and Latin

Americans trade mostly with Latin Americans. Even in more developed regions this practice holds true. Intra-European trade accounts for roughly 60 per cent of all European trade."[15]

Technology and Bigness

The computer and modern technology in general, has certainly played a role in globalisation, though to what extent is debated. Certainly, a vast web of technology aids the international flow and movement of capital markets.

Telecommunications is a central cog in practically all economic activity. Interestingly, global telecommunications remains quite small in relative terms. In a speech in 1998, Dr Pekka Tarjanne, Secretary General of the ITU, made some interesting points. He stated that international telecommunication traffic accounts for less than 10 per cent by value and below 5 per cent by volume of global telecommunications. Comparisons with other sectors of the economy suggest that these figures should be closer to 30 per cent by value.

"The two main, interrelated reasons why comparatively little international telecommunication traffic is traded across borders are high prices for users and restricted market access for service providers," Dr Tarjanne stated. "Consumers pay at least three times more for each minute of international telecommunication traffic than they do for domestic telecommunication traffic, even though the costs of service provision may be quite similar."[16]

Computers and technology in general have a definite influence on globalisation according to Harold Trabold:

There is a close link between technological progress and globalisation...On the one hand, the higher competitive pressure on global markets forces enterprises to apply the most recent scientific findings more rapidly. On the other hand, technological progress itself generates the conditions for further globalisation, e.g. through more efficient communication networks.[17]

While the evidence would seem to suggest that deregulation of national telecommunication markets and the consequent drop in prices will increase international trade and globalisation, this is not an absolute given. As we will see in Chapter 12, *Building Brands Online*, a very important element of commerce remains *trust*. Just because you can phone (or e-mail) an order to a business 3,000 miles away cheaply, doesn't mean you will.

> "I am very sceptical about the claim that technology alone is going to enable globalisation," Dr Francis Fukuyama told Merrill Lynch. "In digital commerce, people are now technically capable of carrying out a transaction, but they are lacking the value-added services that enable them to develop a trust relationship. What globalisation requires is not just network technology, but rather the creation of a whole new series of services that are able to convey the information needed for trust."[18]

The role of technology may sometimes be overstated as a driver of globalisation. However, for globalisation's little brother, merger activity, it can play a central role. Jeff Pelline, writing for *CNET* in June 1998 stated that:

> Technology, not just deregulation, is a catalyst for the spate of recent bank buyouts...Nowadays cost-conscious banks are building state-of-the-art computer networks to link customers and workers as well as to provide banking services on the Internet.[19]

Pelline quoted Hans Schroeder, banking analyst for Hoefer and Arnett as stating that:

> The costs of technology are a principal factor driving these mergers nowadays. If you can consolidate the back office, then you can exact efficiencies and create a more efficient bank. That's definitely a strong trend in pushing mergers throughout the country during the past five years.[20]

In the broader context, technology is playing a significant role, in that it is increasingly automating the work process, allowing more and more work to be shipped to the cheapest environment. This may bring jobs to emerging economies but can create severe pressures for unskilled workers in more advanced economies. This process, if it is carried too far, can destabilise societies, as it further widens the gap between rich and poor.

Harold Trabold, in his paper "Globalisation: Source of Woe or Source of Wealth?" wrote that:

...technological progress has indeed reduced the demand for low-skilled workers for several reasons. First, unskilled workers are easier to replace by machines than the highly qualified. Second, the design and construction of such machines requires even more qualified workers. Third, qualified workers are better able to adapt to changing technical conditions. All in all, technological progress tends to have the same effect on the demand for, and remuneration of, low-skilled workers as foreign trade and direct investment.[21]

The Internet and Bigness

In the early days, the Internet was vaunted as the 'level playing field' where the small players had a chance against the big boys. By 1999, that looked like a cruel myth for many, as the mega-brands, such as Yahoo and Amazon, were dominating.

1998 was a year of consolidation within the Internet space itself. Microsoft flexed its muscles and pushed Netscape into the arms of America Online. In January 1999, @Home bought Excite for US$6.7 billion and Yahoo bought Geocities for US$4.5 billion. We are thus seeing the assembly of Internet mega brands that have extraordinary power and clout.

In other areas, the media was rich with stories of consolidation and mergers. Disney was out doing deals. AT&T and NBC were forging partnerships. WorldCom was as hungry as ever. The Web development, advertising and networking industries were rapidly consolidating.

The Internet is a big idea but is it forever going to be the land of the big? Is the World Wide Web to be dominated by one language – English – and one currency – the dollar?

No, not entirely, anyway.

In some ways, the Internet will be a driver towards globalisation and uniformity. Mega brands will play a central role. However, as the great mass of people use it – those who haven't necessarily a college degree and don't have perfect English – it will become as multifarious as the world itself.

In fact, the Internet facilitates smaller cultures who have for historical reasons been dispersed, to network together. I know, for example, that people interested in the Irish language, but are geographically isolated from other Irish speakers, are coming together on the Internet.

What this means is that the Internet does and will offer room for the niche player who can supply a very specialised market. An example of a niche player would be Kennys Bookstore in Galway, Ireland (www.kennys.ie). Whereas Amazon is a mass market supplier (with some specialist ability, undoubtedly), Kennys has built up 60 years experience in Irish books. There is a genuine friendly professionalism about Kennys. They know their business inside out, they are passionate about what they do, and there is no better place to look for an Irish book.

The Company and Bigness

Why are companies getting bigger and bigger? Globalisation is certainly a driving factor. If your marketplace is global and your competitor has an office in 50 countries, then shouldn't you? If your competitor can offer a 'cradle to grave' range of services, then shouldn't you?

It would seem that much globalisation is occurring simply because it can happen. The computer has caused an increasing commoditisation of production processes, as well as back end administration systems. Companies which under another era would have been a physical impossibility to join together can now be married.

Of course, there is the small matter of the people who work for these companies and how they will get on together. In the industrial age, companies took time to grow. As they matured, they developed strong identities and internal cultures. People stayed with companies for years and could show intense loyalty to *their* company. The type of staff a company had gave it a unique stamp and outlook.

In this period of the digital age, the global, merging company moves so quickly it hardly seems to have time for culture or identity. As was stated earlier, American companies lose an average of half of their workers every four years. Loyalty is unfashionable. Thus, merging is made more feasible.

This is not to say that company culture can be ignored. In fact, the lack of positive and strong company culture could be the Achilles heel of many of these merged entities. In a interview with the *New York Times* in 1998, Ron Bloom, Chairman and Chief Executive of a company which has seen twelve companies merge together advised that:

You have to have a cultural plan to match your fiscal plan,
a cultural plan has to take into account profit and loss,
return on investment and cost of opportunity, just as a
financial plan does.

National identity has historically been a lynch-pin of company
cultural identity. With global merging, this is removed. Peter
Martin, in an article for the *Financial Times* entitled "Tacos and
Ale", wrote about the Daimler/Chrysler merger. He posed the
question:

Which corporate culture will prevail? Will DaimlerChrysler
be engineering-led (like Daimler) or marketing/finance-led
(like Chrysler)? Managers of merging companies usually
argue that neither culture will win: the company will rise to
further greatness on a seamless fusion of the two. The
promise is rarely borne out, but it is probably a desirable
aspiration.[22]

In the industrial age, you could build up something of value over
a long period of time. That's not the case in the digital age. Small
growth and profit figures are not acceptable to many investors
who have grown dizzy on stock markets reaching new heights.
Also, quality workers are scarce and expensive. Instead of focusing on making and selling better products, many companies have
focused on buying their way, through merger and acquisitions, to
those aggressive growth targets.

Of course, the stock markets themselves are there to lend and
eager and helping hand.

"Driving the explosive deals nowadays is Wall Street's bull
market," the *San Jose Mercury* wrote in 1998, "which gives
companies greater purchasing power by using their inflat-
ed stocks as currencies to buy competitors in the quest for
size and efficiency."[23]

It has often struck me that the most brilliant are often the most
blind. There certainly seems to be an 'everyone else is doing it, so
why can't we?' feel to a lot of what is happening these days. Or
maybe it's a need to say that 'mine is bigger than yours'.

Sorry for being cynical, but from what I can observe, a worrying amount of the motivation to get bigger is driven by short-

term and/or reactive thinking. In fact, I would say that the foundation upon which much consolidation is occurring in fundamentally flawed. Where is the customer, staff and long-term view in all the frenzy? Rather, cost cutting and short-term return is king.

The Downside for Companies

If merger activity had to prove itself based on long-term growth, rather than short-term return, there might be less of it happening. Not only that, but there is considerable evidence that mergers rarely achieve the objectives set out for them. In an article in *CFO Magazine* in 1997, Mark L Sirower wrote that "the overwhelming evidence is that the vast majority of these deals will actually destroy shareholder value for the acquirer".[24]

Sirower quoted Warren Hellman, former head of Lehman Brothers Inc., as stating that:

> So many mergers fail to deliver what they promise that there should be *a presumption of failure*. The burden of proof should be on showing that anything really good is likely to come out of one.

According to Dr Laurence J Stybel and Maryanne Peabody of Stybel Peabody, in a paper entitled "The Life Cycle of Mergers/Acquisitions",[25] a number of studies both in the United States and Britain have found that while mergers have a very positive initial impact on share prices, their longer term impact is more dubious.

James Surowiecki writing for *The Motley Fool* in April 1998, titled his article "Mindless Merging".[26]

> "Forget the facts," he wrote. "Today's acquisition-minded CEOs just want to make headlines." Surowiecki went on to point out that, "If there's one thing that is unequivocally true about M&A [merger and acquisition] activity, it's that companies dramatically underestimate how much it will cost and how long it will take to make two companies – with their attendant managerial hierarchies, corporate cultures and computer systems – into one."

Another problem with mergers is that by their very nature they must happen quickly and under clouds of secrecy, thus making it very difficult to get a considered view of both companies. Surowiecki reported that:

> The Citigroup deal, from beginning to end, took less than five weeks. The $60 billion NationsBank-BankAmerica deal took three weeks, and the companies did 'due diligence' in three days. How due, exactly, could that diligence have been?

For those considering merger and global domination, it's worth considering what the chairman of a large American bank told Surowiecki.

> You get big because you're better. You don't get better because you're big.

Bigness and Society

In theory, mergers should get rid of inefficiencies and make the new organisation run more smoothly and, thus, be better for the consumer. In practice, it can often be a leaner, meaner animal, with a reduced focus on serving the customer.

While the merger is happening, disruption of service can occur. In the longer term, decreased competition can mean higher prices, less choice and inferior products.

The *San Jose Mercury* has reported on Senator Dianne Feinstein commenting that since airline deregulation in San Francisco, service has in declined. She also talked about how mergers had caused big banks to "withdraw from their community responsibilities as they develop a national and global vision. Consumers are slapped with more bank charges, and people can't find anyone they know when they walk into a bank".

This is an interesting paradox here. The bigger these companies get the less attention they pay to ordinary customers, particularly if those customers happen to live in small or dispersed marketplaces.

In a *CNET* article, Jeff Pelline commented on how such post-merger behaviour is creating opportunity for smaller banks who do focus on local needs. He quoted Mike Abrahams, analyst with Sutro & Co, as stating that:

> As a result, many community banks are thriving. For exam-

ple, an institution called the Bank of Petaluma in Northern California has expanded by purchasing and re-opening branches previously run by Bank of America. Its motto: 'Perpetuate a unique bank...by providing superior service, innovative products, and timely attention to the needs of the community'.[27]

The broader impact of globalisation is mixed. As Dr Pekka Tarjanne, secretary general of the ITU, pointed out, it can create, "lower prices and more choice for consumers, new market opportunities for suppliers and investors and higher rates of economic growth".[28]

However, for other sections of society, particularly the lower paid, globalisation can have a more harsh reality, impacting severely on women and other minorities. At the 1997 4th World Women's Conference, the point was made that:

...the present scenario of the globalised world is characterised by widening disparities due to unequal access to opportunities and increasing discrimination under various pretexts.

Women – and consequently the family and society at large – are the worst affected as is evidenced in the growing feminisation of the unprotected informal sector, free trade and export processing zones, and of the household industry; together with flexibilisation measures based on gender discrimination.

According to Gerhard Engelbrech, a labour-market expert at Germany's Federal Labour Office:

Much of what hides behind job flexibility is really a devaluation of the employee.

The Limits of Bigness

The bigger things become the more complex they become. The more complex they become, the harder they are to predict and control. Many voices were raised in 1998 warning that while the world system that globalisation was creating might be 'working', nobody was sure anymore *how* it was working. More worrying, nobody was sure how to start fixing it, if it did break down.

Robert J Samuelson, writing for *Newsweek*[29] about the Asian and other crises, observed that:

It is hard to bring coherence to these events, because there is no coherence. The story – the real 'news' – is disorder.

MIT economist, Paul Krugman, made the point that:

Now suppose that you were to buy a copy of the best-selling textbook on international economics. What would it tell you about how to cope with a sudden loss of confidence by international investors? Well, not much. (Trust me – I'm the co-author of that textbook.)[30]

"In a global economy in which billions of dollars move at the stroke of a computer key, ensuring that nice things happen (and that nasty ones don't) is difficult," Michael Elliot wrote in a 1998 *Newsweek* piece entitled "Coming Apart". "The perfect proof of that proposition was offered last week by Alan Greenspan, the Chairman of the US Federal Reserve Board, in congressional testimony on the recent bailout of a large hedge fund, 'Long-Term Capital Management'. 'Given the amazing communications facilities available around the globe,' said Greenspan, 'trades can be initiated from almost any location…Any direct US regulation restricting their flexibility will doubtless induce the more aggressive funds to emigrate from under our jurisdiction.'

"Think about that statement for a minute," Elliot continued. "The most experienced financial regulator in the world's most advanced economy just said that he can't control a few hundred bond traders and mathematicians living (for the moment) in Greenwich, Connecticut. To the question: 'Who's in control of the global economy?' we now have an answer. Nobody."

Many have predicted that globalisation and new technology would usher in for the world a 'long boom', where recession was a thing of the past. 1998 gave these optimists pause for thought. The urge to get bigger and bigger, to drive stock prices higher and higher is creating much nervousness among those who still read their history books.

"The risk of a new 'Great Depression' is greater now than

at any time in the last twenty years," Harold James, professor of history at Princeton University, wrote in the
International Herald Tribune in October 1998. "One indication is the outbreak of financial panic in a wide variety of
geographic and economic settings...It is impossible to
explain the collapse of output at the end of the 1920s in the
industrial countries by looking at their collapsing export
opportunities; by itself, trade does not explain enough.
What made the depression 'the Great Depression' was a
series of financial panics."

In late-1998, *The Economist* predicted that the backlash against
globalisation had already begun.

> As soon as 1999, however, a different but just as wide-
> spread assumption will face its stiffest challenge yet: the
> idea that globalisation is irreversible. No door is too open
> to be closed.
>   "The mix of unstoppable technological change with the
> apparently unanswerable intellectual defeat of central plan-
> ning has made globalisation appear inevitable: only its
> speed and its consequences seem open to debate. Would that
> it were so. The effort to reverse this movement has already
> begun. Next year, most probably, that effort will move into a
> higher gear. The reason, at least, is plain to all, save possibly
> investors in American shares: world recession.[31]

MELISSA AND MONOCULTURE

We may well avoid a world recession in 1999, but I have
absolutely no doubt that there are limits to bigness and that if we
do not reach them in 1999, we will reach them not long into the
new millennium.

Globalisation and bigness go against the natural order of
things, and as those who have seen *Titanic* will be aware nature
has a way of sinking the unsinkable. No matter how important
and superior we think we are as a species, no matter how much
we might conquer and control nature in the short-term, in the
long-term we must obey the fundamental rules of nature or else
we will answer to nature.

One of the most fundamental rules that nature has developed
over billions of years is that the more diversity there is the more
stable and sturdy an environment is and the more capable it is of

surviving in the long-term. Writing about the natural world, *Britannica Online* states that:

> "The increase in species richness and complexity acts to buffer the community from environmental stresses and disasters, rendering it more stable…Diverse communities are healthy communities. Long-term ecological studies have shown that species-rich communities are able to recover faster from disturbances than species-poor communities.
>
>   "A field of weeds containing species only recently introduced to the community is quite different from a rich interactive web of indigenous species that have had the time to adapt to one another," *Britannica Online* warns. "Undisturbed species-rich communities have the resilience to sustain a functioning ecosystem upon which life depends. These communities also are better able to absorb the effects of foreign species, which may be innocently introduced but which can wreak much ecological and economic havoc in less stable communities. The tight web of interactions that make up natural biological communities sustains both biodiversity and community stability."[32]

In some ways, you could say that globalisation is a 'plant' that has been sown rapidly throughout the world over the last 40 years. It has entered into communities that for very long periods had been stable and uniform. As we have seen in Asia, South America and Africa, globalisation has brought with it initial benefit but then has often resulted in great instability. Such instability is a perfect example of what happens in a 'monoculture' environment.

In agriculture, monoculture involves the intensive farming of one particular crop. Rather than using traditional farming methods of crop rotation and leaving fields fallow, monoculture depends on fertiliser and pesticides to allow this intensive farming of the same land to continue year after year.

Monoculture has a number of important benefits, certainly in the short-term. The crop, being uniform, is easier to manage. Greater densities of planting can be achieved, and there are generally high yields. Much of the 'Green Revolution' which started in the 1950s was based on monocultural methods. It was claimed that such approaches would feed the world and help poorer countries raise their standard of living.

However, there is a growing criticism of monoculture throughout the world. Many claim that monoculture delivers short-term gain, while reaping long-term havoc on the environment.

> "Monoculture – growing vast fields of the same crop year after year – is probably the single most powerful simplification of modern agriculture," Michael Pollan wrote in the *New York Times* in 1998.[33] "But monoculture is poorly fitted to the way nature seems to work. Very simply, a field of identical plants will be exquisitely vulnerable to insects, weeds and disease. Monoculture is at the root of virtually every problem that bedevils the modern farmer, and that virtually every input has been designed to solve."

Monocultural practices have lead to the extinction of many crop varieties. Consider the following.

- In the US, over 7,000 varieties of apples were grown at the turn of the century; 80 per cent have disappeared altogether.[34]
- Where once over 30,000 varieties of rice were found in the peasant fields of India, for instance, there are now only a few hundred remaining.[35]
- Current estimates of South American deforestation are in the area of 20,000 sq. km. per year over 500,000 sq. km. have been destroyed in the last century. Modern monoculture farming is responsible for at least 50 per cent of this deforestation.[36]
- Since 1960, over 25 per cent of the rainforest in Central America has been cleared to provide land for cattle ranching.[37]

> "The number one lesson of nature is diversity," geobiologist and author Elisabet Sahtouris has stated.[38] "Nature doesn't like monocultures. The tragedy of our agriculture is monoculture. The tragedy of our culture is that we think we want to clone ourselves, monoculture ourselves...We have extinguished half the languages that were spoken on the earth already, and we are rapidly extinguishing the ones that remain."

> "Monoculture is in trouble," Pollan wrote in the *New York Times*. "The pesticides that make it possible are rapidly being lost, either to resistance or to heightened concerns about their danger."

The Melissa virus which infected the Internet in early April 1999, was a "friendly warning", that exploited a Microsoft monoculture, James Cascio wrote in *Salon Magazine*.[39] Melissa was an e-mail with a Microsoft Word attachment. If you opened the attachment you would see a list of passwords to pornographic websites. However, in the background, Melissa was checking if you had Microsoft Outlook, an e-mail programme. If you had, it sent itself to the first 50 people in your address book. These people would then receive an 'important message' with your address on it. If they opened the attachment, Melissa would spiral onwards.

> "The fuss was, at its root, about organisations mandating a certain operating system, wordprocessor and e-mail program for all of their users," Cascio wrote. "This has become increasingly common. For reasons of efficiency, entire offices – from receptionists to graphic designers to engineers – are moved to a 'standard' platform. Everyone in the company uses the same system, regardless of whether it's the right tool for the job; no platform or software diversity is allowed."

Standardisation has definite advantages. If everyone in a large company is using different systems and software, then support becomes complex and costly. The organisation of information so that it can become widely accessible also becomes extremely difficult. Even basic communication can be difficult.

The Internet has solved many of the above problems, creating a very open system for communication and organisation of information. However, when you combine the Internet with a Microsoft monoculture, you get an environment that is open to attack, as Melissa proved so simply and dramatically.

There are natural limits to how big, centralised and globalised the world can get. We need to understand that:

- bigness can reach a level of complexity where it goes out of control and has as much a chance of moving towards chaos as order;
- just because it's big doesn't mean it's better;
- rapid change brings with it instability;
- uniformity is not good for the long-term viability of any system;
- globalisation can make people hungry for what is their own, for what is unique and local;

- commerce is more dependant on trust and relationships than on any technology;
- much globalisation and merger activity seems to be focused on cutting costs rather than creating a better deal for the consumer;
- it could be said that the need to be big and bigger has become a type of herding instinct for those hungry to drive up short-term profit and stock prices.

We *cannot* predict the future. At the moment, business is getting bigger so that it can maximise itself for one particular type of future. This is unwise. This is a period of extraordinary change. Understanding and managing the present is a difficult enough task. Predicting the future is no better than gambling.

> "The global financial system was teetering on the brink of collapse," George Soros, who wrote in his 1998 in his book, *The Crisis of Global Capitalism: (Open Society Endangered)*. "Russia had defaulted on its treasury bills, financial institutions were extremely risk averse, and the price differentials between various classes of financial instruments were so out of kilter that a large hedge fund, Long-Term Capital Management (LTCM), was nearly wiped out. Since major banks and investment banks were, like LTCM, massively speculating on those differentials, the system literally came within days of a meltdown...The events of the last eighteen months have revealed certain fundamental flaws in the system. Unless we attend to them, the system is liable to disintegrate and we too shall suffer the consequences."[40]

REFERENCES

1. Statement by Alan Greenspan Chairman Board of Governors of the Federal Reserve System before the Committee on the Judiciary United States Senate (16 June 1998), http://www.senate.gov/~judiciary/green616.htm

2. J L Fix, "Latest Megadeals make '80s look tame" *Washington Free Press* (June 1998)

3. J Evans, "Trade Unions and Globalisation: Labour Markets and Structural Change" TUAC Background Paper for the International Seminar in Seoul, (20-21 October, 1997), http://www.tuac.org/news/nbackgrd.htm#begin

4. H Trabold, "Globalisation: Source of Woe or Source of Wealth?" http://www.diw-berlin.de/diwwbe/eb97-07/n97jul_1.htm

5. J Evans, "Trade Unions and Globalisation: Labour Markets and Structural Change" TUAC Background Paper for the International Seminar in Seoul (20-21 October, 1997), http://www.tuac.org/news/nbackgrd.htm#begin

6. P Tarjanne, "Telecommunications and Trade" International Telecommunication Union, Moscow (5 February 1997) http://www.itu.int/plweb-cgi/fastweb?getdoc+view1+itu-doc+4532+0++the%20benefits%20of%20freer

7. Leader, "A Bad Time to be an Ostrich" *The Economist* (19 December 1998)

8. International Institute for Strategic Studies, http://www.isn.ethz.ch/iiss/

9. "The World Welcomes America's Cultural Invasion" *International Herald Tribune* (1998), http://www.iht.com/

10. "Economic Globalization and Culture: A Discussion with Dr Francis Fukuyama" *The Merrill Lynch Forum* (1998) http://www.ml.com/woml/forum/global.htm

11. J Naisbitt, *Global Paradox: The Bigger the World Economy, the more Powerful its Smallest Player* (Avon: 1995)

12. Leader, "Here is the News" *The Economist* (4 July 1998)

13. "How Fast can the US Economy Grow?" *Harvard Business Review* (July/August 1997), http://web.mit.edu/krugman/www/howfast.html

14. H Trabold, "Globalisation: Source of Woe or Source of Wealth?" http://www.diw-berlin.de/diwwbe/eb97-07/n97jul_1.htm

15. "Economic Globalization and Culture: A Discussion with Dr Francis Fukuyama" *The Merrill Lynch Forum* (1998) http://www.ml.com/woml/forum/global.htm

16. P Tarjanne, "The Revolution in International Telecommunications and the Role of the ITU" International Telecommunication Union, Presentation to the Ministry of Information and Communication and representatives of the Korean telecommunications industry, Seoul, Republic of Korea (16 January 1998), http://www.itu.int/plweb-cgi/fastweb?getdoc+view1+itudoc+4579+0++the%20two%20main,interrelated

17. H Trabold, "Globalisation: Source of Woe or Source of Wealth?" http://www.diw-berlin.de/diwwbe/eb97-07/n97jul_1.htm

18. "Economic Globalization and Culture: A Discussion with Dr Francis Fukuyama" *The Merrill Lynch Forum* (1998) http://www.ml.com/woml/forum/global.htm

19. J Pelline, "Technology fuels Bank Mergers" *CNET News.com* (8 June 1998) http://www.news.com/News/Item/0,4,22918,00.html

20. *Ibid*

21. H Trabold, "Globalisation: Source of Woe or Source of Wealth?" http://www.diw-berlin.de/diwwbe/eb97-07/n97jul_1.htm

22. Peter Martin, "Tacos and Ale" *Financial Times*, (27 October 1998)

23. "Dealmaking is Reaching Frenzied Pitch this Year" *The Associated Press* http://www.sltrib.com/1998/jun/06141998/business/38432.htm

24. M L Sirower "Culture Vulture: Think Culture is often to blame for Mergers that fail? Think again" *CFO Magazine* (August 1997) http://www.cfonet.com/cgi-bin/vdkw_cgi/xff8ccfe3-318/Search/2592564/1

25. L J Stybel, M Peabody, "The Life Cycle of Mergers/Acquisitions" Stybel Peabody Lincolnshire, http://www.stybelpeabody.com/lspeech.htm

26. J Surowiecki, "Mindless Merging: Forget the Facts. Today's Acquisition-minded CEOs just want to make Headlines" *The Motley Fool* (23 April 1998)

27. J Pelline, "Technology fuels Bank Mergers" *CNET News.com* (8 June 1998) http://www.news.com/News/Item/0,4,22918,00.html

28. P Tarjanne, "The Role of Telecommunications in Globalization and Regional Integration" International Telecommunication Union, Fourth International Seminar on New Technologies and Telecommunications Services (October 1997), http://www.itu.int/plweb-cgi/fastweb?get-doc+view1+itudoc+4566+1++lower%20prices%20and%20more%20choice

29. RJ Samuelson, "The Loss of Confidence" *Newsweek* (6 February 1999) http://cgi.newsweek.com/cgi-in/nwframe?url=http://newsweek.wash-

    ingtonpost.com/nw-srv/issue/16_98b/printed/int/dept/wv/front.htm

30. *Ibid.*

31. Leader, "A Bad Time to be an Ostrich" *The Economist* (19 December 1998)

32. "The Biosphere and Concepts of Ecology: Community Ecology: Patterns of Community Structure: Biodiversity and the Stability of Communities" *Britannica Online,* http://www.eb.com:180/cgibin/g?DocF=macro/5000/74/39.html

33. G Soros, *The Crisis of Global Capitalism: (Open Society Endangered)* (Public Affairs 1998)

34. K Phanthong & D Patterson, "The Problem Is Plantations" Paper for the Monocultures: Environmental and Social Effects and Sustainable Alternatives Conference (2-6 June 1996) Songkhla, Thailand http://www.geocities.com/RainForest/7813/monpaper.htm

35. *Ibid.*

36. *Ibid.*

37. *Ibid.*

38. S London, "From Mechanics to Organics: An Interview with Geobiologist and Author Elisabet Sahtouris" from the radio series *Insight & Outlook* (August 1996), http://www.west.net/~insight/elsa.htm

39. J Cascio, "The Ecology of Computer Viruses" *Salon Magazine* (7 April 1999) http://www.salonmagazine.com/tech/feature/1999/04/07/melissa/index.html

40. G Soros, *The Crisis of Global Capitalism: (Open Society Endangered)* (Public Affairs 1998)

© Fergal Lawler 1999

12
Building Brands Online

THE NEED TO BRAND

On the Internet, the need to brand is greater than ever, though it can be a very different sort of branding process than the traditional marketer is used to. When building a brand on the Internet, the following needs to be considered.

- The Internet gives much more power and advantage to the consumer than it does to the company.

- The Internet tends to attract an information consumer. They are smart and they are very demanding.

- Consumers are less trustworthy and less loyal today.

- Since the Internet is an essentially sterile environment, consumers who use it will be even less trusting and more questioning.

- Pressurised by a society where time is an increasingly scarce commodity, the consumer, given the right environment, *wants* to trust in a brand as that saves them time.

- Technology is turning products into commodities. Because successful product attributes will be copied quickly, long-term advantage is gained by having a quality relationship with your customer.

WHAT ARE BRANDS?

Originally, brands were used to designate ownership and signify quality: 'these are my cattle', 'this plough was manufactured in my factory', etc. One of the first people to define brands in a modern consumer context was David Ogilvy in 1955 when he stated that:

> A brand is a complex symbol. It is the intangible sum of a product's attributes, its name, packaging and price; its history, reputation and the way it is (promoted). A brand is also defined by consumers' impressions of the people who use it, as well as their own experience.[1]

According to Stephen King in *Developing New Brands*:

> A product is something that is made in a factory. A brand is something bought by the consumer.[2]

Jared Spool of User Interface Engineering, writes about how "branding is the emotional tie – such as the feeling of success, happiness, or relief – that the customer forms towards the brand".[3]

Jerry L Kalman in a New Media White Paper entitled "Branding on the Internet" wrote that:

> Strong brands are well differentiated from their competitors in the minds of the consumer as well as those who endorse them. The actual process of branding assists in making these distinctions. The more strongly differentiated, the easier it is to select and build loyalty to the brand.[4]

Branding is about trust. Branding is about identity. Strong brands are strong – they stand for something. When you hear their name, they resonate with you in the same way that the name of someone you know resonates.

> "A brand is much more than a symbol, name or slogan," the Studio Archetype website states. "It is a 'contract' of trust between a company and its constituencies. Developing a strong and compelling brand identity can create an asset that provides a distinct competitive advantage through the attraction of more customers and investors, higher prices/margins and employee loyalty. These principles of brand are true even in the digital domain."[5]

BRANDS ARE ABOUT TRUST

Brands are indeed about trust. The *Merriam Webster Dictionary* defines trust as an "assured reliance on the character, ability, strength or truth of someone or something; one in which confidence is placed".

The world is a crazy place. It is full of possibilities, full of dangers, full of decisions and choices, full of the good and the bad. We choose well-known brands because we trust them to deliver on their promise to be reliable, to be quality. We know that there are cheaper products available, but we prefer to pay more for these brands because quality and reliability are more important to us. Our brands say something about us too. They reflect the lifestyle we have, or desire to have. They can be – in the truest sense – status symbols. In this sense, we trust our brands to say something important about who we are as people.

In a study published by Studio Archetype and Cheskin Research in January 1999 entitled "eCommerce Trust Study", it was stated that:

First and foremost, it's important to recognise that 'trust' is understood by most consumers to be a dynamic process. Trust deepens or retreats based on experience. The trusting process begins when an individual perceives indications –'forms'– that suggest a firm may be worthy of trust. These indications can include behaviours such as manners, professionalism and sensitivity.

Both consumers and firms understand that these forms are designed to represent trustworthiness. These formal claims to trustworthiness become strengthened over time and are eventually transformed into 'character traits', such as dependability, reliability and honesty.[6]

The "eCommerce Trust Study" isolated six marketplace fundamentals for building and maintaining trust on the Internet, with the brand being at the top of the list.

1. **Brand**: the importance of the company's reputation in the choice to do business with it.

2. **Navigation**: the ease of finding what the user seeks.

3. **Fulfilment**: the process users experience from when they begin a purchase until they receive a shipment and are satisfied with the purchase.

4. **Presentation**: how the site communicates meaningful information.

5. **Technology**: ways in which the site functions technically.

6. **Seals of approval**: symbols that represent companies that assure the safety of websites.

With respect to the brand as a builder of trust, a number of sub-elements were isolated by the study, these included the following.

1. **Overall brand equity**: consumer awareness of what this company does for consumers outside of the Web.

2. **Web brand equity**: how well the company's website fits with consumers' sense of what the company is about generally.

3. **Benefit clarity**: on one's first visit to the site, how easy it is to discern what the site is promising to deliver.

4. **Portal/Aggregator affiliations**: mention of an affiliation to portals and aggregators such as Yahoo, eXcite, ivillage, Lycos, etc.

5. **Co-op third-party brands**: promotion of 'third-party' quality brands.

6. **Relationship marketing**: sending updates and other notices to consumers.

7. **Community building**: facilitating interactions between individual shoppers.

8. **Depth of product offering on the site**: how many varieties of product types the site contains.

9. **Breadth of product offering on the site**: how many types of products the site contains.

Building Trust Online is Difficult

For all its vaunted interactivity, the Internet is an essentially sterile medium. It is an inherently difficult medium within which to develop trust. As Philip E Agre wrote in the *Times Literary Supplement* in 1998:

> People become who they are largely through relationships with others, and information technology increasingly establishes the ground rules under which relationships are negotiated. Yet, as the daily newspaper makes clear, the negotiation of human relationships over the Internet is in crisis. The Internet is currently providing its users with inadequate technical means of constructing the personal boundaries that make relationships possible.[7]

In 1999, the Internet is indeed an inadequate environment within which social relationships and trust can be developed. It is a largely text and minimal graphics environment. These are not exactly the best tools for building trust.

Interactivity and the Senses

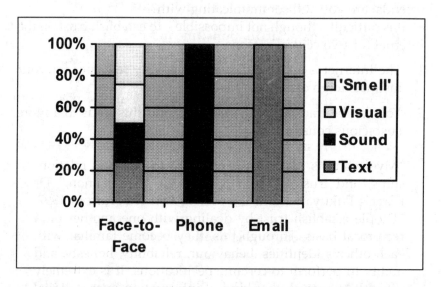

The above chart looks at three communication/interaction scenarios. In a face to face interaction, all the senses are at play: smell, visual, sound, text. This is almost always the ideal scenario for a marketer to get across a message or a sales person to make a sale, or for a company to establish trust. You simply can't beat being in front of the person, shaking their hand, making eye to eye contact. The very fact that you took the time to visit the person can speak volumes in itself.

In a phone conversation you only have voice. This is okay for very straightforward messages or sales processes, where the customer doesn't need that comfort factor of meeting the person from whom they're buying. It is also useful in reinforcing a relationship that has already been established through face to face encounters.

A human voice is more communicative than a textual e-mail. Text alone has been shown to be one of the weakest forms of communication. Professor Fred Hofsteter, Director of the University of Delaware's Instructional Technology Centre, has cited a report that found that people remember 20 per cent of what they see, 30 per cent of what they hear, 50 per cent of what they see and hear, and 80 per cent of what they see, hear and do simultaneously.[8]

E-mail can be a very hard and cold medium. An e-mail communication can very often be like a night-club relationship –

intense and brief. Think back a year. How many of your e-mail 'friends' are you still communicating with?

It is difficult – though not impossible – to establish trust on the Internet for two central reasons.

1. The Internet is a virtual space giving very few cues for your instincts to go on.

2. You can be tracked on the Internet, and this leads to a more suspicious consumer.

"My feeling is that trust is essential to business relation-ships, and trust is basically a social phenomenon," Dr Francis Fukuyama told the Merrill Lynch Forum in 1997. "People establish trust by dealing with one another on a reciprocal basis. Through this, they become familiar with each other's identities, behaviour, reliability, honesty, and ability to perform to certain specifications. It is extremely difficult to purvey that kind of information over a digital network.

"There is a lot of interesting evidence to support this," Dr Fukuyama continued. "There was a study done at SRI in the mid-1960s that examined the impact of long-distance telecommunications on the volume of trans-Atlantic busi-ness transactions. There was actually a very weak relation-ship. Trans-Atlantic business transactions were more strongly correlated with air travel, because most deals could not be consummated without establishing a social relationship."[9]

You can be tracked online. The personal information that you give on a website can be abused and your movements through-out the Internet can be tracked and logged. It is not surprising, therefore, that in 1998, in the acclaimed 8th WWW User Survey, conducted by Georgia Tech, Internet users ranked privacy as their number one concern.[10]

"Fear around money and transactions will probably be surpassed by fear around personal information, identity, and attention," Sean White, CTO of WhoWhere.com told the "eCommerce Trust Study". "If I lose $20, I'll be pissed, but I won't spend weeks trying to resolve it. The time lost isn't worth it and the money can be recovered. Personal information, once released is hard to reclaim and protect. As every aspect of your personal life becomes available online, you'll care much more about it and look for people and services you can trust to protect, hold, it."[11]

While trust is, indeed, difficult to develop on the Internet, and consumers tend to be even more suspicious online because of the fact that they can be tracked and their personal information abused, this is not to say that given the right circumstances, these consumers are not ready and willing to give their trust. Strong brands that work to establish these consumers trust can indeed build that trust.

Donna Hoffman and Thomas Novak, of Vanderbilt University write that:

Web consumers want an exchange based on an explicit social contract built on trust. But commercial websites are their own worst enemies. Contrary to conventional wisdom, product discounts, site access and value-added services don't encourage consumers to reveal information. Most Web users are uninterested in selling their personal data to websites for monetary incentives or access privileges. Consumers don't view their personal data in the context of an economic exchange, despite what many commercial Web providers believe.

Thus, the most effective way for commercial Web providers to develop profitable relationships with online customers is to earn their trust...It sounds ridiculously simple, but allowing the balance of power to shift toward the customer is proving to be difficult for many firms because it departs so radically from traditional business practices.[12]

BRANDS ARE ESSENTIAL ON THE INTERNET

Success on the Internet is all about branding.

It is one of the great myths of the Internet to say that it is a level playing field. In fact, it is the opposite.

With 500 million pages and over 8 million websites in 1999, your brand becomes even more important if you want to stand out and be recognised. To survive on the Internet, you need visitors – the right type of visitors – who will become return visitors, and who will, ultimately, become purchasers and/or advocates of your product. Probably the single biggest problem websites on the Internet face today is getting the right people to visit and visit again.

Offline, all businesses and brands exist within some form of physical *context*. You are a company operating within the Irish market – your 'home' market – and this brings with it certain advantages (and disadvantages). It's that bit easier to sell within your home market, though if that market is small, like the Irish market, you are forced very quickly to sell abroad if you want to expand.

If you are a clothes shop you exist within a context. For example, you might exist within the context of Grafton Street, which exists within the context of Dublin, which exists within the context of Ireland. All of this context gives your shop support and channels people towards it. Grafton Street is a brand that supports you. Dublin is a brand that supports you. Ireland is a brand that supports you.

On the Web you have very little context and you and your brand are basically on your own. When you establish a website it's like setting up a shop in your bedroom or a superstore on the North Pole. Nobody knows you exist.

The Internet is a big sprawling mass of millions of websites, some of which are linked into certain patterns, many of which are outposts. You can happen on the clothes shop by strolling down Grafton Street, but it's a lot more difficult to happen on a website. You can go to a search engine, sure, but search engines and directories are becoming less useful as the Web explodes ever outwards.

Thus, your brand becomes essential. If you have a strong brand, then people will think of you when they require something that your brand delivers. They will not need to go to a search engine. Rather, they will go directly to your website. When they are there, you will not need to work so hard for their trust. They already recognise and trust your brand and if there is a commercial transaction that can occur, they will be more willing to give over their credit card number to you, than to some other website whose brand they do not recognise.

The need for strong brands online is becoming more widely recognised. As *Business Week* stated in 1998:

> Harnessing the Internet to build and maintain brands has become the Holy Grail of marketing.[13]

According to Morris Tabaksblat, Chairman of Unilever:

> The evidence is that the so-called new media – or more accurately, the new proliferation of personal choices that the new media represent – will kill the marketer with the consumer if he doesn't have a well-defined brand.[14]

As Jack Staff, director and chief economist with Zona Research told *ZDNet* in January 1999:

> Around our place here, two or three months ago, some of our analysts believed that as people became more Internet-sophisticated, they would have less use for the portals – that the question of brand was a passing phase. Now we're pretty much in agreement that the brand issue is a big one.[15]

A Pillar in a Virtual Space?

For the average user, the Internet can seem like a very confusing place where it is easy to get lost searching for things. When someone is lost, they often reach for what they know – their brands.

It's all change, as usual. And yet the basics remain the same: look after the customer and the customer will look after you. We need to understand that the customer doesn't like change any more than the company does. In this war of change, give the customer something that they can depend on and trust, and they will give you their loyalty and custom in return.

French philosopher Jean-Jacques Rousseau once made the point that in the modern age, people were being "forced to be free". In the digital age, people are being forced to make *so* many choices. Given the choice, most people prefer *less* choice. They want quality, convenience, value, and a little bit of space and stability in their lives so that they can actually live and enjoy themselves.

This is where a strong brand comes in. A brand can simplify a person's life and if you can do that you can achieve their loyalty. This is where the caring organisation can come in to offer quality advice and support. As marketing expert Richard Segal puts it:

> No longer are brands only the assuring feature of consistency, but rather future certainty in a rapidly changing world.[16]

The problem is that very many of the organisations and brands in the dying days of the industrial age are inherently incapable of offering any of these things.

In this world that is being commoditised as a result of technological progress, the brand can stand out.

> "Today, any advantage based on product or service innovation is short-lived," Barry Patmore and Dale Renner of Andersen Consulting state. "Instead, forging long-term relationships with customers is key to stability in an increasingly dynamic market."[17]

I've often heard it said that we will give our credit cards in restaurants a lot quicker than we will give them over the Internet. There is good reason. By the time you are offering up your credit card in a restaurant, it is likely that you have experienced a satisfying meal. On a website, you are often expected to give up your credit card number in the promise of some future delivery. How do you judge the website is for real? A strong brand is certainly a comforting factor.

In this war of change, the brand can be a pillar of stability. Product and service offerings can – and indeed do – come and go, but the brand can remain the same, giving a sense of security and stability. If we are looking to create trust, remember that people tend to trust in things that have substance and survive.

BRANDING ONLINE IS DIFFERENT

> "The brand heroes are, of course, AOL, Yahoo and Amazon.com," *The Industry Standard* wrote in 1998. "Between them, they now control virtually the entire known world of the Internet: AOL dominating connectivity, Yahoo controlling content, Amazon.com owning commerce."[18]

Although this will change as the market matures, for now the 'brand heroes' are dominating the Internet to an almost unbelievable extent. A 1998 survey by Intelliquest, for example, found that an amazing 56 per cent of Internet users interviewed associated books with Amazon.com.

Visit the websites of these brand heroes – these Yahoo's and Amazon's. They are not 'exciting' places. Visually, they are very simple creatures. What they offer, and how they create their value, is through information and interactivity. They are *useful* places.

As consultant, Scott Kirsner, told CIO.com:

> Offline, branding is about crafting a careful image that potential buyers then passively consume. Online, branding is about an experience. And it's active.[19]

According to Jason Roberts, CEO of Panmedia Corp:

> Building a brand in this medium is all about substance. People want websites to be useful. If you're fulfilling a real need, and you have an honest connection to the audience, then you're bound to do something good.

> "Branding isn't just about image anymore. Everything you do online is part of the brand-building experience," Nick Rothenberg of Reinvent Communications Inc. states.[20]

Jared M Spool, writing about the 1998 "User Interface Engineering" study of the hugely successful trading community, eBay, stated that:

> ...eBay is not a technically sophisticated site. It seemed to us that the site was designed well, but without much flair. It uses few graphics and it has tons of user-supplied text, often all uppercase. We think, rather than the presentation, the most important aspect of eBay is that users consistently found interesting stuff quickly and easily.

> In fact, users, new to computing, told us that eBay will be their first Internet destination, once they get their own computers. This comment led us to believe that eBay has developed the necessary emotional ties that make branding successful. We now think that usability is key for effective branding. It appears to us that any obstacles that the user faces will directly affect how the user perceives the brand.[21]

I feel it is important to repeat that last sentence: *"It appears to us that any obstacles that the user faces will directly affect how the user perceives the brand."* Throw out all your marketing and advertising tricks because they won't work on the Internet. Rather, get down to the mundane, day by day tasks of delivering quality information and developing strong relationships. That's how you build brands on the Internet.

"The Internet is a 'storytelling' medium," Bran Ferren, VP for Creative Technology and R&D at Disney Imagineering, told CIO.com. He stressed that you need to keep things simple.

> Often the Web-experience is frustrating, difficult, convoluted...I can't tell you the number of times I've gone to the Web page of a company and spent ages waiting for dumb graphics to download information. How many times have you seen, for instance, a company that's posted on the Web that doesn't bother to give you a phone number? When I'm on the Web, I want to know about the product you make. This doesn't seem like rocket science.[22]

This, from the company that *sells* imagination? If Disney are keeping it simple on the Web, shouldn't you?

Clement Mok, the design genius who helped give Apple its identity, was asked by *Ebusiness Magazine* what he saw as the key elements in building a successful brand on the Internet.

> First, it's about going beyond the graphics, the logo, and the look and feel being leveraged from the brand. It's about tone and voice, which is implicit in the writing. This is often overlooked. You can have a great looking site but, at the end of the day, if the writing is bad, it can damage the brand.
>
> Second, it's about the efficiency of the experience. If you're doing commerce on the Net, and your download or your shopping cart doesn't work right, you're toast. It's about the quality of the interaction.[23]

Fundamentally, building successful brands on the Internet is about leveraging information and relationships. The traditional brand-builders of image and packaging can in fact create *negative* brand equity online. They are bandwidth hungry, they get in the way of information and relationships.

While branding online is indeed different, it would be a mistake to see it as a totally new environment, where all the rules are thrown out. It's worth remembering that:

- it's far easier to build a brand online if that brand already has a quality reputation in the physical world. Where possible, you should leverage the reputation that your brand has already attained. Remember, there is no such thing as an 'online' or 'offline' brand. It's just a brand that for the moment may exist offline or online or in some mix of the two. In fact, the "eCommerce Trust Study" found that, "better-known e-brands now possess sufficient equity to operate in the physical world, if they choose to do so";

- most major brands spend a considerable sum of money on advertising and promotion. If you want to build a brand online, advertising and promotion is still a key strategy;

- the foundation stone of any brand is the product it represents. If that product is not quality, then you are fighting a losing battle.

The Centrality of Information

Chapters 4 and 5 dealt comprehensively with central role of information in an information society. From a branding point of view, information is the foundation stone upon which you will build your brand on the Internet.

As marketing expert Richard A Segal Jr put it:

> The Internet is where today's business customer 'goes to know'.[24]

James Docherty, President of Hachette Filipacchi New Media has talked about how the information you find on a website – not the medium itself – has "the greatest intrinsic value" for the consumer.

People talk a lot about 'e-commerce', but without information, e-commerce is e-nowhere. John Audette summed it up well when he wrote that:

> As my good Internet pal Jaffer Ali continually reminds me, the Internet is becoming increasingly commerce driven. But as I continually remind him, it may be commerce driven, but it's information led. Which means that those marketing information first, and commerce second, have an advantage over those leading with commerce.[25]

In Chapter 4, *The Three Properties of Information*, I explained how information was made up of three properties: content, structure and publication. Content is the message, structure is how the message is put together and publication is how you get the message to your target audience. The formula for information value is as follows.

Information Value = Content x Structure x Publication

It should be the objective for every brand to maximise its information value. This is achieved by making each property of information a priority focus. There is simply no point in having great content if it is badly structured on a website. A content-rich, well-structured website is equally useless if its target market is not attracted to visit it.

Quality information is the bedrock of any branding exercise on the Internet. It is information that is the door opener for a relationship with the consumer. They may have a question, they may want more information, they may want to buy from you as a result of the information they have already received. If a website does not have comprehensive information then it will be very difficult to develop relationships.

People make Relationships

Denis Beausejour, Vice President of Worldwide Advertising for Procter & Gamble, has talked about how:

> At the end of the day, brands are about relationships. They are about trust and service and insight into what people need.[26]

James Docherty, President of Hachette Filipacchi New Media has echoed this belief when stating that:

> Brands demand a relationship between product and consumer.

A relationship has got to be a two-way process. The company provides the product and the service. What does the customer provide?

"The customer's contribution to the relationship is simple

– loyalty – expressed in terms of purchased product,"
according to The Pubs Group. "In our business every time
we lose a customer it represents not the natural order of
things, but a branding failure. Make no mistake about it.
You do all the work in the relationship – from a corporate
and a product standpoint – and the customer provides all
the reward."[27]

Barry Patmore and Dale Renner, when commenting on the 1998
EIU/Andersen Consulting study on customer relationship management (CRM), stated that it "clearly indicates that the ability to
systematically build and maintain customer relationships is
rapidly becoming a competitive necessity. These relationships
are key to moving beyond the cost-cutting and streamlining of
the past to an era of growth".[28] (Unfortunately, it would seem
that much of the drive of CRM is about statistically analysing
customers, rather than attempting to develop long-term relationships with them.)

Gary Heil in his book *One Size Fits One*[29] points out that "relationships are the currency of the future" and that you build
"relationships one customer at a time". His rules for creating a
solid relationship with today's information consumer include
the following.

- The customer rules for a one size fits one world.

- The average customer does not exist – get to know us.

- Make our experience special: give us something to talk about.

- If something goes wrong, fix it quickly.

- Guarantee our satisfaction.

- Trust us.

- Don't take us for granted.

- Our time is as important as your time.

- The details are important to us – they should be to you.

- Employ people who are ready, willing and able to serve us.

- We care whether you're a responsible corporate citizen.

Words are funny things at the best of times. The word 'relationship' is used constantly in today's marketing and branding

speak. But what exactly do we mean when we say that someone has a relationship with a brand?

At one end of the spectrum we have the romantic relationship or attachment. I doubt even the most fervent marketers would expect their customers to be so entranced and entangled. At the other end of the spectrum is a basic connection between two entities. In strict terms, such relationships can be very fleeting – 'out of sight, out of mind'.

What the brand tries to do is create a strong connection at the point where you start thinking about the product category, or better still, at the point where the purchase decision is made. When you think of cornflakes, you think Kellogg's, when you're thirsty, you think of Coke, when you're hungry and want some fast food, you think of McDonald's.

James G Barnes and Darrin M Howlett, in paper entitled "Predictors of Equity in Relationships between Financial Services Providers and Retail Consumers", explored the definitions of relationships. They identified:

> . . .two characteristics which should be present for an exchange situation to be characterised as a relationship.
>
> 1.   First, for a relationship to exist, it has to be *mutually* perceived to exist; that is, acknowledged by both partners.
>
> 2.   Second, the relationship goes beyond occasional contact to some special status, suggesting that a relationship is difficult to define, but the partners will know when one exists.

The Relationship Online

How do you create a relationship – a strong connection – online? The bedrock of any online relationship is information. To further that relationship, you need to open up an interaction between the consumer and your company. We know that the ultimate interaction is a transaction whereby the consumer becomes a customer as they buy one of your products. From there you try to establish a pattern of repeat purchase, evolving into brand loyalty. The stronger the relationship you can have with your customer the greater likelihood that brand loyalty will develop.

In an online environment, direct relationships begin with encouraging e-mail interaction and move to their most complex structure in the form of communities (see Chapter 6, *Community Feeds Commerce*). Communities will create the most loyalty, but they are very expensive to create and maintain, and are not suited to many brands. A basic rule here would be that if the brand does not emotionally engage consumers offline, then it is unlikely that it will engage them online.

There is a belief that technology can efficiently automate relationships. Instead, I would say that technology has demeaned relationships to the point where the consumer is deeply suspicious of anything purporting to be a relationship, believing – quite rightly – that the "Dear Gerry" and blue hand-written signature, is no more than a clever wordprocessing trick. I remember almost throwing a very important letter in the bin because I had become so used to receiving phoney junk mail. I don't know about you, but I don't get a warm feeling when a piece of software calls me "Gerry". I'd prefer it was kept formal. At least that's more honest.

Technology can support relationships, but it alone cannot deepen or maintain them in any long-term sense. You need people there watching out for the exceptional case, ready to the help the confused consumer, ready to enter into a dialogue, ready to care about the consumer.

Here lies the rub of the digital age. *The Internet demands more human interaction, not less.* Companies, so used to downsizing and head count, find this so difficult to deal with. The promise that technology has always given to them is that it will cut costs, cut people and increase profits. The idea of a technology such as the Internet requiring more people – in certain parts of the business anyhow – is anathema to the information technology philosophy that has gripped business over the last twenty years.

Be prepared to change your way of thinking! If you want to reap the benefits of the Internet on a long-term basis, then you must invest not just in technology but in two types of people.

1. Those who can create information.

2. Those who have the capacity to enter into long-term relationships with your customers.

The Communication Frequency Spectrum

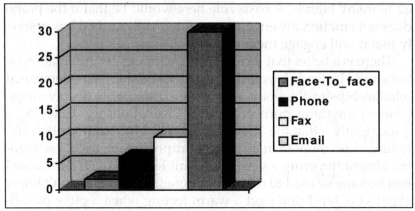

It is generally e-mail, and not your website, which will be your main tool for helping support the establishment and maintenance of relationships. As the above chart illustrates, e-mail can greatly increase the frequency of communication you can have with your customers.

Let's say you have an hour communicate. With face to face, you might meet two people. With phone, you might reach six and maybe leave a few voice mails. With fax you might send ten, if the paper isn't out and there isn't a queue at the fax machine. In an hour, you could send 30 short e-mails. If you had a mailing list you could send 30,000 or 300,000.

E-mail, therefore, allows you to communicate much more frequently and used effectively this can allow you to reach customers with communication more regularly and to reach those customers that you simply wouldn't have had to time to reach if you were using other means of communication.

This is a very significant change in communication capacity and opens up a much broader channel between company and customer that should be actively exploited so as to deliver information and establish stronger relationships.

Relationship Value

It is worth repeating: the best and most long-term relationships involve people interacting with each other. In trying to establish a way of measuring relationship value, the following factors need to be taken into consideration.

1. *The history of the relationship*: How long has it been in existence? How strong is it?

2. *The current status of the relationship*: Is it active or dormant? Has there been a weakening or strengthening of the relationship?

3. *The current nature of the relationship*: How is the relationship being carried out? How much time and energy is being currently spent on the relationship?

Taking the above into account, I would propose the following basic formula:

$$\text{Relationship Value} = \text{Time} \times \text{Energy} \times \text{Touch}$$

Relationship value is thus measured by the time and energy that has and is being spent on it. What I mean by 'touch' is how physically close the relationship has been. No matter how many e-mails you have sent someone, you cannot beat physically meeting that person to deepen the relationship.

The Relationship Cost

'You don't miss your water till your well runs dry' is an old saying. Relationship and one to one marketing theories were not 'new' developments for marketing and business. They were a reaction to the trend away from relationships. They were attempting to say that mass marketing was not the Holy Grail for every product. That even though relationships are expensive in time and energy they still could deliver value. That, yes, even though they were 'inefficient', in that relationships involve people, they still were the best way of establishing loyalty and trust.

And what good is trust and loyalty, you might ask? Well, research has shown what common sense dictates – that loyal customers increase a company's profitability and help consolidate its long-term future. Research results from the Harvard Business School have found that it costs around five times as much to get a new customer, as it does to keep an existing one. The research also found that a 5 per cent reduction in lost customers every year can add up to 75 per cent to an organisation's profits.

Modern marketing has been obsessed with getting customers, rather than keeping them. Information technology has been obsessed with cutting costs, rather than keeping customers. In the caring economy, these two trends must be reversed.

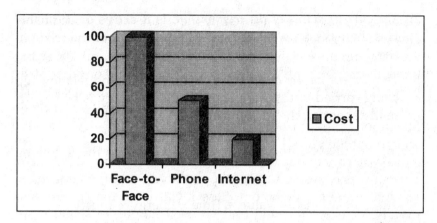

Let us now look at the example of a banking relationship so as the explore the relationship cost – and benefit – inherent in its every transaction with its customers. Let's say that if somebody comes into your bank and transacts with you the cost is £1. Let's say that if you can carry out that transaction over the phone the cost is 50p, and if it's done over the Internet the cost is 10p, as the above chart illustrates.

To those focused on cost reduction in a bank or other institution, such scenarios are eminently pleasing. Saving 90p sounds absolutely wonderful. The Internet is a great thing surely.

The world is never that simple. Hidden in the £1 is a substantial 'relationship cost'. The bricks and mortar, the lovely tiles, the desks, the pleasant and friendly people (hopefully, anyhow) who chat about the weather to the customer, are all part of a relationship cost. So, great, the cost cutter responds, let's close all our branches.

However, for all the technical gee whiz, physical bank branches are still fundamentally important to banking.

"Most literature that discusses channels tends to focus on changes that will lead to branch closure and/or physical alteration to meet the new needs of the customer," Michael Meltzer wrote in *Using the Data Warehouse Effectively for Channel Management*. "Most studies in the US (PSI, MEN-TIS and others based on customer research) view the branch as still playing a major part in delivery channel strategies even as we move into the next century…In their 5th annual report that discusses 'technology in banking', Ernst & Young reported that every bank they surveyed intended to open new branches."[30]

Okay, so staff are rarely as friendly these days as they used to be. However, a branch is where you get to know your customer. All the data mining and market research in the world can't beat that basic interaction with the customer. Once a bank, or other institution, begins to look at a customer purely from a transactional point of view, customers will begin to look at banks and other institutions purely from a transactional point of view. Loyalty will go out the virtual window.

So, you cannot just move from £1 down to 10p and not incur a penalty. Because you have stopped investing in relationships, your customers will become less loyal. Customer churn will rapidly increase. You will find yourself having to spend more and more marketing pounds to attract new customers. Very quickly you will discover that it is cheaper to keep a customer than to get a new one. The vaunted cost reduction promise will prove illusory; costs will merely have been displaced.

So, let us look at that £1 face to face cost again. Let's just say that of that £1, 50p relates to pure transactional costs – the mechanical costs of processing the transaction that occurs. Let's say that the other 50p relates to the relationship cost – the cost of interacting with the customer. For the 50p phone cost, let's say that 25p is transactional and 25p is relationship. For the Internet, let's say that entire 10p is transactional.

Following the above scenario, we could say that because the relationship cost has been halved in the phone to phone, brand loyalty has also been halved (certainly in a long-term perspective). In the Internet scenario, there is no relationship budget at all, therefore no relationship, therefore no loyalty.

If you agree with the above, then the 'correct' cost for a phone transaction is in fact 75p per transaction and for the Internet is 60p.

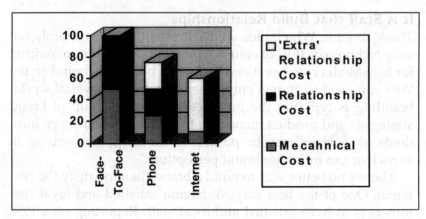

The central point I'm making here is that an organisation needs to isolate how much of the transactional cost is purely mechanical transactional and how much is a relationship cost.

The organisation that reduces its relationship budgets, reduces its relationships and thus weakens its brand loyalty. Relationship costs are hidden in all sorts of budgets, whether they are marketing, advertising, public relations or transactions.

On the Internet, you can spend your relationship budget in a variety of ways. For example, the customer may be actively encouraged to send e-mails with any questions they have. It may become company policy that every customer is contacted by e-mail at least once a month. Physical get-togethers may be organised. Experts may be paid to host regular chat forums. Whatever the approach, that relationship 50p budget needs to be spent. Otherwise, you'll spend your relationships.

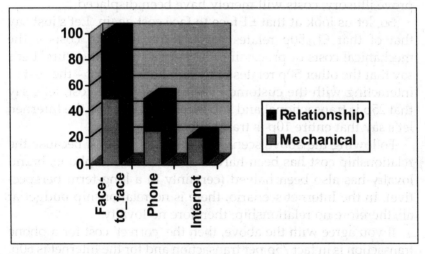

It is Staff that Build Relationships

Think about it: Who builds your relationships? It's certainly not your technology. It is, of course, your staff. Peter Jerram, writing for NewMedia.com has stated that when building a brand on the Web you need to "target employees first. In the physical world, branding is typically the province of a small group of brand strategists and product managers. In cyberspace, however, hundreds of workers may be posting to the corporate website in ways that can influence brand perceptions".

There's no better way to build a brand than to satisfy the customer. One of the best ways of having satisfied and loyal customers is to have satisfied and loyal staff. Reporting on a 1998 study by Towers Perrin for the *1to1 Marketing* newsletter, Britton Manasco wrote that:

> The research suggests that companies with employee turnover rates of 10 per cent or less have as much as a 10 percentage point customer retention advantage over companies with employee turnover rates exceeding 15 per cent. The implications are huge. Increasing customer retention just two percentage points can add 6 per cent, or $60 million of value to a typical insurance agency with $1 billion in revenues, according to the study. A five-point improvement can add $140 million in value.[31]

US corporations are not doing a very good job of holding onto their staff, according to *The Loyalty Effect*, a 1996 book by Frederick F Reichheld.

> US corporations now lose half their customers in five years, half their employees in four, and half their investors in less than one.[32]

Interestingly, a 1998 study of America's *Fortune 25* companies by Hally Enterprises, Inc. found that employees are the biggest audience for the corporate website.[33] Despite that fact, the study found that companies rarely take their employees into consideration when building the public website. I remember a conversation I had with a manager in Microsoft who stated that he (and most others he knew) had taken to going to the Microsoft public website for much of his information.

> "While naturally targeting customers, the media and investors with their websites, corporations may be missing a huge productivity bonus by not recognising what they can do with the source of their real market power – the company staff," the Hally study stated.

> "When you develop a brand program, the primary audience is employees," Ken Morris, president of corporate communications firm Siegel & Gale states. "They must understand what the brand promises so that they can translate and interpret."[34]

Barry Patmore and Dale Renner, when commenting on the 1998

EIU/Andersen Consulting study on customer relationship management, make the point that many corporations are becoming more and more aware of the need to "increase the skill levels and abilities of front-line employees, giving them the tools and power to enhance customer relationships".[35]

According to The Pubs Group:

> ...the corporate side of branding is a significant cultural act. Your corporate culture – the way everyone in your company thinks, feels and acts about their role in the relationship – forms a critical side of the triangle. This will manifest itself in the way you structure customer service, in how you make difficult changes to the way you do business, in how you include your customers in your business decisions and how you reach out to your current and prospective user base. You can't fake this with clever copywriting either. Corporate culture starts at the top, permeates throughout your company and manifests itself at every point of customer contact. For better and for worse.

In the technological haze that has been whipped up over the last twenty years, some fundamental truths have been lost. Looking after your staff, using them as brand builders, shouldn't need to be something learned from a textbook.

The Loyal Customer

The objective of any relationship with a consumer online is to create a loyal customer. The loyal customer is worth their value in gold. Loyal customers do more than buy your product. Loyal customers:

- want you to succeed and will stick with you through some rough patches, as they have invested their loyalty in you;
- are less price sensitive;
- will be more inclined to buy other products from you;
- will give you feedback and help you develop better products, more suited to their needs;
- will act as a word of mouth champion for you.

We don't give our loyalty easily. It takes time and good experience to become loyal to anything. However, once something has achieved our loyalty, we have made an emotional investment in it, and we want it to succeed. Its success says something about our good judgement; its failure speaks of our poor judgement.

If I am loyal to a product then I am less likely to switch from that product just because a competitor has reduced their price. If I have become loyal to a particular company as a result of buying one of its products for a period of time, then I am more amenable to buying other products from that company. These are simple rules of human nature.

The information consumer can be a powerful advocate for your brand. Yahoo is one of the Internet's most successful brands. A key factor in its early success was positive word of mouth.

> "We benefited from a lot of incredibly positive word of mouth," stated Karen Edwards, director of brand management for Yahoo. "Until we went public, there was no paid advertising at all."[36]

In a User Interface Engineering study of eBay, the world's largest person to person trading community on the Internet, with over 1 million users, it was found that most respondents had discovered eBay through "word of mouth. They had heard about it recently from a colleague who endorsed the site".[37]

In 1996, GISTICS, a research and consulting firm, released the results of a survey of 4,000 brand management, creative and production professionals on behalf of Apple Computers. A central benefit that the survey found in building a brand online was the improved feedback loop between customer and company which helped ensure that future products more suited customer needs.

> "As customers investigate, buy and use products and services in an interactive market space," the survey stated, "they spin off preview-demand and usage satisfaction profile data informing producers what to build, for whom, how many and for what price, creating an absolute competitive advantage."[38]

Your website can thus be an extension of your research and development lab; a place where your customers and your product developers interact on an ongoing basis.

> "Interactivity, and the opportunity for collaboration with

the consumer that occurs when using the Internet, is the single most important take-away for the branding process," Jerry L Kalman states in his article "Branding on the Internet". "If the customer doesn't become involved with the company or its message, it was a wasted branding effort.

"Nothing is more important to understanding the power of the new media and the use they play in building a strong brand presence than realising that not only is time-to-market severely compressed but also the time horizon for market cycles is collapsed," Kalman continues. "The Internet does more to collapse the process leading to success or failure in branding than any other medium has or will have because of its immediacy and the power with which it increases collaboration between enterprise and customer...or expands the gulf between them."[39]

Loyalty Programmes

A loyalty programme is about building loyalty with the objective of increasing profitability, particularly long-term loyalty. It's saying to the customer that you as an organisation value their loyalty and are going to reward them in some meaningful way for that loyalty. It's saying to the customer that you believe loyal customers are special and should be treated in a special way. It's about making a commitment to and entering into a partnership with your customer.

Loyalty must be a two-way process: your customer is loyal to you and you are loyal to your customer. A loyalty programme must result in both parties profiting. Otherwise, it is no more than a marketing trick. The customer will ultimately find out. They will feel conned by the process. They will feel that you have abused their loyalty. Those who hold these feelings most strongly will feel abusive towards you – they may want to get their own back. Remember, that the Internet empowers the consumer more than the company, and thus that the Internet is a powerful tool in the hands of a (former) customer with a grudge.

The basic principle of a loyalty programme is that a customer is rewarded every time they purchase a product. Many loyalty programmes have graded award systems, whereby the reward rises the more you purchase and/or the longer you are a member. Loyalty programmes generally take the form of clubs, identification cards, information newsletters, gift certificates. What we term as 'online communities' are in many ways a natural evolution of loyalty programmes.

Loyalty programmes should not be entered into on a whim. They are slow to build and once established should last for a long time. As Brian Skirving of Loyalty Magic states:

> It must be remembered that loyalty programmes, unlike short-term promotional campaigns, are very much long-term if not permanent marketing strategies, that can be difficult to back away from once they have commenced operating.[40]

Ray Jutkins of Power Direct Marketing states that:

> Personalised relationships with customers is not a here today gone tomorrow concept. The idea must become a part of you – you the organisation, your products and services...and most importantly, your people." Jutkins goes on to discuss another key function and attribute of loyalty programmes: measurement. "If you can't measure it you can't improve it. Database direct marketing allows you to learn more, to do more, to serve more. And most importantly, to earn more, too."[41]

Loyalty programmes are all about interaction with the customer.

> "In every instance, we have learned that frequency/loyalty/retention programs are not passive," Jutkins explains. "They work best when there is lots of action...things going on for your customers to enjoy, to benefit from. Communication is a must.
>
> "The Web, of course, is a communication/interaction medium, and thus can be a powerful tool for a loyalty programme."[42]

The following are the key benefits of establishing a loyalty programme.

1. The customer is more loyal, will buy more and will be less likely to switch to a competitor.

2. The customer is more understandable, you will be able to observe their behaviour patterns better, thus allowing you to create more targeted offerings to that customer in the future.

3. Through two-way communication process, you are more understandable to your customer. They will become more aware of the broad range of products you offer and may well help you develop future products that match their needs better.

4. Less needs to be spent on mass marketing activities, since you have an increased ability to better reach your target market.

Probably the key success factor in any loyalty programme is the commitment of the organisation – from top to bottom – to its philosophy of getting closer to the customer. In this sense, it's very much down to people. If the people in your organisation are not good at, nor interested in establishing relationships and loyalty, then no matter how fancy your databases or data mining technology is, you are doomed to failure.

Having said that, a well-planned database is central to the success of a loyalty programme. Planning a database is not really a technology issue. The central questions that needs to be asked are:

1. What sort of information do I want to store on my customers?

2. What sort of information do my customers wish me to store on them?

3. How am I going to use this information to reward my customers?

4. How am I going to use that information to create better future offers to my customers and thus establish deeper loyalty?

There are significant costs involved with loyalty programmes. The main cost area include the following.

*   **Planning and set-up costs.** Planning for the database is essential, as poor planning will mean that you will not be able to properly use the data you are gathering, thus negating a central reason behind starting a loyalty programme.

*   **Launch costs.** A loyalty programme will generally require a substantial amount of initial marketing expenditure, so as to

raise awareness and interest among the target market. This is because to get someone to join a loyalty programme is a significant enough decision, particularly in its early stages, when it hasn't built up much word of mouth momentum.

- **Interaction costs**: Many of today's streamlined organisations simply do not have the staff, who have either time or the social skills, to interact on an ongoing basis with customers.

- **Reward/Incentive costs**. The incentives given needs to be sufficient to make it worth the customer's time to participate in the loyalty programme. However, if they are too high they can create a major financial strain.

Partner Relationships
Partnerships and alliances make a great deal of sense on the Internet, as the Internet is all about creating links and connections. As Scott Kirsner told CIO.com:

> Partner relentlessly. A lot of old-line brands fail to understand that partners are everything in this medium. Never underestimate the impact of sharing content, swapping links, bartering for ad space, entering into co-marketing agreements or partnering in other creative ways.[43]

The major brands, such as Yahoo and Amazon, have all been aggressive about establishing partnerships so as to create a wide a net as possible to catch the consumer surfing on the Web. Partnerships are particularly appropriate when you are creating complex developments, such as communities. Any community worth having requires a huge range of skills and resources – the partnership route is the ideal strategy here.

For brands that have weak Internet potential, the partnership or sponsorship route may be the best way forward. It may make a lot more sense to sponsor a particular community website that is already up and running and attracting your target market, than to build such a community from scratch, which even if it is a success, will deliver minimal return for the investment required.

THE DRAWBACKS AND CHALLENGES
OF BRANDING ONLINE

Aside from the fact that trust is difficult to build online, there are a number of challenges that branding on the Internet faces. These include the following.

- Spam relationships.
- Word of mouth – the negative side.
- Globalisation.
- Relationships are expensive.
- The diminished role of packaging.

Spam Relationships

Much of modern-day direct marketing has been a process of trying to trick people into thinking that they are being communicated with on a one to one basis, rather than being part of a mailing to thousands. Everything from "Dear John" to the scanned signature being in a different ink, attempts to create a sense of personalisation. It is nothing but trickery.

Certainly, this trick marketing has worked in some situations. For products or services where we don't require a lot of interaction or further information to make a decision, any communication proves as a reminder and a call to action. However, the vast majority of people must be getting jaded when they get yet another mass mailing telling them that they've been "specially selected" yawn, yawn...

'Spam' is perhaps the most notorious form of direct marketing being practised on the Internet. Because of the structure of the Internet, it is very easy and cheap to send mass mailings of e-mail. Spammers either buy or 'harvest' thousands if not millions of e-mail addresses, and then send e-mails to these addresses promoting everything from sex websites to get rich schemes.

Spam is different from direct mail in one very important way: it generally *costs* the receiver. If you or me are receiving spam, then it can cost in two ways. Firstly, it can cost with regard to our telephone company's charge for the time it takes to download the spam. Secondly, your Internet service provider may charge us by hour of usage.

While the above can be genuine costs, the real cost of spam is the time it wastes and the way it clogs up and interferes with normal e-mail. Dealing with an ever-increasing flow of information is a constant challenge for people. Spam pollutes that flow.

Word of Mouth: The Negative Side

In Chapter 9, *Think Network*, I discussed negative network value, giving the example of how it impacted on Intel as a result of the Pentium bug. The information consumer has a powerful weapon in their hands in the form of the Internet. On the Internet, if this consumer becomes angry they can punish the company and brand in a way that was never before possible.

The Internet is the ultimate grapevine, the ultimate word of mouth, and angry customers are embracing it. Gary Heil, author of the book *One Size Fits One*,[44] in a 1998 speech, gave the example of how Starbucks and United Airlines and Nynex had been actively targeted by angry customers, who used everything from websites to 1800 numbers to get their point across.

A 1999 article by Stephanie Armour in *USA Today* entitled, "Companies Grapple with Online Gripes", opened by stating that:

> Emboldened by new technology, consumers are taking new steps to air their gripes by posting them on the Internet...Rogue Web pages, often launched by irate consumers or former employees, have taken on a range of big-name companies, such as BMW, Apple Computer and Burger King. There's 'Down with Snapple' and 'Wal-Mart Sucks'.[45]

Nike is the quintessential, hugely successful marketing organisation. However, as the digital age matures and the Internet gathers pace, a company such as Nike is finding that some consumers and public are 'just doing it', but in a way Nike had not intended.

If you go to Yahoo! and search for 'Nike' you will find an entire section entitled 'Anti-Nike'.[46] People who are opposed to some of Nike's practices are networking together to put pressure on Nike to change. Their websites have titles such as: 'Boycott Nike', 'Internet Anti-Nike site', 'Just Do It! Boycott Nike!', 'Nike Sucks! Ring'.

The *USA Today* article wrote about how:

> Nike still is reeling from an Internet hoax that swamped the firm with more than 7,000 pairs of used sneakers. Whole schools sent in children's shoes because of an Internet rumour saying they'd get new Nike's in return.

'We just kept getting smelly old shoes,' says Scott
Reames at Nike. 'We quickly felt the power and influence
of the Internet. It's frightening. It certainly caused
headaches'.[47]

Coming down like a tonne of bricks on someone who is attack-
ing you on the Internet is rarely the right approach. You've got
to fight rumour with fact. (Or fact with fact. Or fact with apolo-
gy.) You've got to inform. You've got to engage energetically
with the consumers on the network. Often, your critics start off
in a mild way. It is your lack of attention to their complaint that
can feed their resentment and make them more annoyed and
perhaps ultimately vindictive. If you interact with them at an
early stage, there is the potential to win them over, turning them
into an evangeliser for your brand rather than a bad-mouther of
it.

Gary Heil summed it up well in *One Size Fits One*.

The only business objective that makes any sense is a long-
term relationship with each profitable customer. Today's
customers have vast power to collaborate with you to
build your businesses...but if they're not happy, they will
walk away faster than ever before – or actively undermine
you.[48]

Globalisation

A traditional pillar of branding has been the nation from which
it originated. 'Made in Germany cars' signified quality. 'Made in
Japan televisions' signified reliability. Coca-Cola and
McDonald's were about the 'American Dream'. I remember
when I was young I drank Coke, partly because I was thirsty, but
partly because I wanted to be 'with it'.

The Internet can be seen a reflection of the movement towards
the global village. But all is not as rosy in the village garden as
might be expected. Peter Martin in a 1998 article for the *Financial
Times* entitled "Tacos and Ale", wrote about how:

Companies with a dissonance between their national and
corporate identities face a difficult challenge.

British Airways, seeking to build a global identity as
'the world's favourite airline', has had to grapple with the
knowledge that British national characteristics (especially

a perceived reserve and cool professionalism) alienate some potential customers. Its attempt to project a less national identity has managed to annoy British traditionalists without, as yet, making much of an impact on the wider world. If British Airways and American Airlines are able to consummate their planned alliance, they will face an even more complex branding challenge.

To be able to make a simple national statement is a significant marketing advantage...But in a world of crossborder mergers, it is an advantage many of the biggest, most ambitious companies will have to live without.[49]

Relationships are Expensive

"Years ago, retailers, bankers and auto dealers had real customer relationships," The *McKinsey Quarterly* wrote in 1995. "They knew their customers personally, understood what they wanted, and, as best they could, satisfied their needs through personalised service. As a result, they earned loyalty and a large share of their customers' business. But this was a costly and inefficient system, and eventually it gave way to mass marketing. Customers traded relationships for greater variety and lower prices."[50]

Perhaps one of the most misleading myths ever peddled about the Internet is that it is cheap to develop for. Creating information and interacting are not cheap activities. They require skilled people and people are expensive.

In a 1998 article for *Crain Communications*, Alice Cuneo wrote that:

For all its value, analysts and marketers also point out that brand building in cyberspace is not cheap, easy or foolproof.

"Supporting this vehicle for a brand is an enormous obligation once you start to get involved in it," said Emily Green, Director of People and Technology Strategies, Forrester Research.[51]

The 1998 Arthur Andersen study on online communities found that "online communities require a significant investment of time and effort to maintain. This is almost always greater than that required to launch the community".[52] The study also found that managers almost always underestimated this cost.

The price of loyalty is not cheap. However, as Geoff Mott, managing partner of McKenna Group, accurately summed it up:

> The big prize is not reduced cost, but customer loyalty.

The Diminished Role of Packaging

In the same way that Marshall McLuhan talked about how "the medium is the message", it could be said that for many brands, "the package is the product". Not so on the Internet.

Although packaging has become very closely associated with branding, its original core function has been to protect the product. Packaging something on the Internet, in the form of graphics, can be a time-wasting exercise for the consumer. If there's one thing you don't want to do with the information consumer, it's waste their time.

When you go into a supermarket, you don't go looking for the actual Kellogg's Corn Flakes. Instead, you look for the red Kellogg's box – package – that contains the corn flakes. Pre-purchase, the package is the product. However, if you go to the Kellogg's website, you go there because you believe it contains information that will be useful to you. Getting a big red box of an image that takes ages to download is not exactly information.

Avoid packaging on the Internet at all costs. Remember, the Internet is an information and interactive medium. People don't come to your website for packaging, but rather for facts. As The Pubs Group put it:

> Your customers – typically knowledgeable and informed – will jump over a ton of packaging to get next to a good branding relationship.[53]

INTERNET BRAND AUDIT

Not all brands are suited to a comprehensive Internet presence, in the same way that not all brands are suited to television advertising. To find out whether your brand is suitable or not for such a presence, an Internet brand audit needs to be carried out. The following are the basic stages for such an audit.

1. Brand scope.

2. Situation analysis.

3. Information audit.

4. Relationship audit.

5. Brand new thinking.

Brand Scope

You need to get an initial scope of the brand's Internet potential so as to establish whether it is worthwhile pursuing a full brand audit. This involves some broad discussion and research on the brand, as well as asking the following questions.

- Is there comprehensive information available on the brand?

- Does the consumer require comprehensive information when buying the brand?

- Are there any indications that the consumer is not getting enough information presently?

- Is the brand's visual image translatable into information?

- Is the consumer's emotional involvement with the brand quite strong?

- Does the organisation already engage in strong relationships with its customers?

- Can the brand tell its story and engage its consumer without its packaging?

- Do you presently have a loyalty programme for your brand?

The more positive answers to the above questions the more likely it is that the brand is suitable for a comprehensive Internet presence. As a general rule, I would say that the more image and packaging intensive a brand is, the less suited it is to the Internet. The more information rich it is and the more relationships that can be developed around it, the more suited it is.

Situation Analysis

This would involve an investigation of the following.

1. **Consumer analysis**. Is the brand's target market online and if so how are they behaving? (*Primary consumer research may be required here.*) If not, can a new online audience be developed?

2. **Competitor analysis.** What are competitors doing online, with a particular focus on innovative developments?

3. **Industry/Marketplace.** What's happening with regard to the overall industry/marketplace on the Internet.

Brand Information Audit

Before examining how we measure the brand information environment, I would like to revisit the primary characteristics of information, as defined in Chapter 4, *The Three Properties of Information*.

These are:

- information is made up of three essential properties: structure, content and publication – the three properties of information;

- information is a process or activity, and not an object – it is the communication of knowledge and intelligence;

- information is a type of evolving knowledge-based order, with the opposite of information being chaos.

In measuring the brand information environment, key questions that we need to ask at every stage are as follows.

1. How does what we have before us measure up against the three properties of information: content, structure, publication?

2. Is what we find in the environment already communicating intelligence or knowledge to its intended audience?

3. What within the environment has the potential to become information, particularly because of the Internet?

A brand's information environment is made up of two basic sections.

- Brand/Company information.

- External information.

Brand/Company Information

The first question that needs to be asked here is: What information is presently available on the brand? Where this present information would be found is: on the packaging, in brochures and fact sheets, white papers, manuals, on a website if there is one, in a help desk if there is one.

Remember, information is a verb, not a noun. It is the *act* of communicating intelligence or knowledge. If it is not reaching or reachable by its intended audience, it is *not* information.

This leads to the second question: What information exists within the company which is presently regarded as 'secret' or 'confidential' and is therefore not released? Remember, in the industrial age, information was like gold and was closely guarded. We are not in the industrial age anymore. Today, information is like milk. We need to use it quickly or else it goes off. In the industrial age, information had to go through an arduous process to prove that it was 'safe' to release to the public. Today, it should be the rule that information has to go through an arduous process to prove that it should be *kept secret*. In the digital age, information acquires more power the more it flows.

Competitive advantage in the digital age is not based on what you know, but rather on what you do with what you know. It is based on action. The computer is commoditising intelligence, putting knowledge on a chip. As I have articulated again and again throughout this book, one of the only things that has the possibility of remaining unique, no matter what the computer commoditises, is a genuine relationship with a customer. One of the key ways of establishing and consolidating that relationship is in releasing as much information to that customer as possible.

Question three is: What is there within the company environment that has the *potential* to become information? Most companies are full of wonderful knowledge about the brand. The intelligence resides in the minds of the company's staff, from the research and development people to the marketing, sales and support staff.

I remember once talking to a manager in an engineering firm. He was bemoaning the fact that an engineer was retiring. This person, the manager told me, had 40 years' experience of the company's products. Whenever they had a difficult problem, they went to him. Now he was retiring and much of his wonderful knowledge and experience was going to be lost.

To get a true measure of the information potential within the company you need to do two basic things.

1. Interview key people who know the brand.

2. Examine documentation/content on the brand to see which of it, if properly structured and publicised, could become information.

The fourth question is: What are the costs of turning potential information into real information, or in releasing what was historically confidential information? Undoubtedly, the costs are substantial and they are ongoing.

This leads us on to the fifth question: What are the benefits? Remember, this is the age of information. If you believe that, then you must accept its implications. Information is the fuel. Information is the resource. Information is what makes you rich or poor. If information consumers buy your brands then the future of your company becomes increasingly dependent on delivering information to them.

External Information
This information relates to the following.

- Competitor information.

- Media information.

- Marketplace information.

- General information.

- Consumer information.

- Associated information.

Competitor information refers to what information your competitors are providing. *Media information* refers to that provided by newspapers, television, etc. *Marketplace information* refers to that information provided by the marketplace or industry, by professional associations, bodies, etc. *General information* is information that relates to the brand that comes from the wider environment. It would include government information, EU Regulations, etc.

Consumer generated information has historically been very weak. While consumers might have had a number of strong opinions on brands, their ability to communicate such opinions has been relatively limited. Consumers may also have acquired valuable information in relation to new uses and unintended benefits of the brand. For example, individuals may have come up with innovative recipes that use a food brand's ingredients.

The Internet is an environment where consumer-driven information has the potential to thrive, in that it allows it to flow and
be organised. It may also be true that the increased interaction
between the company and consumer online, as well as the interactions that occur between consumers of the same brand, has the
ability to create new sets of information.

It may be that the brand's information environment is quite
weak. If this is so then it should be explored whether that brand
has been or can be *'associated'* with a richer information environment. For example, has the brand been associated with soccer? Is
there some potential there? Can the brand be associated with a
particular attitude?

When examining the information environment, it is important at all times to keep in mind how the Internet can or is changing this environment. It is in the change that the Internet is bringing about where the greatest opportunity and threat lies.

Brand Relationship Audit

We have already examined in detail the range of brand relationships that can occur. Here are some of the questions that need to
be asked in order to carry out a successful brand relationship
audit.

1. What are the number of relationship connection points that
    presently exist between the organisation and customer?

2. Have these increased or diminished over the last five years?

3. How often does a member of the organisation interact with a
    customer in a year? (This may need to be broken down by cus-
    tomer type, as some customers are more valuable than others.)

4. Has this increased or diminished over the last five years?

5. How brand loyal do customers feel towards the brand?

6. Has this loyalty weakened or strengthened over the last five
    years?

7. Do you have or have you had loyalty programmes for your
    brand?

8. What would it take for a customer to switch to a competitor?

9. What are the key switching costs that the organisation has
    established?

THE FUTURE OF BRANDS ON THE INTERNET

If the Internet stands for information and interactivity, instead of image and packaging, will it in time change the nature of what we mean by a brand? Some brands will always remain image driven, but others – those that are more information rich and interactive – may find that their brands evolve in a positive manner on the Internet. Those brands that totally ignore the medium may find that disgruntled consumers (or disgruntled former employees) are taking the brand to task.

Morris Tabaksblat, Chairman of Unilever NV, has written about how:

> We shall have to learn how to build a complete environment for our brands. Create a brand experience if you like. See to it that a brand embodies an attitude that's relevant.[54]

Marketing expert Richard Segal has talked about how:

> Going forward, brands must stand for ideas. They must be the compass that guides the customer through an increasingly blurring world of speed, connectivity and intangibles...Brands are increasingly becoming the reference point of insight and intellectual value. Unlike the brands of old that have served as stages for the announcement of invention, new brands are the interfaces through which customers gain insight.[55]

The Internet demands brands. Technology has turned products into commodities. Brands embody history, identity and a sense of style.

> "Every brand, whether well developed or not, has a personality," Jerry Kalman wrote in a 1997 New Media White Paper entitled "Branding on the Internet".[56]

If you don't brand yourself on the Internet, then you're just a commodity, and commodities have little value in the digital age. Some, such as Dwight Gibbs of *The Motley Fool* believe that everything will be branded on the Internet. As Gibbs puts it:

> The brand will be everything and individuals are going to start branding themselves.[57]

REFERENCES

1. D Ogilvy, *Ogilvy on Advertising* (Random House: 1987)

2. S H M King, *Developing New Brands* (out of print)

3. J M Spool, User Interface Engineering, http://world.std.com/~uieweb/

4. J L Kalman, "Branding On the Internet" New Media, http://www.new-media.org/

5. Studio Archetype, http://www.studioarchetype.com/

6. "E Commerce Trust Study" Cheskin Research and Studio Archetype (January 1999), http://www.studioarchetype.com/headlines/etrust_frameset.html

7. P E. Agre, "Yesterday's Tomorrow" *Times Literary Supplement* (3 July 1998) http://dlis.gseis.ucla.edu/people/pagre/tls.html

8. F T Hofstetter, University of Delaware http://www.udel.edu/fth/index.html

9. "Economic Globalization and Culture: A Discussion with Dr Francis Fukuyama" *The Merrill Lynch Forum* (1998) http://www.ml.com/woml/forum/global.htm

10. GVU's WWW User Surveys, http://www.cc.gatech.edu/gvu/user_surveys/

11. "Ecommerce Trust Study" Cheskin Research and Studio Archetype (January 1999), http://www.studioarchetype.com/headlines/etrust_frameset.html

12. D Hoffman and T Novak, "Trustbuilders vs. Trustbusters" *The Industry Standard* (11 May 1998), http://www.idg.net/idg_frames/english/content.cgi?vc=docid_9-60444.html

13. J Berst, "Secrets of Spiral Branding" *ZDNet AnchorDesk* (13 November 1998), http://www.zdnet.com/anchordesk/story/story_2745.html

14. M Tabaksblat, Chairman of Unilever NV, *Smart Routes to the Smart Consumer*, http://www.unilever.com

15. M Broersma, "E-shoppers go Bonkers for Brand Names" *ZDNN* (4 January 1999), http://www.zdnet.com/zdnn/stories/news/0,4586,2181624,00.html

16. R A Segal Jr, "Get in Touch with your Intangibles" FutureFocus '98 (7 May 1998), http://www.hsr.com/futurefocus/ff1998/intouch.html

17. A B Patmore and D H Renner, "Closer to the Customer, Closer to the Goal" Andersen Consulting (1998) http://www.ac.com:80/overview/Outlook/over_2nov97.html

18. M Wolff, "Defeating Net Gods" *The Industry Standard* (16 October 1998) http://www.thestandard.net/articles/opinion_display/0,1266,2086-0,00.html

19. S Kirsner, "Branding Tall" *CIO Magazine* (December 1998) http://www.cio.com/archive/webbusiness/120198_main.html

20. *Ibid.*

21. J M Spool, User Interface Engineering, http://world.std.com/~uieweb/

22. A Jahnke, "Tomorrowland" *CIO Web Business Magazine* (December 1998) http://www.cio.com/archive/webbusiness/120198_qa.html

23. R Mathieson, "Branding on the Net: The Clement Mok Interview" *Ebusiness Magazine* (May 1997) http://www.hp.com/Ebusiness/may/s_archetype.html

24. R A. Segal Jr, "Get in Touch with your Intangibles" FutureFocus '98 (7 May 1998), http://www.hsr.com/futurefocus/ff1998/intouch.html

25. J Audette, Multimedia Marketing Group, http://www.mmgco.com

26. D Beausejour, "The Promise of Interactive Advertising" Procter & Gamble Worldwide (1998), http://www.4interactivemarketing.com/digitrends/dtonline/features/promise.html

27. "Branding and Brand Loyalty" The Pubs Group http://www.pubsgroup.com/Branding.htm

28. A B Patmore and D H Renner, "Closer to the Customer, Closer to the Goal," Andersen Consulting (1998) http://www.ac.com:80/overview/Outlook/over_2nov97.html

29. G Heil, T Parker, D C. Stephens, *One Size Fits One: Building Relationships One Customer and One Employee at a Time* (John Wiley & Sons: 1996)

30. M Meltzer, "Using the Data Warehouse Effectively for Channel Management" CRM.Forum (1998) http://www.relationship-marketing.com/homepage2.htm

31. B Manasco, "Key Correlation: Customer and Employee Loyalty" *Inside 1to1* (17 September 1998), http://www.1to1.com/articles/i1-9-17-98.html#a3

32. F F Reichheld, *The Loyalty Effect: The Hidden Force Behind Growth, Profits and Lasting Value* (Harvard Business School Press: 1996)

33. Hally Enterprises Inc., "The Primary Audience of US Corporate Websites is Employees" Nua Internet Surveys
http://www.nua.ie/surveys/?f=VS&art_id=896457399&rel=true

34. *Ibid.*

35. A B Patmore and D H Renner, "Closer to the Customer, Closer to the Goal" Andersen Consulting (1998)
http://www.ac.com:80/overview/Outlook/over_2nov97.html

36. P Jerram, "Born on the Web" *NewMedia.com* (1998)
http://newmedia.com/NewMedia/97/07/fea/born.html

37. J M Spool, User Interface Engineering, http://world.std.com/~uieweb/

38. A Z Cuneo, "Cyberbrand Study: Web Branding opens Links to Customers" *NetMarketing* (10 January 1996), http://www.netb2b.com/cgi-bin/search_articles.pl?search=Cyberbrand+study&stype=netb2b

39. J L Kalman, "Branding on the Internet" New Media
http://www.newmedia.org/

40. B Skirving, "Developing your own Loyalty Programme" Loyalty Magic
http://www.loyalty-magic.com/develop.html

41. R Jutkins, "What IS a Loyalty Program?" Power Direct Marketing
http://www.rayjutkins.com/mma/mma020.html

42. *Ibid.*

43. S Kirsner, "Branding Tall" *CIO Magazine* (December 1998)
http://www.cio.com/archive/webbusiness/120198_main.html

44. G Heil, T Parker, D C. Stephens, *One Size Fits One: Building Relationships One Customer and One Employee at a Time* (John Wiley & Sons: 1996)

45. S Armour "Companies Grapple with Online Gripes" *USA Today* (26 January 1999), http://www.usatoday.com/life/cyber/tech/ctd479.htm

46. Anti-Nike, http://dir.yahoo.com/Business_and_Economy/Companies/Apparel/Footwear/Athletic_Shoes/Brand_Names/Nike/Consumer_Opinion/Anti_Nike/

47. S Armour "Companies Grapple with Online Gripes" *USA Today* (26 January 1999), http://www.usatoday.com/life/cyber/tech/ctd479.htm

48. G Heil, T Parker, D C Stephens, *One Size Fits One: Building Relationships One Customer and One Employee at a Time* (John Wiley & Sons: 1996)

49. Peter Martin, "Tacos and Ale" *Financial Times* (27 October 1998)

50. P Child, R J Dennis, T C Gokey, T I McGuire, M Sherman, M Singer, "Can Marketing Regain the Personal Touch?" *The McKinsey Quarterly* (April 1998), http://www.pfsmckinsey.com/canmark.htm

51. A Z. Cuneo, "Cyberbrand Study: Web Branding opens Links to Customers" *NetMarketing* (10 January 1996), http://www.netb2b.com/cgi-bin/search_articles.pl?search=Cyberbrand+study&stype=netb2b

52. Next Generation Research Group, Arthur Andersen http://www.ngrg.com/

53. "Branding and Brand Loaylty" The Pubs Group http://www.pubsgroup.com/Branding.htm

54. M Tabaksblat, Chairman of Unilever NV, *Smart Routes to the Smart Consumer*, http://www.unilever.com

55. R A. Segal Jr, "Get in Touch with your Intangibles" FutureFocus '98 (7 May 1998), http://www.hsr.com/futurefocus/ff1998/intouch.html

56. J L Kalman, "Branding on the Internet" New Media http://www.newmedia.org/

57. A Orr, "Internet Gurus predict Rough Road to Digital Future" *Reuters* (19 November 1998), http://www.techserver.com/newsroom/ntn/info/111998 /info9_19727_noframes.html

© Fergal Lawler 1999

13
Internet Business Principles

WE NEED A DIGITAL AGE PHILOSOPHY

If this is indeed a 'new age', then, by definition, we all need a new philosophy, a new way of thinking about and embracing this new age. For some of us it may require a realignment, for some a radical shift, for some perhaps a blossoming of already strongly held beliefs. But all of us need to find the space to stand back and question in a most fundamental way the world around us and our role in that world. To carry on regardless, as if nothing has or is happening, is to behave in a foolish, short-sighted manner.

Before looking at some key business philosophies and principles, it is important to understand that what makes this age different is that it is a 'digital' age. Things digital are fluid, rapidly changing things. Software is everywhere.

The early signs of the digital age are that it is an unstable, unpredictable place. For many of us, it feels like we are living through a war of change. Whether in time this war will ease or this digital landscape will forever shift on it fluid foundations, we are not to know. However, for now we must learn to deal with change or else it will deal with us.

It Pays to Care

A foundational tenet of such a new philosophy is that it pays to care.

Although it is technology that makes the digital age possible, the digital age is not about technology. The digital age is about people. Technology has gone to our heads. In the process, many of us have lost sight of some of the core reasons why we do things. We are not robots and automatons. We are feeling, living people, and our customers are feeling, living people too.

The obsessive information technology focus on cost-cutting, commoditisation, automation, cheapest price and removing humans from the environment of human contact, is quite simply not what many people want. To be human involves strong engagement and interaction with other people. Part of the purchase process is to enjoy the human interaction that occurs during that process. A human is like a battery that is constantly recharged by their interaction with other people.

The Internet, which has become the foundation stone of the digital age, is about communication, interaction and the sharing of information. These are very human activities and while technology can be a great support to communication and the sharing of information, it is people who make great communication and great information possible.

Too many of us have been blinded by the shiny promise of the latest version of the fastest chip that mysteriously doesn't end up making things all that faster after all. Computers may have put a lot more gadgets in our offices and homes, but they have signally failed to deliver the 'paperless office' or the 'leisure society'. There is more paper than ever and we are working longer hours than ever.

Something is seriously wrong. The modern human is like a rat on a technological treadmill of our own making. We have embraced technology for technology's sake, believing the hype that it will solve all our problems. Technology is always going to make things more efficient. Technology is always going to result in cost savings. Technology makes more mergers possible and, therefore we should merge. Technology allows for more globalisation and therefore we should globalise. Have we all become slaves to the 'great technology swindle'?

Do you dread the idea of anything you own breaking down? I know, I do. Everyone is over-stretched. Nobody has any answers. Nobody knows how to fix anything anymore. So very few even care. So, this is the 'information society'? Well, I'll pass on it, if that's OK with you.

Why this almost fanatical obsession with reducing cost? What about value and service? It must be recognised that, no matter how smart your technology is, there is a point beyond which reduction in costs result in reductions in value and service.

The dumbing down of marketing to the lowest common denominator of the lowest price does service to nobody. It may be a little known secret, but a lot of people have money these days. The whole explosion of the convenience, leisure and entertainment industries shows that people are not that price sensitive – they will pay for things that they like, for things that make life easier.

The digital age organisation must stop focusing on cost and start focusing on value. The key Internet business principle here is to put the needs of people – staff and customers – back into the centre of the business equation. It needs to be recognised that the only real way you can do this is with people. With technology turning every product into a commodity, it is good people who will make the difference. That means having a happy and motivated staff, because a happy staff will make for a happy customer and that will make for more profit in the long-term.

Think Digital

In a digital age, we need to think digital. Software is wrapping itself around our world. In how it is created and marketed are many important lessons for us to learn. Open source software is a phenomenon that on the surface looks technical and distant, but is really reflective of an ancient and co-operative way of thinking. We need to understand and learn from software, because it is at the cutting edge of our digital world.

Keep it Simple

The scarcest resource today is time. People are under pressure, working longer hours and confounded by choice. There is always a newer version of something that takes time to learn and at the end of the day is questionable with regard to what genuine value it delivers.

Everyone is shouting about complexity but beneath the surface the consumer yearns for quality and simplicity. A founding Internet business principle is therefore not to get caught up in the hype. Keep it simple.

Learn to Play

For many of us, arriving in the digital age is a bit like arriving at a tourist resort expecting to go skiing, but instead finding sun-drenched beaches; we've a lot of baggage that we need to let go.

We need to stand back from things and take nothing for grant-ed. We need to get into the mode of learning again, and that, to at least some degree, requires childlike attributes of inquisitive-ness and playfulness. Play releases the unpredictable, brings with it surprises and reveals the truths that lie just under our nose. There is room for heresy too; the need to really challenge the unchallengeable, to think the unthinkable.

As much as we might want it, there is little point in rigid long-term planning in an environment that is just leaving chaos and seeking order. Sometimes, we will need to take risks that in another area of business we would not contemplate. We need to let things flow a little. The benefit may not come from the project at hand, but rather from learning about the envi-ronment through carrying out the project. (This doesn't mean we shouldn't plan but plans need to be more flexible and adaptable than previously.)

Evangelise

A philosophy is a state of mind. Once you are on the road to a new way of thinking, it becomes necessary to bring many others along that road. No individual or organisation will change their business and/or personal philosophy as a result of some overnight enlightenment or weekend seminar. It's a slow process and constant evangelism is required to raise awareness and enthusiasm.

Long-term Vision

When so much is focused on the short-term and dealing with this war of change that we find ourselves caught up in, it is even more vital to have a long-term vision. What does the organisa-tion want to stand for and do into the future?

Without a long-term vision, it is probable that the organisa-tion will be dragged all over the place, as it reacts to short-term demands. It will become this and that and the other, and nothing at the end of the day. With all this out-sourcing and downsizing and virtual corporation stuff, you really have to figure out what your core principles and strengths are.

Inform

In a society driven by information the *story* of what you are producing can be as important as what you are producing. It is certainly no longer enough just to make things–you have to inform.

Information is the act of communicating knowledge. If you cannot master information, the digital age will pass you by. Mastering information means becoming skilled in its three properties: content, structure and publication. You must have good content, but it must be well-structured and reach its target audience effectively .

Information in the industrial age was like gold, and hoarding and controlling it did make sense. It is more like milk in the digital age. You need to use it quickly and let it flow. Much of the advantage of the digital age is acquired by your ability to learn, not by some specific set of knowledge you have right now. The advantage goes to those who have the momentum.

Of course, one of the most critical problems facing people today is information overload. Getting your information to stand out is an increasingly difficult task. But it is a task that you must undertake.

Create Structure

The Internet, like the universe, may have been born in chaos, but the challenge today is to create structure. Consumers don't like chaos. The vast majority of people seek stability and order.

The Internet is indeed a vast, expanding space (just like the universe). But those who are succeeding on the Internet – Amazon, AOL, Yahoo – are busy establishing structure. They are creating 'homes' and centres where consumers can gather to find out things and buy things.

At a larger level, countries are faced with the challenge of creating super-structures for the Internet. They need to create national information infrastructures and national e-commerce infrastructures. Just as today, countries are judged by their road, electricity and telecommunications infrastructures, so in the digital age will they be judged by the quality of the Internet infrastructures they create.

UNDERSTAND COMMUNITY

The foundation stone upon which modern commerce is built is community. Practically every product you buy has a label that states that it was 'made in...' some particular country. National identity has thus been a core selling attribute. Companies have grown strong within their own home/national markets, and only then expanded internationally. Companies have been their own communities, developing their own unique cultures and work practices which allowed them to effectively achieve their objectives of creating products and services. Community had become so central in the business landscape that it had become taken for granted.

It would seem that so much of this is so easily and conveniently forgotten by those who wish to make short-term profit today. Globalisation and merger mania is eroding the very foundations of what has made so many of the world's greatest companies great. National identity is becoming a joke, or at best a slick marketing trick. Company culture is going out the window as workers realise that it's everyone for themselves. Many companies don't know what they stand for and couldn't care less.

It all adds up to a destabilised, uncertain world, and nowhere will this uncertainty and instability be more evident than on the Internet. The Internet, for all its promise, is a sterile, cold environment. It is *not* an ideal environment within which to build communities. But it is an environment within which communities *must* be built by those organisations that wish to survive in the long run.

Community brings with it staff loyalty. Community brings with it customer loyalty. Community delivers a stable marketplace. Community brings with it a better relationship with the wider public and with the environment. Community brings with it a closer understanding of the needs of the marketplace.

Organise around the Consumer
A major new business model that is rapidly emerging on the Internet is one where the company organises around a specific set of consumers, rather than around a set of products and services. This is what America Online, Amazon and Yahoo are doing – they are creating communities online that will consume online within the community space that these companies have helped nurture. Microsoft, a company that has had an uncanny ability to see and adapt to key trends, is also now pursuing such a strategy.

Focus on the Niche

There will only be a handful of Amazon's and Yahoo's. However, there will be thousands of specialist niche market opportunities on the Internet. Some of them could be described as 'communities of interest': gay communities, U2 fans, vintage car enthusiasts, etc. Niche marketing will become a much more developed science online, because it will allow these communities of interest – who are spread far and wide in a geographic sense – to gather together and share their interests and enthusiasms on a website or through e-mail lists. To succeed in these emerging market niches, companies will have to truly understand their customers and deliver unique product offerings and first-class service and support.

EVERYONE IS THE CENTRE OF SOMEWHERE

The Internet empowers the individual, employee and consumer more than it empowers the company and organisation. The Internet is a network and on this great network, everywhere/everyone is potentially a powerful centre. You can fight against the Internet or you can go with the flow and this means following a strategy of empowerment. Empower your employees by listening to them, by treating them with utmost respect and by creating a genuine team atmosphere. Empower the consumer and individual by listening to them, by treating them with respect, by creating products and services as much *with* them as for them.

The Internet is also reflective of a larger trend in society: the growth in importance and empowerment of what were historically dis-empowered elements of society: old people, women, children. Old people will make up a significant block of the digital age society. They will have major spending power and will demand a major voice. Women are constantly working their way forwards and upwards. They too have major spending power and equally will demand that their voice and concerns will be heard. Children have a voice and a purchasing influence and power that was hitherto unknown. Children have great potential in the digital age, but equally they have great needs that must be properly addressed. Old people, women and children are three key engines in *The Caring Economy.*

DIVIDED WORLDS

The way things are going, the digital age will not narrow the great divide between rich and poor but will rather widen it.

Today, more than half the population in the world have as much chance of landing on the moon as getting connected to the Internet. Even within advanced economies, the divides are widening, between those who live on low and high incomes, between those who live in rural and urban areas. In these economies, as much as 30-40 per cent of the population may remain outside the gates of the information society for many years to come.

In 1999, we have seen in Kosovo, the impact of the political 'butterfly effect'. No country or region is too small or remote to have an impact on the global village. Forget about the moral imperative of creating a more stable, just world. The world is becoming increasingly connected and intertwined. Allowing injustice and human despair to fester will ultimately bring a payback, even to those who might think they are most immune from it.

THINK NETWORK

The Internet, of course, is the great 'network of networks'. The best way to succeed on the Internet is to imitate what made the Internet a success. To do this we must think Internet and that means thinking network.

The Internet has global potential and reach, but it needs to be understood that much of the world revolves and will continue to evolve around what is local. It also needs to be clearly understood that just because the network itself has a global reach does not give any automatic global reach to an entity that uses it. What it does mean, however, is that a global competitor can reach in more easily.

Networks are about creating connections and interacting. They are about co-operation and collaboration. Whereas in the industrial age it often made sense to hoard things and keep secrets, in a network the direct opposite can often apply. By working with the network and sharing, much can be achieved.

A network is an exponential environment. Things can grow very quickly within it. Therefore, a network is not something that you can easily take for granted. You need to be always active within it and always watching how it and the entities within it are developing.

Like all things digital, networks are versatile. They are also measurable. Things can be tracked. This measurability is raising very significant issues that need to be clearly addressed. From an organisation's point of view, it is good to be able to track a consumer, but the consumer tends to guard their privacy jealously. Getting the balance right is very important here.

Not surprisingly, networks are complex environments. They require a lot of attention. They also tend to be insecure environments. Yes, you can close everything down and make it incredibly difficult to get in and get out. But that runs contrary to the co-operative and sharing potential of the network. Vigilance is what is required.

The Internet has proven without doubt what a network can achieve if it is open in thinking and open in operation and design. It is the openness of the Internet that has been the foundation stone for its success. It would do well for those who want to succeed on the Internet to copy where possible the principles upon which the Internet has thrived.

BRAND

The Internet is a virtual space and we all have to work hard to create credibility and trust within what can be a very sterile and cold environment. Brands are of central importance on the Internet because they give context and can act as pillars in this virtual space for the consumer.

Brands are about trust and building brands on the Internet is about building trust through the consistent delivery of quality information, and through the interaction and relationship building that occurs every time you respond quickly and accurately to an e-mail, for example.

You are seriously deluding yourself if you think software and technology alone will build lasting relationships. Databases and customisation will help but there must always be the guiding hand of management and employees committed to the customer.

RESOURCE PROPERLY

At the heart of every good Internet development are good people and good brands. Good people, as we well know, are hard to come by and are expensive. Good brands are equally expensive to build and maintain.

Developing for the Internet is not some once-off gesture but rather an ongoing commitment. It requires a long-term view and a long-term investment of substantial resources of both time and money. It is not cheap to develop for the Internet.

The Internet has still not fully matured and therein lies the opportunity and the challenge. The opportunity is to establish brands for the future. The challenge is to resource these brand while they grow to maturity.

INTERNET BUSINESS PRINCIPLES

The following is a summary of the 'Internet Business Principles' which *The Caring Economy* has explored and developed. They are meant to help you guide your thinking and your actions in an age that is revolutionising the world around us.

The Caring Economy's set of 'Internet Business Principles' are:

1) *Care*. Care about your customers. Care about your staff. Care about all those connected with you. Put people first because people are where you will find your unique competitive advantage.

2) *Empower* all those connected with you and where appropriate create communities which allow you to organise around the consumer, rather than around a product or service offering.

3) *Champion and focus on old people, women and children* who are three key engines in *The Caring Economy*. Also, focus on niches and communities of interest, delivering unique products and services. In the digital age, it will pay to specialise.

4) *Focus on the value you deliver*, not just the costs you save. Remember, the Internet is not cheap to develop for, requiring quality brands, quality people and substantial ongoing investment.

5) *Let your information flow by focusing on the three properties of information: content, structure and publication.* Use information quickly and gain value from the momentum it creates.

6) *Keep the communication of your information as simple as possible.* Cut through the hype and don't fall into the trap of being complicated in a complex age.

7) *Think digital and study the lessons that are being learnt in software development.* Learn from the Internet too. Remember, the

best way to succeed on the Internet is to imitate how the Internet itself became a success and this means thinking network.

8) Learn to play, challenge the unchallengeable, think the unthinkable and encourage the heretic. Evangelise and bring other people with you. Embrace change and flow with the age.

9) *Protect and build your brand and good name*. Trust is not easy to establish on the Internet and those who gain the consumer's trust will reap the long-term rewards.

10) *Have a long-term vision of where you want to go*. Don't forget the information poor consumer. Remember that we are citizens of an increasingly connected world. For the long-term stability and prosperity of our world, we cannot continue to ignore the injustice, poverty and famine that so many of our fellow citizens must daily endure.

Go n-éirí an bóthar leat.
(This is the Irish for good luck on the journey.)

New Thinking
Gerry McGovern writes a free, weekly e-mail entitled 'New Thinking', which seeks to contribute to a philosophy for the digital age. To subscribe, send an e-mail to:
newthinking-request@nua.ie
with the word
subscribe
in the body of the message.

For back issues of 'New Thinking' please go to:
http://www.nua.ie/newthinking/

Index